BUILDING THE WOODEN FIGHTING SHIP

BUILDING THE WOODEN FIGHTING SHIP

James Dodds and James Moore

Illustrations by James Dodds

Facts On File Publications
New York, New York ● Bicester, England

First published in the United States of America by Facts on File, Inc., 460 Park Avenue South, New York, NY 10016

First published in Great Britain by Hutchinson & Co. (Publishers) Ltd

ISBN 0 87196 979 3

Printed in Great Britain

10 9 8 7 6 5 4 3 2 1

Edited by Sue Hogg
Designed by Roger Walker

Detail on page 127 from: Glorious First of June, de Louthesbourg, National Maritime Museum, Greenwich.

Detail on page 113 from: David Steel, Elements of Mastmaking, Sailmaking, Rigging, etc., 1794

Details on pages 39, 51, 57, 89 and 109 from: 'A Geometrical Plan and North East Elevation of His Majesty's Dock Yard at Deptford; with Part of the Town', by Thomas Milton, 1753. National Maritime Museum, Greenwich

Details on pages 13 and 21 from: W.H. Pyne, *Microcosm*, 1824

1 George I surrounded by his ships. From William Sutherland, *Shipbuilding Unveiled*, 1717. Photo: National Maritime Museum, Greenwich. By 1717 the fleet included 129 large men-of-war (first to fourth rates)

CONTENTS

2 The capture of *Princessa* by *Kent*, *Orford* and *Lenox*, 1740. Oil painting by P. Monamy. National Maritime Museum, Greenwich. It was from this Spanish ship and later French prizes that the design of the English 74-gun man-of-war was evolved

1

THE ORIGINS OF THE 74

In April 1740 *Princessa*, a Spanish man-of-war, was captured, after a six-hour chase, by three English ships, *Kent*, *Orford* and *Lenox*, each of 70 guns. Although *Princessa* also carried 70 guns, she was much larger than any of her pursuers, being nearly 20 feet longer overall and 500 tons heavier. Her guns were heavier than those of the English ships, and she carried them higher above the waterline. She was a fine example of the general superiority of foreign over English ships of comparable armament and the British Admiralty decided to use her as a model for future ships. So, with the collaboration of several master shipwrights and in accordance with the Establishments of 1719, *Royal George* was laid down to her lines at Woolwich in 1746. Despite her 70 guns, *Princessa* was considered too large to be the basis of a third or second rate; *Royal George* was to be a first rate, with 100 guns. Subsequently, two intermediate sized ships were constructed on similar lines: *Princess Amelia*, with 80 guns on three decks, was laid down in 1751, and *Blenheim*, with 90 guns, was laid down in 1756, both at Woolwich. They were designed by Sir Thomas Slade, who became Surveyor to the Navy from 1755 to 1771. It was Slade who was to be responsible for future developments in the design of the English man-of-war.

At the time ships were rated according to the number of guns they carried, from the largest – first rates – with 100 guns to the smallest – sixth rates – with only 20 guns. A system of rates had been laid down by the Navy as early as 1650, and although the standardization was in terms of armament, there were attempts to rationalize design in the interests of economy and efficiency. It was Admiral Lord Anson, now regarded as the father of the Navy, who brought a measure of order and discipline to the British fleet that was eventually to make it supreme in Europe. He recommended that no vessel smaller than a 64-gun

3 Sir Thomas Slade, Surveyor to the Navy, 1755–71. Artist unknown. National Maritime Museum, Greenwich. The designer of *Victory*, Slade was responsible for the development of the English 74

ship should fight in line of battle. This, he believed, was the smallest class of vessel that could fight effectively in the line.

The classification of rates established by Anson in 1754, and modified in 1792, is as follows:

Rate	1754	1792
First	100 guns	100 guns and over
Second	90 guns	90–98 guns
Third	70–80 guns	64–80 guns
Fourth	50–60 guns	50–60 guns
Fifth	40 guns	32 guns
Sixth	20 guns	20–30 guns

There was very little difference in the length of English first, second and third rates. The largest vessels had virtually reached the maximum length in relation to weight and strength that could be achieved in timber construction. By the beginning of the seventeenth century, in fact, shipwrights had built the largest ships possible with all-wood construction, and from then until the early years of the nineteenth century the industry seems almost to have stood still. Improvements were made, but it was the details of the design that changed rather than the size or method of construction. It was not until the end of the eighteenth century that the more extensive use of iron fastenings, knees and later cross-bracing enabled the length of vessels to be increased. These developments meant that less weight of timber could be used, thus giving a lighter construction, yet at the same time strengthening the hull.

In first and second rates the guns were carried on three decks; third and fourth rates had two gun-carrying decks; and fifth and sixth rates only one. In the case of two- and three-deckers, what was called the gun deck proper was the lower, or lowest, of the gun-carrying decks, and was just above the water-line. This was where the heaviest guns were carried, the main armament. The largest guns used by the Navy at this time were 42-pounders, the figure referring to the weight of shot fired by the breech-loading cannons. A third rate, for example, would have twenty-eight 32-pounders, each weighing 55 cwt. Thus the gun deck had to be immensely strong both to support the armament and to withstand the shock of recoil when a broadside was fired, all the guns on one side of the vessel being discharged virtually simultaneously. First and second rates were higher, beamier and generally bluffer in the bows than third rates to provide the additional displacement required to compensate for the third deck. With only two decks, third rates had a lower centre of gravity and were, on the whole, lighter in construction, thus making them faster and easier to handle. They gave a good balance between fast hull shape and number of guns.

It was the two-decker with a total of 74 guns that turned out to be the ideal fighting ship, becoming, in the second half of the century, the backbone of the British Navy. Compared with the three-deckers, she was more manoeuvrable, and also less vulnerable in that she presented less of her hull to the enemy. For a vessel of her size she had a good turn of speed, reaching 10 knots in a fair wind. Compared with the single-deckers such as the frigate, she was certainly slower and more cumbersome, but she could deal much heavier blows in battle and was more comfortable in heavy weather, the upper deck, forecastle and quarterdeck, on which the handling of the ship under sail took place, being that much farther away from the water and thus less likely to be swept by heavy seas. The gun deck also was protected from the elements and clear of the confusion of ship-handling.

All in all, the two-decker had a great many advantages, although the frigate, one of the finest looking sailing ships of the time, had claims later in the century to be the darling of the fleet, mainly because of the daring exploits accomplished in such vessels. One of the most famous was the frigate *Pallas*, which sailed as a privateer under Captain Lord Cochrane in 1805.

In 1760 there were 397 ships in the Royal Navy, of which seventy-five were third rates of 74 guns. By 1800, out of a total of 800 ships, 139 were 74s. At the peak in 1804 there were only nine first rates and twenty-two second rates in service, which meant that the bulk of the Navy's work fell fairly and squarely on the 74s, ably assisted by the frigates, which eventually outnumbered them. Due to her popularity, the 74 had a great deal of attention lavished on her design and construction, and represents the finest vessel that the eighteenth-century shipwright could achieve building in wood alone.

Ironically, the ship that was eventually to give England supremacy of the seas was based on French designs. During the first half of the eighteenth century English skills in naval architecture did not match the capabilities of her shipwrights. Although English yards could build strong, seaworthy vessels, these were old-fashioned, showing little advance on ships of a century before. It was the French who perfected the 74. By 1744 only one English 74 had been ordered: *Culloden*, built at Deptford and launched three years later.

In 1747 an event of great significance for the development of the English 74 occurred. No less than four French 74s were captured by the Navy: *Magnanime*, *Le Monarque*, *Invincible* – which was captured by Admiral Lord Anson – and *Terrible*. They were surveyed the following year, *Magnanime* at Plymouth in March 1748, and the others at Portsmouth in June and July. The surveys were carried out, as was customary, to ascertain whether the ships were suitable for purchase by the Admiralty. The net proceeds of such purchases went to the officers and men of the ships making the capture, and to the admiral commanding the squadron, as prize money. It was for such rewards that seamen went so willingly into action against the enemy.* Captains and officers could become wealthy men overnight, especially if the prize was carrying a valuable cargo. Anson, in his voyage round the world between 1740 and 1744, succeeded in taking Spanish ships in the Pacific yielding over £500,000 in treasure. In May 1762, two English ships, *Active* and *Favourite*, captured *Hermione*, a Spanish vessel from Lima, off Cadiz. The net proceeds from this prize were £519,705, the captains receiving £65,000, the lieutenants £13,000 and the seamen £484 each.

*The gunners' job was not to sink the enemy vessel, but to dismast her, thus rendering her helpless so that the marines could board and capture her. The crew had the cost of the damage they inflicted deducted from their prize money.

Survey Report on Terrible, *15 June 1748*

This vessel was taken by a squadron of His Majesty's ships under the command of Sir Edward Hawke (later Lord Hawke and one of England's most famous and successful admirals). The survey report was drawn up by the master shipwright at Portsmouth, P. Lock.

In hold	There are no Fish, Brandy, Steward and Sail Rooms, Captains, Marines, Gunners, Boatswains or Carpenter's Storerooms, Surgeon or Pussers Cabins. The well wants repairing.
Orlop	There are no Clamps, the beams butting against the footwales. Five beams with knees require to be added. There is no platform on the beams for the cables to lie on.
Gun Deck	One beam rotten. Two pieces of spirketing on the starboard side ⎱ Shot; require One piece of spirketing on the larboard side ⎰ shifting The main capstan unserviceable. Requires to be new. There is but one pair of bitts. The fore hatchways require to be altered. Ladders, Gratings and Garlans for shot want repair.
Upper Deck	One half beam rotten Two pieces of clamp ⎱ On the Four pieces of spirketing ⎰ starb'd side One piece of spirketing ⎱ On the One piece of string in the waist ⎰ larboard side Shot Require shifting Several pieces of quickwork One beam requires shifting in the jeer capstan room There are no jeer capstan, no fore hatchways, nor Furnace for dressing provisions The Ladder, Gratings & Kevils want repair.
Forecastle	The topsail sheet bitts The cathead ⎱ Shot One piece of spirketing on the larboard side ⎰ Require shifting The grating and scuttle over the furnace and fireplace wanting The after breastwork and Belfry want repair There are no fore jeer bitts

Negotiations over prizes were handled by an agent, appointed by the interested parties (the captors), whose function was simply to act as middle man and see that there was fair play. Not every ship captured was purchased, since a survey might reveal her to be so in need of repair as to be uneconomical. One such vessel was a French frigate captured in 1760. A laconic note in the Admiralty Board minutes records that she required too much work to make her suitable for service in the Navy. The captain and crew who captured her must have been extremely disappointed.

The surveys on the four French vessels were most revealing as they pinpointed the basic differences between English and enemy vessels. French methods of design and construction could be studied, and it was from the lessons learned from *Magnanime*, *Le Monarque*, *Invincible* and *Terrible* – and from the earlier prize, the Spanish vessel *Princessa*, the model for *Royal George* – that draughts for a whole new generation of ships were drawn by Sir Thomas Slade. *Shrewsbury*, *Norfolk* and *Dublin*, followed by *Resolution*, *Mars* and *Warspite*, were originally ordered as 70s but were changed to 74s, the first three in November 1755 and the latter in April 1756. Excluding *Culloden*, the first ships designed as 74s – *Hero*, *Hercules* and *Thunderer* – were all ordered in July 1756. *Hero* was built at Plymouth, while her sister ships, *Hercules* and *Thunderer*, were built at Deptford and Woolwich respectively. *Triumph* and *Valiant* were both ordered on 11 January 1757: 'to build a ship of 74 guns … by the draught of the *Dublin*'. This was amended on 21 May 1757 to 'by the draught of the *Invincible*', the French prize captured by Anson. *Bellona* and *Dragon* followed in 1758. Thus it would seem that there were three main draughts on which the new 74s were based: those of *Dublin*, *Hero* and *Invincible*.

The design of English vessels was not only influenced by the practical discoveries from French and other prizes. In his *Treatise on Shipbuilding* (1754), Mungo Murray, a shipwright at Deptford and later a ship's carpenter on *Weymouth*, states: 'I have written this book containing all the discoveries I could make, either by my own observations or gatherings from the writings of French authors.' And William Falconer, in his introduction to *An Universal Dictionary of the Marine* (1769), refers to the works of two French writers, M. Saverien and M. du Hamel, and a Dutchman, M. Aubin. These, he notes, 'are voluminous'.

The new generation of 74s represented good value for money.

The *Triumph* of 74 guns though the most enlarged dimensions, required a considerably less quantity of materials to construct her, than even the *Mars*, which was three hundred tons less than herself: while on the other hand, the *Thunderer* of 74 guns only required nearly eighty [172] loads of timber more than the *P. Amelia*, which was in the class or rate above her.★

In fact *Triumph* took less timber than the previous 74s, and 500 loads less than the *Princess Amelia*, yet carried only six fewer guns, on two decks instead of three. Small wonder that, with all her other advantages, the 74 became the dominant ship of the line. Only five 70s were launched in England after 1750, three 68s (in 1750 and 1768), one 66 – *Lancaster* – in 1749, and two 64s – *Prudent* in 1768 and *Intrepid* in 1770.

The new 74s were relatively smaller than their French and Spanish counterparts, though of more solid construction. The enemy vessels were generally longer, slimmer and hollower in section behind the gripe (forefoot), the poop deck was higher – a feature left over from the previous century – and the French in particular had much more elaborate decoration on the stern. The difference in size between French and

Quarter Deck	The foremost beam	
	The breastwork on the larboard side	
	Three strakes of the flat (deck)	Shot
	The quickwork	Require shifting
	The planshires and kevils	
Roundhouse	One piece of spirketing. Shot; requires shifting	
Withoutboard	Two pieces of channel wale on the starboard side	Want
	One piece of channel wale on the larboard side	repair
	Several planks on the sides and two fenders	
	The head, stern, galleries, channels and ports	
	All the joyners work requires to be new	
	A fore hatchway requires to be made on the upper deck	

She wants a new suit of masts and yards

Her bottom appears to be a little touched by worms and fastened with nails. By the best account we can get, we learn that she is about eight years old. Her hull measures 1590^{28}/$_{94}$ tuns. Parts of a sum at £8. 10s 0d per tun £13,517 10s 7½d. But judge her repairs and works necessary to put her in good condition will come to about £2300 0s 0d with the charge of materials supplied from His Majesty's magazines for securing her when she ran aground after she came into harbour amounting to the sum of £5 19s 7½d.

The workmen employed thereon being paid by the agents of the captors together the sum of £2305 19s 7½d ought to be deducted off the value.

Value	£13,517 10s 7½d	
Deduction	2305 19s 7½d	
	£11,211 11s 0d	

Herewith we send you her dimensions and scantlings.

Length of keel	133 ft 11 in
Breadth extreme	47 ft 3 in
Depth of hold	20 ft 7½ in
Tuns	1590^{28}/$_{94}$

★John Cranock, *History of Marine Architecture*, vol. 3, 1851. The comparative tonnage, loads of timber and costs are shown on page 36. Although *Thunderer* took more timber, she cost less than *Princess Amelia*.

The Development of the English 74-Gun Ship

Prizes

	Guns	Length	Breadth	Tons	Captured	From	Order to be Surveyed
Princessa	70	178.0	51.9½	2046	8.4.1740	Spain	6.2.1740
Invincible	74	171.3	49.3	1793	3.5.1747	France	5.7.1748
Terrible	74	164.0	47.6	1590	14.10.1747	France	15.6.1748
Le Monarque	74	174.10	47.2½	1707	14.10.1747	France	5.7.1748
Magnanime	74–70	173.7	49.6	1832	31.1.1747	France	30.3.1748
Téméraire	74	169.0	48.0	1685	18.8.1759	France	4.3.1760

Ordered as 70s then changed to 74s while building★

	Length	Breadth	Tons	Order to change	Launched	Yard
Resolution	165.6	46.10½	1546	13.4.1756	14.12.1758	Bird†
Lenox	165.6	47.0	1579	8.4.1756	25.2.1758	Chatham
Shrewsbury	166.1	47.1	1594	1.11.1755	23.2.1758	Deptford
Norfolk	165.6	46.8	1556	1.11.1755	28.12.1757	Deptford
Dublin	165.6	46.9	1561	1.11.1755	6.5.1757	Deptford
Mars	165.6	46.8	1556	13.4.1756	15.3.1759	Woolwich
Warspite (renamed *Arundel*)	165.9½	46.11	1580	13.4.1756	8.4.1758	Deptford

The first English 74s designed as 74s★

	Length	Breadth	Tons	Ordered	Begun	Launched	Yard
Culloden	161.4½	46.3	1487	31.12.44	23.5.45	9.9.47	Deptford
Hero	166.6	46.8	1564	7.7.56	2.8.56	2.3.59	Plymouth
Hercules	166.6	47.0	1608	15.7.56	15.7.56	15.3.59	Deptford
Thunderer	166.6	47.0	1609	15.7.56	17.9.56	19.3.60	Woolwich
Bellona	168.0	46.11	1615	31.1.58	10.5.58	19.2.60	Chatham
Dragon	168.0	46.0	1603	28.12.57	28.3.58	4.3.60	Deptford
Valiant	171.6	49.0	1799	11.1.57	1.2.58	10.8.59	Chatham
Fame	165.6	46.7	1565	13.4.56	28.5.56	1.1.59	Bird†
Superb	168.0	47.0	1612	28.12.57	12.4.58	27.10.60	Deptford
Triumph	171.6	50.0	1825	11.1.57	2.1.58	3.3.64	Woolwich

★All English draughts by Sir Thomas Slade. †Private yard.

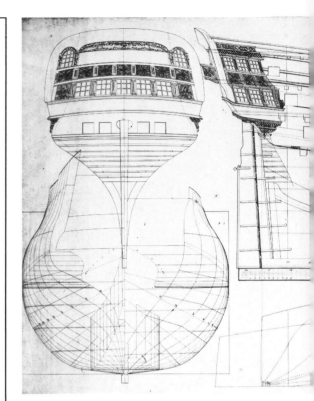

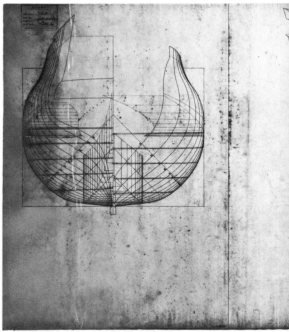

English ships persisted throughout the century.

Slade's draughts for *Hero* are extremely detailed (Figure 4), while those for the virtually identical *Hercules* (Figure 5) and *Thunderer* (see Figure 37) are much more rudimentary. Although Slade is not regarded as an originator among naval architects, his designs show his excellent common sense. He will never be forgotten while *Victory* still exists, for it was he who designed her. His assistant, John Henslow, who later became Surveyor to the Navy, is credited with having made the sketched *Thunderer*'s figurehead (see Figure 115).

We have a good idea of what *Thunderer* looked like. Thanks to the custom of building models of all important ships before they were approved and the

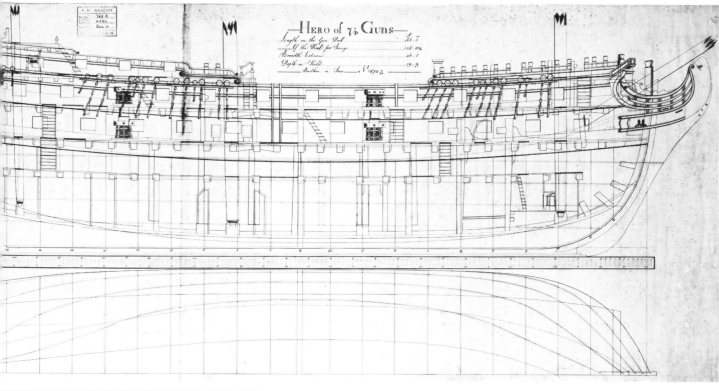

4 Draughts of *Hero*, designed by Sir Thomas Slade, 1756. National Maritime Museum, Greenwich. The first English ship designed as a 74 was *Culloden*, in 1744. *Hero* was the first of a series of 74s and her draughts were copied for *Hercules* and *Thunderer*

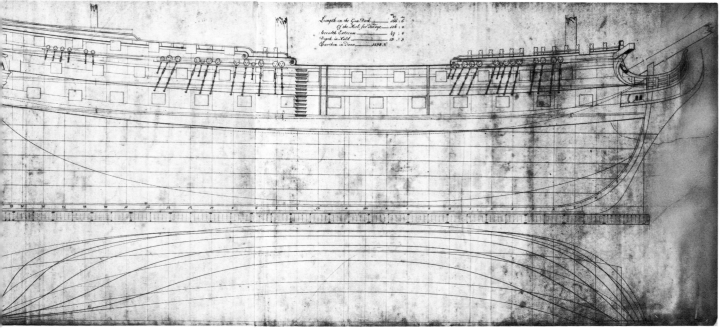

5 Draughts of *Hercules*, designed by Sir Thomas Slade, 1756. National Maritime Museum, Greenwich. These draughts are much less detailed than those of *Hero* on which they were based

order to build was given, we can examine the beautifully detailed contemporary model of *Hercules/Thunderer* in the National Maritime Museum at Greenwich (see Figure 38). Her hull length was 166 feet 6 inches, but her bowsprit would have given her an overall length well in excess of this. On the keel she measured 136 feet, and she had an extreme breadth of 47 feet 2 inches. Her depth in the hold, effectively the distance from the main deck to the top of the keelson, was 19 feet 9 inches. She had a burthen of 1609 tons. (All her main measurements are set out in her hull plan; see Figure 37). *Victory*'s measurements, for comparison, were 186 feet hull length, 150 feet on the keel, an extreme breadth of 51 feet 6 inches, and a burthen of 2161 tons. If the two vessels were to be placed side by side, *Victory* would easily be seen to be the larger ship, accounted for in part by the fact that she was a three-decker. *Thunderer* was among the largest vessels of her time, but would have looked more streamlined than a first rate, and would have been a faster sailer. *Victory* was a well-mannered ship, much liked by her captains, but she was no racehorse. (From early on in the eighteenth century the performance of all Admiralty vessels was recorded on a special form, and later entered in the log book.)

In common with all large sailing vessels of the period, *Thunderer* was ship-rigged. This means that she had three masts, all of which were square-rigged. This was the most popular type of rig until the advent of larger sailing craft in the 1860s, when the four-master became a common sight.

The main part of her armament, the twenty-eight 32-pound cannons, was carried on the gun deck. On the upper deck were twenty-eight 18-pounders, on the quarter deck fourteen 9-pounders, and a further four 9-pounders on the forecastle. In addition to the considerable weight of her guns, ammunition and stores, she took on ballast in the form of 160 tons of shingle, which was distributed in the bilges.

The cost of her construction is known to the last penny. The dockyard and Admiralty officers were meticulous in keeping complete financial records. From these it is possible to learn a great deal about the pattern of building, fitting-out and operation of the fleet. Also recorded are the names of the yard officers, the builders (all trades from master shipwright to scavelman), the riggers, and the officers, crew and marines. Written in the exquisite copperplate handwriting of the eighteenth century, the paybooks, orders for timber and stores, and many log books kept by captains and officers have survived to tell a vivid tale.

The total cost of building, rigging and equipping *Thunderer* was £39,155 16s 9d, of which the hull accounted for £33,044 7s 2d, and £6111 9s 7d went on rigging and stores. In 1760 this was a vast sum of money. Comparisons with an earlier age are always difficult but, assuming something like a hundred times inflation, the equivalent cost today would be over £3 million. However, in an age when the national income in real terms was much lower than it is now, expenditure of such sums on ships of war must have been an enormous burden on the nation's wealth. There was no opportunity for public discussion of defence and war budgets; an autocratic government simply raised the money by taxes and through loans mostly in the form of 3 per cent consols. In 1750 the national debt was nearly £80 million and it rose to £244 million by the end of the American War of Independence. However, the period we are considering was one in which real wealth was growing at an unprecedented rate, certainly faster than in modern times. Against this background, the national debt and high government expenditure do not appear so frightening. The national debt was more or less easily absorbed and it certainly enabled Britain to become a major trading and industrial nation with a vast overseas empire. Even so, in the 1750s a tight rein was kept on naval expenditure which was running at a budgeted £5 million odd per annum.

Up to October 1772 *Thunderer* cost £23,290 14s 1d for various repairs, rerigging and drydocking. Gales could play havoc with wooden ships. In the late summer of 1778 she limped home to Plymouth with much of her rig in a state of shambles after a storm in the Bay of Biscay. On this occasion she gave her main yard to *Victory*, which was not so badly damaged, so that the latter could remain on station off the French coast. Between October 1772 and July 1777 *Thunderer* was at Woolwich for what were called 'large repairs' or virtual rebuilding. This time the bill was £28,160 14s 3d, of which only £3089 5s 8d went on rigging. Before she sailed on her last commission to the West Indies in 1780, a further £16,555 16s 6d was spent on refitting and repairing her. Indeed, the wooden man-of-war required seemingly endless expenditure to keep her in fighting fettle. *Thunderer* was in no way exceptional in this respect; maintaining the fleet was a constant drain on the Navy's resources and some vessels cost even more, especially those which saw a lot of action or spent longer periods on patrol. Much of the trouble was caused by the use of inferior timber in shipbuilding by this time, and this, plus the heavy demands on the Navy, meant that the wooden ship, despite the finest workmanship, could not stand up to the consequent wear and tear.

Thunderer's complement for most of her service at sea was 650 officers and men, though at times the full complement was not mustered. On occasions she carried marines; the muster tables give, for example, figures of 123 in August 1766 and 131 in June 1778. The complement was cut to 600 in the first half of 1778, either for reasons of economy or because, with the American War in full flood, there was a shortage of men. A third rate was reckoned to need between 450 and 600 officers and men for a full, efficient crew when she was on a war footing. The organization of victualling and accommodation was considerable, and a great deal of thought went into the design of the ship so that the crew plus marines could be adequately housed. However, it was inevitable in a ship of this size that the crew should have been accommodated in overcrowded conditions. Herein lay part of the disquiet that led to the great mutiny of 1797.

The order to build *Thunderer* was given on 15 July 1756 and is recorded in a Navy Office letter of that date. In a Navy Office memorandum dated 13 August 1756, on the state of naval ships being built in the King's and in private yards, her completion date is given as December 1758, six months after *Hercules*. In the event, her completion was put back for reasons we cannot trace but which were probably due to lack of suitable timber. She was finally launched on 19 March 1760.

2

THE TIMBER TRADE IN THE EIGHTEENTH CENTURY

Throughout the seventeenth and eighteenth centuries, there was a dramatic growth in the shipbuilding industry. The major European powers were developing their navies, while the opening of world trade routes, colonial expansion overseas and the beginnings of the industrial revolution gave a huge impetus to merchant shipping. The consequent demand for first-quality timber – both for shipbuilding and for house building – rose to such heights that the timber trade attained a level of importance equivalent to that of the oil industry today. In western Europe timber became the premier raw material, and the trade formed the basis of many business fortunes, including those of John Major and the Hennikers. Oak, elm, and fir were consumed in such vast quantities by shipbuilders that supply barely kept pace with demand. Indeed, with the onset of the Seven Years' War (1756–63), the Navy's requirements began to place severe pressures on the sources of supply.

For large pieces of timber, especially oak, the Navy's demands were paramount. The third, second and first rate fighting ships were the largest vessels of their times. Merchant ships were usually smaller, with the exception of the East Indiamen, which were effectively a kind of warship with cargo-carrying capacity. By the end of the eighteenth century there were about 15,000 ships in Britain's mercantile fleet alone, while the Royal Navy at its peak mustered some 600 vessels.

The size of these ships, considering that they were built entirely of wood, is impressive and was achieved by the use of massive timbers. It is difficult to convey just what the timbers of a large wooden sailing vessel were like; only a visit to HMS *Victory*, the one fully preserved warship from this period, can give a true idea of the scale of the frames and knees, the stem and sternposts, and the planking. Rigidity and strength

in the hull were achieved by placing frames close together – some fifty were used in *Thunderer* – so that the overall result, once the 4-inch planking was applied, was a solid wall of timber some 2 feet thick.

Part of the reason for such solid construction lay in the need to provide a wide margin of safety against the ravages of dry rot, the main enemy of the wooden ship in the eighteenth century, but another consideration was to obtain a structure strong enough to withstand the enormous strains of firing the guns and withstanding enemy fire in return. In this respect, French ships, which had lighter hulls, were certainly more vulnerable. Undoubtedly the more solidly built vessels of the British Navy, though they were frequently criticized for so being, were able to stand up better in action. This, combined with superior gunnery, was a major factor in the success the Navy enjoyed against the French, as the number of enemy ships captured or disabled testifies.

Various contemporary accounts give an average consumption of between 1½ and 2 or more loads of timber per ton of warship. English shipyards were towards the upper end of this scale – hence the tendency for British ships to be relatively heavy and slow – and allowed 2.3 loads per ton of ship, but this quantity probably took account of wastage. By contrast merchant ships, which were smaller, lighter vessels constructed on more basic lines with fewer decks and less reinforcement, needed only 1 to 1½ loads per ton. The amounts of timber required for *Thunderer* are shown on page 14.

In this instance the timber of over 3400 fully matured oak trees was used in the construction of a single ship. Between 1751 and 1761 Woolwich dockyard used approximately 40,000 loads of timber to build sixteen vessels, at a cost of approximately £380,000 (see page 36). In addition, contemporary records indicate that the growing merchant fleet was using up to three times as much timber as the Navy, although this does not imply direct competition for the choicest and largest pieces, except in the case of the East Indiamen.

Of all the timber used in shipbuilding, oak was the most important, being regarded by the British in particular with a certain reverence as a symbol of strength and endurance. After all, oak trees may adorn the countryside for two centuries or more, and their majestic appearance implies immense stability. For the British Navy there really was no other choice but English oak. Due to its slow growth it is a tough, durable wood which works well – and for that reason was much liked by shipwrights – and it provided a high proportion of compass pieces. Imported oak was used only as a last resort.

In earliest times the relatively low population enjoyed an abundance of natural forests and did not have to husband their resources to any marked

Amounts of Timber Used in *Thunderer*'s Construction

	Loads	% of total
Oak timber, straight	723	
Oak timber, compass	1892	
	2615	70.43
Elm	50	
Fir	121	
	171	4.61
Knees, square	68	
Knees, raking	79	
	147	3.96
Thick stuff:		
10 inch	19	
9 inch	59	
8½ inch	–	
8 inch	81	
7½ inch	–	
7 inch	29	
6½ inch	16	
6 inch	136	
5½ inch	18	
5 inch	70	
	428	11.53
English oak:		
4 inch	128	
3 inch	62	
2½ inch	3	
2 inch	3	
	196	5.28
Danzig oak:		
4½ inch	1	
4 inch	86	
3 inch	10	
	97	2.61
Danzig elm:		
4 inch	58	
3 inch	2	
	60	1.62
Total	3713	
	= 185, 650 cubic feet	

Thick stuff: plank over 4 in thick and up to 12 in wide.
1 load = 50 cubic feet = 1 average oak tree.
Note the high proportion of compass oak.

White Oak   Elm   Fir   Spruce   Hemlock

extent. It was not until the fifteenth century that the idea of plantation silviculture was introduced (by a monk, it is said), and was taken up by landowners to whom the prospect of long-term investment was appealing. There was ample land available for such enterprises, especially after the dissolution of the monasteries and the distribution of their estates among the King's favourites. In the seventeenth century John Evelyn's *Sylva* (1664) had an enormous influence on the development of forestry as an industry.

The main area for oak was the south of England, particularly the counties of Sussex, Surrey, Hampshire and Kent. Another important region was the Forest of Dean. Sussex oak was judged to be best by a short head.

The growing of oak was often a well-regulated affair, groves of trees being regularly thinned and replanted. There were two basic types of grove. In what were known as the high woods, giant oaks stood in small groups, maturing together. The other kind of grove was the copse, which contained a mixture of old and young trees. Old trees were known as standards – a term still used as a measure of timber and equal to 50 cubic feet. Every so often the smaller trees were thinned out to allow the standards to grow to maturity. By this method about fifty standards could be grown to the acre. Hedgerow oaks, the humbler, less tended trees, provided timber suitable for compass pieces in general.

The length of time required to produce an oak tree of peak size varies considerably, depending on soil and climate conditions. English oaks grow quite slowly in the relatively tough climate of these isles, but were thought, in consequence, to have a harder wood which was resistant to rot. The best oaks take between eighty and 120 years to reach a diameter of 2–3 feet, which gives a useful amount of heartwood; sapwood was avoided in shipbuilding since it is softer and more prone to rot. For the largest ships the size of trunks required to make stem- and sternposts would have entailed a growing life of up to 150 years.

The high demand for compass oak was difficult to meet. It was used for knees and shaped pieces where the natural curve of the timber ensured greatest strength. Bending wetted or steamed timber was no substitute for the naturally grown curve. To some extent growers could predetermine the curvature of a piece of timber by chaining branches down so that they grew to a high radius, and the effort was certainly worthwhile since compass oak fetched the highest price.

Experiments were also carried out to establish if timber cut in the winter was better than timber cut at any other time of the year. Some vessels were planked on one side with winter-cut oak, and on the other side with spring, but no firm conclusion was reached. In general, it was held that the best timber was wintercut, when the sap was not flowing, and this was the course that was always followed.

Deciding when a great or standard oak was ready for felling was a highly skilled job, calling for a great deal of experience and intuition. The obvious temptation was to maximize one's profit, but a tree left too long could become *bois passé*, a French term for wood past its prime. The best oak is unmistakable by its strong, clean smell of tannic acid and its fresh, reddish colour. It should not, therefore, have been too difficult to decide whether a felled tree was good timber. But in standing or felled timber there were no less than sixty-five possible defects known to the eighteenth-century fellmonger.

Over the years the cultivation of oak for shipbuilding was the centre of conflicting interests in Britain. The demand of the Navy for the best and biggest pieces, and for compass oak in particular, implies a systematic approach and long-term investment on the part of landowners. However, the best oak needs the best soil for cultivation, so a landowner had to decide whether to grow wheat or oaks. With an increasing population, the demand for staple foodstuffs forced up the price of wheat, especially as the industrial revolution gathered momentum; thus, the quick return on cereal crops made them an attractive proposition. With a minimum time of eighty years needed to produce useful timber, and a maximum of 150 years for a fully mature oak, there was no quick return on investment, but a landowner's descendants might inherit an excellent legacy. Indeed, there were patriotic, businesslike men prepared to make the

6 The different types of timber used in shipbuilding in the eighteenth century. From left to right: white oak, elm, fir, spruce, hemlock. A ship the size of *Thunderer* used approximately 3700 loads of timber, of which 95 per cent was oak. Elm was used below the waterline for the keel and the garboard strakes. Fir was used for masts and spars, decking, and cladding the hull below the waterline

7 The forest areas of southern England that supplied oak for shipbuilding

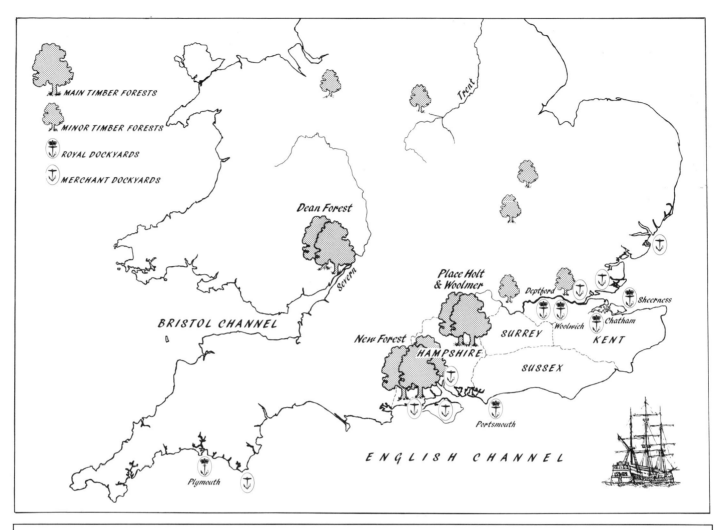

8 The different types of timbers that can be cut from different types of oaks. On the left are two hedgerow oaks, from which futtocks, breast-hooks and transoms, and curved pieces for frames and knees were cut. Straight pieces suitable for stem- or sternposts and beams came from forest oaks, or standards as they were known. Oaks grown in copses provided curved timbers for the basic framework of the ship

Hedgerow Oaks

Forest Oaks

necessary investment with their families' long-term interests in mind.

In an age of landscape gardening on a grand scale, some landowners preferred to see the largest oaks adorning their estates. Such trees, naturally, went beyond maturity and their massive pieces of timber were lost to shipbuilding. Instead, their angular branches stood gaunt against the skyline as a part of the scenery.

Another profitable use for oak trees, and one that did not require them to be grown to maturity, was for making charcoal. This was used extensively for smelting iron. At one time it seemed that these islands would become completely deforested to provide the needs of the industrial revolution. Help was at hand, though, in the person of Abraham Darby. His invention of a method of making coke from coal revolutionized the iron industry and preserved the oak as an indigenous species. Unfortunately, his discovery came too late to save many trees which would have reached maturity in the middle and later years of the eighteenth century, just when they were most needed by the Navy. In the end Britain practically ran out of homegrown oak at a time when it was most in demand for building ships to fight the French and Napoleonic wars.

There was certainly a need for a national policy on growing shipbuilding timber in England, but despite much debate guidelines were never forthcoming, even at times of greatest strategic necessity. The royal forests set a very bad example, providing a miserable amount of oak. Their capability was probably in the region of 40–50 per cent of the Navy's requirements, but they only managed to provide about 10 per cent. In 1759 the Royal Society of Arts instituted gold and silver medals to be awarded annually for the largest plantations of trees, but this was small incentive.

The lack of any policy did, indeed, have serious consequences in that it led to an incredible decline in the length of time ships remained in active service. This was partly a direct result of the increasing use of imported timber, particularly from Stettin in the Baltic, which accelerated the ravages of dry rot. Baltic oak was known to be prone to rot, but its extensive use after the Seven Years' War was inevitable.

The situation was exacerbated by the use of unseasoned oak. Oak takes three years to season, but such was the urgency to get ships built that shipwrights were forced to use green timber. This was estimated to halve the life of a ship. There was, however, a very good practical reason for using green oak: it was easy to steam into shape. A piece of oak

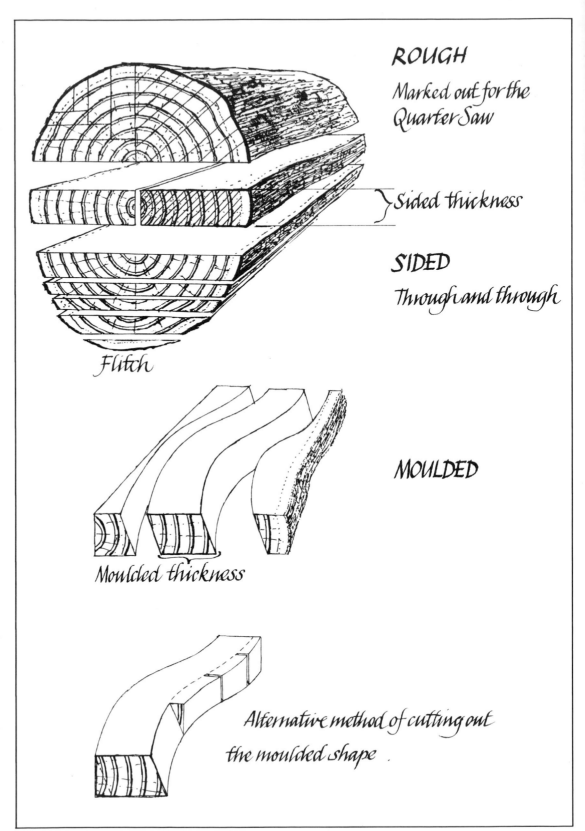

ROUGH
Marked out for the Quarter Saw

Sided thickness

SIDED
Through and through

Flitch

MOULDED

Moulded thickness

Alternative method of cutting out the moulded shape.

9 The conversion of timber from baulks to sided and moulded planks. The timber was first cut to its sided thickness. The moulded shape was either cut directly by the sawyers following the lines marked on both sides of the plank, or if the bevel (angle of cut) was acute the plank was cut square to its largest dimensions and the bevel trimmed off with an adze

10 Compass timber was cut from crooks in which the natural curve in the wood provided maximum strength

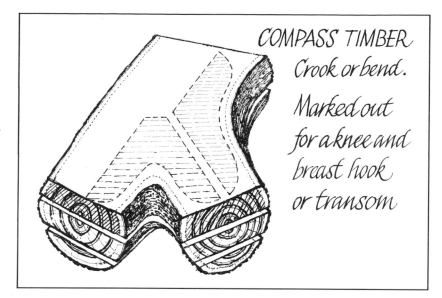

COMPASS TIMBER
Crook or bend.

Marked out for a knee and breast hook or transom

The Navy set very high standards for timber. The Royal Purveyor examined trees before felling, and the cut timber was subjected to close inspection in the yards once it was delivered, the inspectors often reducing the price to the vendor if the timber was found to be defective. To prevent concealment of defects, standards were laid down for how the timber should be cut and what dimensions it should have.

The purchasing contracts were hand-written, usually on printed forms, and were simply for outright purchase. However, we have come across one example, and there might well have been others for private yards, where the purchaser undertook to return sound timber to the original owner if and when the ship was finally broken up. The intention was to use such timber for house building. Oak that had survived that long and was still sound would have been exceedingly hard and durable, ideal for roof timbers, floor joists and staircases.

The average price of oak for naval contracts during the inflation-free years of the eighteenth century was £4 5s 0d per load. In the 1750s naval dockyards were using as much as 30,000 loads of oak every year, representing the largest single item in the naval budget. Oak was always ordered in mixed loads, the Navy requiring a certain proportion of compass and great pieces with every load of straight. The various sizes and shapes of timber were individually priced according to their relative scarcity, but the average price still held good until 1792 when an overall scarcity pushed prices up considerably.

A small detail of the purchase of general interest concerns the mark placed on the felled trees. A broad arrow was stamped on the butt, this being the mark for all naval and military stores (later it was used on prisoners' clothing). The arrow appears in the crest of Henry Sidney, Earl of Romney, who was Master General of the Ordnance in the seventeenth century, and he introduced it as a stamp to signify government property. In 1698 an Act was passed imposing heavy penalties on any unauthorized person found in possession of goods marked with the broad arrow.

When the fellmonger had selected the trees and the Royal Purveyor had given his approval, they were felled by axe – a laborious task lasting several days when there was a giant oak being cut. Contrary to the practice in France and many other European countries, little of the timber was converted on site. Although sawyers would occasionally work in specially dug sawpits in the forests, most of the timber was transported as raw logs to the dockyards. This meant that large pieces of oak for shipbuilding rarely came from a site more than twenty miles

1 inch thick was said to be capable of being bent to a 1-inch radius. Had ships been built under cover, any green timber would have seasoned satisfactorily *in situ* on the hull, but few, if any, ships were built under cover in England. The constant exposure to inclement weather, alternating with periods of drying out, resulted in the rapid spread of dry rot.

Not that this went unnoticed. Many British naval architects and shipwrights were aware that there were covered yards on the Continent (Chapman's yard at Karlskrona was a fine example, and there were covered yards at Brest and Venice) and they advocated that vessels should be built in this way, allowed to dry out thoroughly and then fastened up tight on their bolts. Regrettably, no action was taken to put this into effect, and despite the appearance of great efficiency, the English naval dockyards, at least in this important respect, lagged behind their continental rivals.

There is also evidence that the use of iron was regarded as contributing to the spread of dry rot in wooden vessels. The whole question finally came under close scrutiny during the French and Napoleonic wars, when the enormous strains placed on the Navy found many of the ships sadly wanting and constantly in need of major repairs. It was finally recommended that copper fastenings should replace iron. In view of the high cost of copper, this recommendation would not have been made had not the circumstances warranted it.

The records show that the average life of a naval ship declined dramatically as the century drew to a close, reaching an all-time low of eight years by 1792. When *Thunderer* was built in the middle of the

century the figure was more like twenty years. However, very few ships escaped a large repair during their lifetime, when a vessel was so badly racked and rotted that nothing short of a complete rebuild could save her. A high proportion of frames usually had to be replaced, as well as numerous knees inside the ship, especially near the waterline, the area 'twixt wind and water. It was clearly thought to be more effective to repair an existing vessel than to build a new one, but this must have added almost as much to the demand for good oak as building anew. Although *Thunderer* does not appear to have had a very strenuous seagoing career, during her lifetime she cost in terms of repair something like two and a half times her original price. Her loss in the great hurricane of 1780 can have had little to do with her overall condition as she appears to have been a seaworthy vessel. She was simply overwhelmed by extreme weather, which also accounted for several other ships at the same time.

There are numerous records of earlier ships lasting many years. Examples are *Royal William*, which was built in 1719 and was in service for nearly a hundred years, and the vessels of Phineas Pett, which were built at Deptford in the seventeenth century and of which the best known is probably *Sovereign of the Seas*. These ships were built of English oak, thus giving credence to the belief that it had superior qualities, but another factor may have been significant in contributing to the life of Pett's ships: he instituted the practice of having a vessel's timber cut to size in the forest, choosing each piece with great care. This admirable procedure seems to have been abandoned in later years.

distant from a river or seaport. To move massive baulks by land over longer distances would have been too expensive and there were few rivers suitable for transporting bulky cargoes. As it was, the task of moving huge trunks was an arduous and lengthy business. Several pairs of horses or oxen would be used to draw wagons – known as tuggs – over the unmade tracks and roads, with the largest trunks slung beneath the axles.

Once the timber had been cut there was a fair level of wastage due either to natural flaws or to bad storage, which fostered rot. Another cause of waste, in part a facet of the corruption rife in the eighteenth century, was the practice of allowing shipwrights to take home chips. In theory, these were lengths of timber 3 feet or less which were unsuitable for shipbuilding, and they were regarded as a perquisite of the shipwright. Inevitably, the privilege was abused and there are reports of shipwrights at Woolwich stopping work one hour early to saw useful timber into chips. It is not recorded what these were used for, but doubtless many ended up in pieces of furniture, or as parts of houses, or were simply used as firewood.

Corruption was an accepted part of business ethics in the seventeenth and eighteenth centuries and the Navy Board and naval dockyards were no less affected in this respect than any other establishments. The timber trade in particular, because of its great importance and the volume of business, involved large contracts which were frequently the occasion for generous presents for favours received. Possibly the best account of such transactions is to be found in Pepys's *Diary* where he recorded details of presents made to him as Clerk to the Navy Board. By the end of the eighteenth century attempts were made to clean up whole establishments and eradicate bribes as supplements to inadequate salaries. With the costs of naval warfare reaching alarming proportions after the Seven Years' War, it became essential to ensure that the whole system was efficiently and honestly run.

As the century progressed it was the lack of large pieces for stem- and sternposts that became the greatest problem. Vessels often had to be built with smaller pieces joined together, thus weakening the structure. Ships built in this way often became cranky sailers. Several frigates were actually built entirely of fir, but the experiment was apparently not a great success. Eventually, in the early nineteenth century, larch – first used in 1792 – became recognized as a suitable alternative to oak for planking. It has proved to be the best conifer to be grown in Britain and the huge tracts of Forestry Commission plantations that can be seen today consist mainly of larch trees.

After oak, the most important timber used in shipbuilding was elm. In the main this came from English sources, although French elm was highly thought of. Elm was not grown in groves in the same way as oak, but was found singly or in small groups of half a dozen or so trees.

Elm has two distinct advantages for shipbuilding: its close, twisted grain holds fastenings such as bolts very well and it does not rot if constantly immersed in water. It was never, therefore, used above the waterline – except for cabin furniture and panelling – or 'twixt wind and water as it does not take kindly to being alternately wet and dry. In medieval times it was used for underground water pipes and whole sections from medieval London have been found still intact.

Because of its properties, elm was used for the keel and the garboard planks – the first three planks from the keel outwards. (Beech was sometimes used for the latter, though rarely.) The average length of a piece of elm was 24 feet, which meant that the keel could not be formed from one piece, especially in the larger vessels, but was made up of smaller lengths scarphed together. For rigidity the aim was to have as few pieces as possible, but great efforts were made to ensure that the scarphs were really close joints, through-bolted with eight bolts and made tight, with flannel and tar liberally applied. *Thunderer*'s keel was probably made up of six pieces; *Victory*'s consisted of seven separate pieces.

For masts, spars, decking and underwater cladding of the hull, fir – Scots pine (*Pinus sylvestris*) – was used. Firs grow to an enormous size, taking up to a hundred years to reach maturity. Fir cladding served to protect the oak planks from marine borers, the idea being that the cladding could easily be stripped off and replaced as it became worn. At best, this practice can only have worked tolerably well. It was not until copper sheathing was introduced in the 1770s that the problem was really solved to anyone's satisfaction.

The main source of fir and associated byproducts such as turpentine and tar, which were used extensively in shipbuilding, was the Baltic. The timber trade had flourished there since the Middle Ages and was so well established that it continued to dominate the international markets even though equally good or better timber could be obtained from alternative sources such as the Mediterranean and North America. The main timber ports were Danzig, Memel, Riga and Stettin, although a certain amount of wood came through St Petersburg (now Leningrad). Pride of place went to Danzig, whose top-quality products were highly thought of by the Navy Board. Stettin was virtually the sole exporter of oak planking, which formed a large part of the trade after 1756.

The best pole and deals (1–2 inch boards) came from the Baltic. Baltic spars were commonly known as hand masts from the practice of measuring their circumference by palm widths. They came in three sizes: great, middling and small. The quality of the timber was established by a system of inspection known as bracking. Brackers worked in every Baltic port, their integrity being well recognized by the Navy. They placed marks on the butts to denote port of origin and quality, and timber is still marked in this way to this day. An example of eighteenth-century marking can be quoted from Danzig. There, first-grade timber was marked with a K, second-grade with a B, and third-grade with a B B. The system was widely accepted as a guarantee of quality, but this did not prevent the Navy from appointing its own agents or sending inspectors to ensure that standards were maintained and that the brackers were not falling prey to bribery. As the volume of trade was so high, this precaution is understandable. Moreover, it was certainly in the interests of the Navy Board to see that it was getting the best in competition with countries such as Holland and France.

Many of the Baltic merchants traded exclusively in timber and ships' stores and all the major powers, including Britain, had representatives there in the form of agents, purveyors and merchants. In time of war these rather dreary towns with their grim façades became centres of intrigue, with foreign nationals acting as spies on behalf of their own countries, sending home details of enemy shipments. Reports from English agents resulted in action by the Navy and French cargoes of masts fell into British hands. In the latter half of the eighteenth century the Baltic and its approaches became the happy hunting ground for British naval patrols.

The basis of the Baltic trade was the great forests that flourished across the whole of northern Europe as far as the Ural mountains and extended far inland. Some timber, especially oak, even came from as far afield as the Carpathians. Forestry was well developed and well organized, although it appears that arboriculture as such was little practised. New trees were allowed to grow naturally, but were systematically culled and thinned. Villagers tended the forests on their own or on the landowners' behalf. Felling began each November, the trees being cut by groups

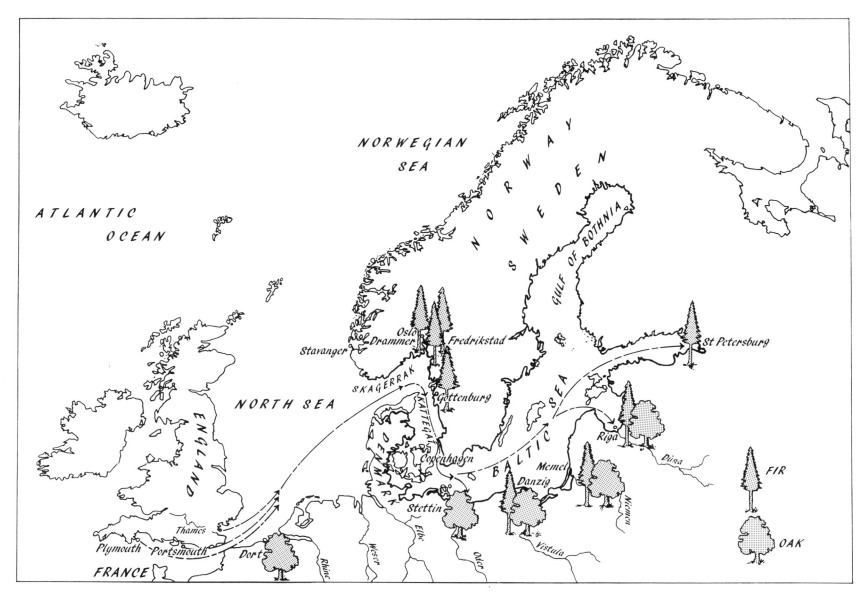

11 Northern Europe, showing the main areas that supplied oak and fir and related products to English yards

of villagers, and proceeded throughout the winter.

The whole of northern Europe is pierced by a number of large rivers which provided an ideal means of cheap transport for the unconverted tree trunks. Each of the main ports lay on or near a river mouth, and the timber was rafted down in the spring or early summer when the snows had melted and there was a good flow of water. The Vistula, Dvina, Nieman and Oder became scenes of great activity as the tree trunks, stripped of their bark, were chained together to form rafts, having been dragged to the water's edge over the winter snows. A mild winter could result in a lower output than usual as there were no roads or usable tracks over which the timber could be hauled by other means.

Oak was almost invariably brought down river with the lighter fir, a certain number of logs to each raft. It floated much deeper than the fir, and perhaps the reason that it was so prone to rot was because the logs were allowed to lie for long periods in fresh water before being shipped, and remained damp in the holds of transport vessels en route to England. If the subsequent seasoning was inadequate, it is hardly surprising that the timber acquired a reputation for being of inferior quality. Much of the timber was converted in the watermills along the course of the rivers or in the seaports. Here, unlike England, there was no prejudice against mechanization. A high proportion of wood, however, found its way onto the ships in a raw state.

The ships that carried the timber from the Baltic were a motley collection of vessels, usually between 300 and 400 tons burthen. This was, in fact, the average size of a merchantman at this period, although it seems very small, and was certainly much smaller than any of the Navy's rates. Roughly one ton of cargo was carried for each ton of burthen. Some ships were especially built to carry timber. They had bluff bows, flush decks and ports in the transom and bows for loading. The heavy timber such as oak went in the hold, with the longest pieces of fir on the top of the pile, but timber was also stacked high on deck.

12 The Thames at Wapping, 1762–71. Watercolour by John Hood. National Maritime Museum, Greenwich. Timber ships from the Baltic are shown discharging their cargo onto timber rafts and barges. The small portholes in the stern are for loading and unloading long baulks of timber

The size and shape of the cargo made it difficult to stow and keep in place, and the voyages were often hazardous, with the ships racked and strained by the rough waters of the Skagerrak and the North Sea. They were often leaky and cranky, but this did not deter the skippers, who drove their vessels unmercifully. During the relatively long voyage from Riga or Danzig to the London river – between 1000 and 1500 miles – the crew would build boats on deck. Presumably this was a perk of the job, just as chips were for the shipwrights.

With the length of the voyage, the costs of Baltic timber were high. The transport cost more than the timber. It is said that a tree felled in Poland and having a value of 5s was worth as much as £5 5s by the time it arrived in one of His Majesty's dockyards.

Apart from the Baltic, a certain amount of timber came from Norway and Sweden, particularly through the port of Gothenburg. However, it was considered to be inferior and was not much used by the Navy despite its relative cheapness, a result of the shorter sea voyage.

The American continent provided timber of a very high quality. From the New England states came white and red pine, and even oak, and from the Southern states and Central America came lignum vitae. This is a hard, durable, heavy wood, brownish green, even yellow, in colour, which, since it has a high wax (fat) content, is ideal for marine purposes. It was used extensively to make pulleys, shafts and bearings where the amount of wear was considerable, and also for mallet heads, particularly caulking mallets. The North American timber trade did not develop to any great extent until the nineteenth century, however, and was badly disrupted by the American War of Independence; overall the Baltic trade remained supreme.

It is difficult to emphasize too strongly the importance of the timber trade, especially in the eighteenth century. It was the key to successful war at sea, to international power, and it lay at the root of expansion into the modern world.★

★The best account of the timber trade, particularly in the Baltic, during the seventeenth and eighteenth centuries is to be found in Robert Albion's admirable treatise *Forests and Sea Power* (Harvard University Press, 1926). Although a scholarly work, it is extremely readable and cannot be recommended too highly for anyone wishing to delve further into the subject.

3

THE PURCHASE OF SHIPS' STORES

Because of its proximity to London – a major manufacturing centre in the eighteenth century – and to the Navy Office, the naval yard which held the largest and most comprehensive supply of ships' stores was Deptford. For example, most of the Navy's sailcloth requirement was delivered to this yard and then allocated to other yards. Occasionally, however, stores in transit would be redirected to other dockyards when they were needed urgently.

Each yard kept meticulous records, reporting regularly to the Navy Board on the state of their holdings of stores. One record shows the four yards on the Thames reporting jointly; Portsmouth and Plymouth are the subject of another; but Portsmouth – the largest and most important dockyard, and the major victualling yard in the eighteenth century because of its location and accessibility – also reported separately.

The scale of business done on behalf of His Majesty's yards was extensive, quite beyond that of most other kinds of commercial activity. In addition, there was a considerable amount of trade arising from private shipbuilding. It was the naval contracts which were the plums, however. A single contract for, say, masts, spars and deals might be worth £250,000 to a merchant in one year, equivalent to perhaps £25 million today.

The Navy Board controlled the purchase of all materials and stores. Each item was open to tender, or 'treaty' as it is referred to in the Admiralty records. First, the Navy Board would note the prices that had been paid for previous contracts; it would then set a price that it was willing to pay on a new contract and rarely did it have to exceed this amount. In the middle of the century prices remained remarkably stable. At times the Board tried to reduce the amount it was willing to pay for a contract; in 1755 and 1756 it offered less than had been paid previously, possibly

because it had done its homework and detected a glut or an increase in supply over demand of certain goods.

Often the Board set two prices, a maximum and a minimum, which, on paper at least, indicated a willingness to bargain within tight limits. Suppliers were then invited to submit tenders. Sadly, this elaborate system seems to have been largely a charade. In theory every supplier stood the same chance, and no doubt in some cases this was so, but there is evidence that bribes for contracts were the order of the day. Certainly, large contracts for timber went repeatedly to the same suppliers even when their quotations were not the lowest. Evidently bargaining went on behind the scenes and the records of treaties were merely window dressing.

A typical treaty is shown in Figure 13. Dated 26 February 1755, it shows that John Major, a leading timber merchant, had won the previous contract and was awarded this one, offering prices that in one or two cases substantially undercut those of his competitors. He had to be content with £61 13s 6d per load for his Danzig crown plank, as against £61 15s per load the previous year. The prices he accepted match the Board's offer for each item, although they were consistently lower than what the Board had paid before. So far as the Danzig crown plank is concerned, his original bid was so far below that of any of his competitors that one cannot but suspect that he had been advised what price to tender.

Where the timber was to be delivered is not specified in the treaty, but two thirds of the order was to be delivered by or before Christmas 1755 and the remainder by or before Michaelmas 1756.

An interesting feature of the treaty is the provision made for the extra costs of transporting the timber to Portsmouth and Plymouth if required. Prices quoted in the contract are for the London river, but supplements of £5 and £6 respectively were payable if cargoes were redirected to the two latter ports. The supplements were to be raised to £9 and £11 if conditions of war should prevail.

There were usually between three and six bidders for each contract, depending on the materials concerned. In this particular treaty the competition was between five merchants, whose names appear frequently on other treaties and contracts. One regular supplier of oak was John Richardson & Son. John Henniker was another important merchant, with the lion's share of the North American mast trade. He, and possibly others, chartered his vessels to the Admiralty during the Seven Years' War for transporting stores to North America and Europe.

Occasionally details of the bidding are to be found in the margin of a treaty. One such, in October 1755, concerned turpentine, and the bids were all well above the price set by the Navy Board. In August of the same year the Board had paid £7 2s 6d per barrel and now it wanted to pay only £6 10s. Eventually a Mr Hambledon accepted the price, although originally he had asked over £7 per barrel (of 32 gallons).

All goods were described exactly in the treaties, and their quality carefully specified. They were inspected on delivery to the yard by the Royal Purveyor, who reported his findings to the clerk of the cheque. Timber was measured and checked by a shipwright, or a number of shipwrights, whose specific task this was; other goods were presumably also examined by specialists before the Purveyor made his report. As with timber, the Navy Board reserved the right to reject inferior stores, or to reduce the prices paid for them.

In the main, contracts, certainly the big ones for timber, were granted for one year (twelve months) certain and six months' warning. Generally contracts were negotiated six months ahead of first delivery, most specifying the intervals of delivery, normally each quarter. Contracts were always made on behalf of a particular yard rather than for a particular vessel actually building there. However, it is possible to deduce that large pieces of timber, for example, were probably for the keels of ships being laid down at or near the time of delivery.

Occasionally long-term contracts were made. There is an excellent example on record, dated 28 May 1755, with John Henniker for New England masts. This agreement was for five years, and specified three or four loadings each year with at least seventeen loadings between Lady Day 1756 and Lady Day 1761. The specifications include some very large spars – masts of 30–37 inches and bowsprits 30–37½ inches in diameter.

After timber, the most important raw material was hemp, from which rope, cables, and canvas for sails, boat covers, wind funnels and the like, were made. Every ship used many miles of rope and cables in its rigging, had a sizeable sail area, and carried a good quantity of spare rope and canvas for repairs at sea. Today manmade fibres have virtually replaced hemp in shipbuilding, but in the eighteenth century it was the strongest, most durable material available for the purpose.

Hemp came from the Baltic, imported in hundreds of tons every year from Riga and St Petersburg. It was widely grown in Russia and Poland, where the sandy soil was particularly favourable to it. The plant was sometimes grown for its seeds, which yield an oil used in making paints and varnishes, but the stalks

13 Navy Office treaty showing rival tenders for supplying timber, 26 February 1755. Public Record Office, Kew

	Charles Dingley	Francis Wynant	John Major	
...nk & prussia Deals.				
.0	7. 2. 6	7. 7. 6	6. 15. 0	
			6. 13. 6 +	
7.0	0. 17. 6	0. 17. 3	0. 17. 0	
16.0	0. 16. 3	0. 16. 3	0. 16. 9 +	
			0. 15. 9 +	
15.0	0. 14. 9	0. 14. 6	0. 14. 0	*The Board agreed with Mr Jnᵒ. Major*
			0. 13. 9 +	*at the prices Corps wch'd ⅔ whereof*
14.0	0. 14. 0	0. 14. 0	0. 13. 0	
			0. 13. 3 +	*to be deliver'd by or before Xmas 1756,*
14.0	0. 15. 0	0. 14. 3	0. 14. 0	*and the remainder by or before*
			0. 13. 9 +	*Michˢ 1756 .*
13.0	0. 13. 9	0. 13. 6	0. 13. 0	
			0. 12. 9 +	
12.0	0. 12. 6	0. 12. 6	0. 12. 6	
			0. 12. 3 +	
11.0	0. 10. 9	0. 10. 3	0. 10. 6	
			0. 10. 3 +	
9.6	0. 10. 3	0. 9. 6	0. 9. 6	
			0. 9. 3 +	
9.0	0. 9. 3	0. 9. 0	0. 9. 3	
			0. 8. 9 +	
9.6	0. 0. 6	0. 0. 6	0. 0. 6	
			0. 8. 3 +	
0.0	0. 0. 0	0. 0. 0	0. 0. 0	
			0. 7. 9 +	
7.6	0. 7. 9	0. 7. 6	0. 7. 6	
			0. 7. 3 +	
---	7. 0. 0	6. 10. 0	5. 0. 0 +	
			9. 0. 0 if a war	
---	0. 0. 0	7. 10. 0	6. 0. 0 +	
			11. 0. 0 if a war	

produce straight fibres, or *line*, up to 6 feet in length which are ideal for rope and canvas.

The imported hemp was converted into canvas by private spinners and weavers, the contracts attracting keen competition. A treaty for canvas dated 20 February 1756 lists no less than nine bidders, all of whom were asking more than the Navy Board offered of 15s 4d per bolt for No. 1 canvas, which was the heaviest weight and used for sails of the largest vessels. Eight grades of canvas are listed: 44 oz (No. 1), 41 oz, 40 oz, 35 oz, 32 oz, 29 oz, 24 oz and 21 oz. The contract in this case was for Deptford from where the canvas was distributed to the various yards.

Rope and cables were produced in the Navy's own rope yards, the one at Woolwich being a reasonably large operation in its own right. Records show that the Navy also bought considerable quantities of cordage from private manufacturers such as John Shakespear, Griffith Hare and Charles Eve, whose names appear on treaties for Woolwich at this time.

Old, discarded rope was unpicked to make oakum – another important commodity – for caulking the seams of vessels to make them watertight. Much of the old cordage would have been already tarred to preserve it, but white oakum, from untarred rope, was also used. It was essential that no rotten cordage was unpicked for oakum.

Goat and cow hair, mixed with tar, was used to pay ships' bottoms and as caulking between the fir cladding and the oak planks of the hull. The hair came in both spun and loose form, spun hair being the more expensive. Goat hair, which is finer and therefore superior to cow hair, was preferred, although the treaty specified that up to 50 per cent cow hair could be supplied. Presumably goat hair could not be obtained in sufficient quantities to be used exclusively.

Tar was used as a general preservative on both the hull and the cordage. Considerable quantities came from the Baltic where it was produced as a byproduct in the distillation of turpentine. It was described variously as Stockholm tar (possibly the best-known name), plantation pitch (presumably because it was manufactured in the great forest plantations of Russia and Poland), and East Country tar. It was commonly mixed with tallow, brimstone and oil as a crude form of antifouling. Diluted with turpentine or mixed with oil or red ochre, tar was used to paint a vessel's sides, to protect the planks from splitting in the sun and wind. In *Thunderer*'s case, only her bottom and wales were tarred.

Tar was supplied in barrels of 32 gallons, known as *lasts*, an old Dutch measure. A common order would be for 1000 barrels. In the mid-century Andrew Lindgren, whose name occurs frequently in treaties of the time, was paid £12 12s per last.

Tallow, which is insoluble in water, was also used to treat timber. Described as winter-melted town tallow in the treaties, it was made from rendered beef and mutton fat. Masts were payed with it to stop any shakes collecting water and rotting. According to Falconer, hogs' lard and butter were sometimes employed for the same purpose. Tallow was also mixed with tar for paying the bottom of vessels. A specific use of tallow was as 'boothose tops' (now called boot topping): the top three strakes of planking below the waterline were payed with tallow as it was thought to make the ship slide through the water more easily. Tallow is no longer used for this purpose, but the practice remains in the custom of painting a different band of colour along a vessel's sides at the waterline. Most of the tallow was home produced, although some may have been imported in time of shortage.

Turpentine was used extensively as thinner for tar or wax and resin for paying a vessel's sides. As it hardens on exposure to air, it may also have been used as a simple varnish on cabin furniture. It was distilled from the resinous exudation from the bark of pine and fir trees, and formed a major byproduct of forestry in the Baltic countries. Although the Navy's requirement was large, turpentine must have been produced in sufficient quantities as bargaining for naval contracts was keen. Thus, in 1755 the Navy was able to buy at a price of £6 10s per barrel. The specification laid down that it should be double refined, so it may have been bought for medical purposes. For many centuries it was used as a liniment for sprains and bruises, and for rubbing on the chest against bronchitis and pleurisy. Most of the turpentine seems to have been delivered to Deptford from where it was distributed as required.

As a general varnish, resin, a gummy extract of pine trees, was mixed with turpentine for paying topsides, ship's boats and blocks. Again, double refined, 'without drop, clean and good', was specified by the Navy, but the description includes the word 'English', which implies that the double refining was carried out in this country, although the crude resin was imported. Unlike other commodities, its price seems to have fluctuated rather markedly around the middle of the century. In 1743 the Navy was only paying £6 15s per ton, but the price rose to £16 per ton in 1750, then fell to £7 in 1753. In April 1755 a quantity was bought from Peter Fortes & Son for £6 15s per ton. The Navy's annual consump-

tion seems to have been in the order of between 10 and 20 tons.

Falconer mentions the use of oil mixed with tar for paying the topsides. This must be what is called 'trayne oil' in the records. This was refined whale oil and was probably used as a lubricant and for cleaning iron guns to keep them free from rust.

Sulphur, described as 'brimstone' in the records, came from Spain and was an ingredient in the mixture used to pay ships' bottoms. It was thought to poison the worm which attacked the planking, but was not terribly effective. The problem was only really solved when copper sheathing was introduced in the 1770s. Powdered sulphur, or flowers of sulphur as it is commonly known, is a mild disinfectant. Burnt in a confined space, it was used to cleanse the interior of ships after long periods at sea or after an epidemic. It was almost certainly a standard item in the surgeon's limited supplies of medicine, both as a general disinfectant and as a laxative administered in weak solution in water, for which purpose it is still sold by chemists today.

An increasingly important material in shipbuilding as the years went by was iron. In 1756 it was still a very expensive commodity. Wrought iron could only be made in small quantities until the invention of the puddling process by Henry Cort in 1784. Until then, wrought iron, the purest form of iron which is malleable, not brittle, was made by hammering out the impurities, a slow and laborious process. Its all-important use on ships such as *Thunderer* was as fastenings and in forging the anchors. High quality was essential; and the best iron came from Sweden ('Best Swedes Iron'), being made from ore which contained very little impurity. Swedish iron came from Oregrund (spelled Orgrounds in the naval records), a small port just north of Stockholm. High-quality metal was also imported from Spain and a little came from North America. A small amount was produced at home. It is described as 'bar iron' or occasionally 'billets' in the records.

Around this time cast-iron ballast was coming into use. A certain amount was bought in by the yards, though the price of £27 5s per ton compared unfavourably with the cost of the normal shingle ballast. There is no evidence that iron ballast was used on *Thunderer*, though it is possible that some was used for trimming. Its great advantage was ease of handling: it took up less space and was easier to move than mountains of small stones when the ship needed to be inspected. Shingle must have been an undesirable form of ballast, harbouring wet and fostering decay, but it was easily obtainable and very cheap.

A slightly unusual item of ships' stores was glass, used for lanterns and for the windows in the after cabins. At this time sheet glass was made by the laborious and highly skilled method of blowing long 'bottles' which were then laid on a cast-iron slab and cut so they could be flattened. The size of the sheets, therefore, was limited by the size of cylinder a glass blower could blow. The description of the Navy Board's requirements makes interesting reading. The glass had to be stone ground to make it smooth, to be 'London glass in all respects', and the panes had to be well ground, well polished, clean, clear, substantial and good. The thickness required was a sixth of an inch, and the length from 7 inches to 16 inches, with a breadth within 2 inches of the length. The price varied from 1s for the smallest size up to 7s for pieces 16 inches square. A charge of 2d a piece was made for cutting. Glass was, therefore, an expensive item.

Among the small, ready-made items which were bought in very large quantities were treenails and hewed wedges. Treenails (or trunnels) were the commonest form of fastening used in shipbuilding at the time. They consisted of wooden pegs, rather like dowels, from 12 to 48 inches long, with a diameter of between ½ and 2 inches. To ensure a straight grain, they were split, rather than cut, from billets of close-grained Sussex oak, and then mooted, i.e. rounded, by hand to the required diameter. Once driven home, they provided a very tight fastening, the wood swelling as it became wet. In the middle of the eighteenth century they were cheaper to produce than iron fastenings.

They were supplied in their thousands by the large timber merchants and were finished outside the yard by freelance mooters working piece rate. A typical shipment into Woolwich in 1757 from Thomas and Henry Mills included eight different sizes of treenails varying in price from £1 2s 6d to £20 15s 0d per 1000.

Hewed wedges were also supplied in a finished condition. They were used extensively in ship construction, particularly to force planks into place. They were made from oak, elm or ash, and one treaty gives the following specification: 3½–4 inches at the head, and none to be less than 3 inches thick or under 16 inches long. The Navy Board paid £3 per 100 for those delivered to Woolwich.

Treenails were not the only items supplied by outside labour. Launching blocks, deadeyes, snatch blocks, trucks for flag staves, and blocks for running rigging were bought in as required. In addition, there was sail thread by the pound weight, lamp oil, coal, sand, chisel rods, and a hundred and one items without which the yard could not function smoothly.

4
THE DOCKYARD

In selecting a vessel to represent the wooden fighting ship, we naturally turned to the records of the British Admiralty where we were able to draw from first-class archive material carefully preserved since the eighteenth century. Thus it was that we settled upon *Thunderer*, a vessel built in what was perhaps the most famous of the royal dockyards: Woolwich, a microcosm of the larger yards.

It would be wrong to claim that the royal dockyards were exemplary institutions in the way in which they were organized and run. High productivity was not one of their virtues. In the middle of the eighteenth century the time taken to build substantial vessels was affected by the shortage of large pieces of high-quality oak, but it is hard to explain a ten-year building programme for the *Royal George* at Woolwich, or even a four-year programme for *Thunderer*,* by this fact alone. No records give reasons that can account for the delays. The Navy Board was riddled with dishonesty and there was probably a fair degree of slackness in the yards which must in part have contributed to the long building programme. Also, building was often interrupted by the ever increasing number of ships requiring repair. Private yards were probably more efficiently run of necessity, in order to remain in business.

However, such was the reputation of English shipyards in the eighteenth century that shipwrights came from all over Europe to improve their skills and learn about the organization of the operation. Frederick ap Chapman, an astute businessman who is widely regarded as the father of the science of naval architecture, worked in yards on London's river as a shipwright from 1741 to 1743. Chapman later established his own yard in Sweden and built up the Swedish royal dockyard at Karlskrona into a model of

*It should have been possible to build a 74 in half the time.

14 George III (1760–1820). Oil painting by Thomas Gainsborough. National Maritime Museum, Greenwich. In 1774 when *The King's Book* on the state of the Navy and royal dockyards was prepared, George III had a fleet of 338 ships, 143 of which were first to fourth rates. Of these, the largest number – fifty-seven in all – were 74s

its kind. The main countries involved in ship construction on any scale at this time were Sweden, Holland, France, Spain and England.

It is thanks to Samuel Pepys in the seventeenth century and to the increasing awareness of the need for rationalization in the eighteenth century that records of all kinds of activities were so carefully maintained, in particular those involving expenditure. There were detailed job specifications prepared for yard officers, records of purchases of timber and stores, payrolls listing everyone from senior yard officials down to the rat catcher, voluminous correspondence between the yards and the Navy Board, and careful minutes of Navy Board meetings, although these are not as full as one would like, recording only conclusions rather than discussions. In addition, there are the logs of captains, officers and masters, and detailed reports from yards and naval stations overseas. Altogether this adds up to a formidable amount of documentation. There are one or two serious gaps, however: some activities were not considered worth recording, and certain documents such as the yards' daily reports did not survive the clearout of the Record Office that took place at the beginning of this century. Nevertheless, enough material remains for us, drawing also on several of the excellent handbooks on shipbuilding that graced the eighteenth century, to form a good idea of how shipbuilding was conducted in the royal dockyards.

An invaluable account of the general state of the royal dockyards and the Navy in 1774 is contained in a report prepared for King George III, recorded in a beautiful leather-bound volume known as *The King's Book*.

The principal and largest yard was Portsmouth, its main advantage being the spacious roadstead, the largest in England or, for that matter, in the known world at the time. The report refers to the easy entrance for capital ships, while the dockyard, being situated on an island in the harbour, was easy to defend and was, in fact, heavily fortified. With the developments in naval warfare in the second half of the eighteenth century, indeed, even to the end of the Napoleonic Wars, Portsmouth was ideally situated to serve the fleet operating in the Channel and the Bay of Biscay. There was also a huge naval arsenal at Portsmouth, employing twice as many men as Woolwich and providing all manner of services and repairs.

Plymouth was only established as a royal dockyard in 1689, but grew to be the third largest in the kingdom. It was clearly the best port in the United Kingdom for squadrons cruising the Western Approaches, an aspect of naval activity that increased rapidly in importance with the expansion of the North American colonies. Plymouth is criticized in the report of 1774 only in respect of the narrow, crooked passage into the harbour, although it was not as disadvantageously sited as Chatham.

Chatham was the kingdom's second dockyard and, until the onset of the French wars brought Portsmouth to the fore, the main naval arsenal. It was founded during the reign of Queen Elizabeth I and remained of considerable importance despite the ravages inflicted by the Dutch during the reign of Charles II. It provided a safe, sheltered anchorage, especially after Sheerness was fortified on the orders of Charles II to guard the mouth of the Medway during the Dutch wars. A natural protection to the approaches to Chatham was the navigational hazards of the Thames Estuary, although they held no fears for the Dutch who had traded these waters for centuries. The Medway is a tricky river to negotiate and the large, eighteenth-century square riggers found its 15 miles of twisting channel difficult to navigate. For ships of the line (third rates and above) there were only 6 points of the compass on a favourable wind to sail down river to the Thames Estuary. Sailing up river was a little easier, with 10 points of the compass on a favourable wind. Even then there were only a few days per month during the spring tides when the water in parts of the channel was deep enough for the larger vessels. Tucked away in the correspondence in the middle of the eighteenth century is a plaintive note from the resident commissioner at Chatham to the Navy Office in London asking for permission to work on Sunday so

15 *Buckingham* on the stocks at Deptford, 1752. Oil painting by John Clevely the Elder (1712–77). National Maritime Museum, Greenwich. Clevely trained as a shipwright at Deptford before becoming a painter. His twin sons, Robert and John, also trained at Deptford, as shipwright and caulker respectively. Both later became artists. To the left of *Buckingham* can be seen the sheer legs for raising the stern assembly of a ship at an earlier stage of construction than *Buckingham*. Beyond is a team of four horses drawing a baulk of timber which has just been unloaded from a timber barge, and beyond them is a house or donkey crane. On the right are the gates to the graving dock, with sawpits in the background. At the river edge, in the foreground, is a latrine

that *Captain*, a third rate, and another similar sized vessel could be brought in and docked, thus enabling the yard to take advantage of the spring tides and save a whole month. Chatham continued in importance despite the more advantageous position of the Channel ports. Sheerness remained subordinate to Chatham, but helped relieve the problems posed by the navigational difficulties of the Medway.

The most remotely situated from the sea, Deptford performed the crucial function of grand magazine for the fleet and for other yards. All manner of naval stores were delivered in bulk to Deptford and redistributed to other yards and to naval stations overseas such as Halifax, Nova Scotia, and Gibraltar. The river at Deptford must have been a very busy place, with warships coming and going, and merchantmen unloading timber and other commodities from the Baltic and elsewhere. It was at Deptford that Peter the Great studied shipbuilding in 1697, and it would have been the natural yard for important foreign visitors to be attached to.

According to the 1774 report, neither at Deptford nor at Woolwich was it considered necessary to have a resident commissioner as the Navy Office was so near at hand. Both yards were under the immediate inspection of the Comptroller and Surveyor to the Navy. It is reported that the Navy Board had frequent occasion to send for officers from the Deptford yard for information and advice. The same practice must have extended to Woolwich, making these relatively small yards important in influencing shipbuilding policy. At Deptford the master shipwright was certainly asked to estimate costs of repairs to warships so that the Navy Board could assess tenders from private yards for undertaking the work.

As Deptford lay a long way up river on the narrowest reach below London Bridge, its building programme tended to concentrate on smaller vessels, although third rates such as *Hercules*, *Thunderer*'s sister ship, were built there. The river at that point has a relatively high fresh-water content, to the detriment of any vessel lying there for a long time – the bottom planking deteriorating faster in fresh water than in salt.

Woolwich, the first royal dockyard to be established, is referred to as the 'Mother Dock' in the 1774 report. It was regarded as more conveniently sited than Deptford for getting ships down river after they were launched. It was smaller than Deptford and 'will not contain a proper quantity of Timber suitable to the Works that otherwise might be carried on for Building and Repairs of Ships.' Nevertheless, many famous ships were built there.

The yard was founded by Henry VIII for the building of the greatest ship in his navy, the *Henry Grace à Dieu*, more colloquially and better known as *Great Harry*. In 1515 she was the largest vessel afloat. She represented a great feat of shipbuilding and established the reputation of the yard, which was to prosper, turning out some famous vessels over the years.

The status of Woolwich in the seventeenth century was due to the genius of the great shipwright, Phineas Pett, who was appointed master shipwright there in 1607. He was born at Deptford on 1 November 1570 and his first important appointment was as assistant master shipwright at Chatham in 1601. His skill in designing ships soon came to the attention of James I and he was appointed master shipwright at Deptford in 1605. His swift move to Woolwich was undoubtedly due to the fact that larger ships could be built there, thus providing more scope for his talents. These were not long in finding expression in the shape of one of his finest designs, *Prince Royal*, a very large vessel, said to be the first three-decker ever built. She started her career with 56 guns, but her armament was increased to 90 guns when she was rebuilt. The development of the three-decker was significant because it was to become the standard for the largest battleships in the fleet, with an armament of 100 or more guns.

The pinnacle of Pett's success as a naval architect came, however, in 1637, when *Royal Sovereign* was launched at Deptford. She was originally to have been called *Soverayne of the Seas* (and indeed, she is still referred to as such in some reference books). She was the largest vessel to have been built in England at that time, being 127 feet on the keel. This would have given her an overall length of around 160 feet. Her construction was the result of a whim on the part of Charles II, and was opposed by the Navy Board which thought she would be too large to be manageable. These objections were swept aside and, with all the flair and imagination of the skilful Pett, she took to the water as a three-decker, armed with 100 guns. At the time she was the most powerful warship in the world. In *The Ship* Bjørn Landström comments that she was ahead of her time so far as size was concerned. This refers to the limitations that the materials and methods of 1637 imposed on the skills of shipwrights. They were moving into a new era, but not without problems. Indeed, the breakthrough in

16 'Geometrical Plan and North Elevation of His Majesty's Dock Yard at Woolwich with Part of the Town', by Thomas Milton, 1753. National Maritime Museum, Greenwich

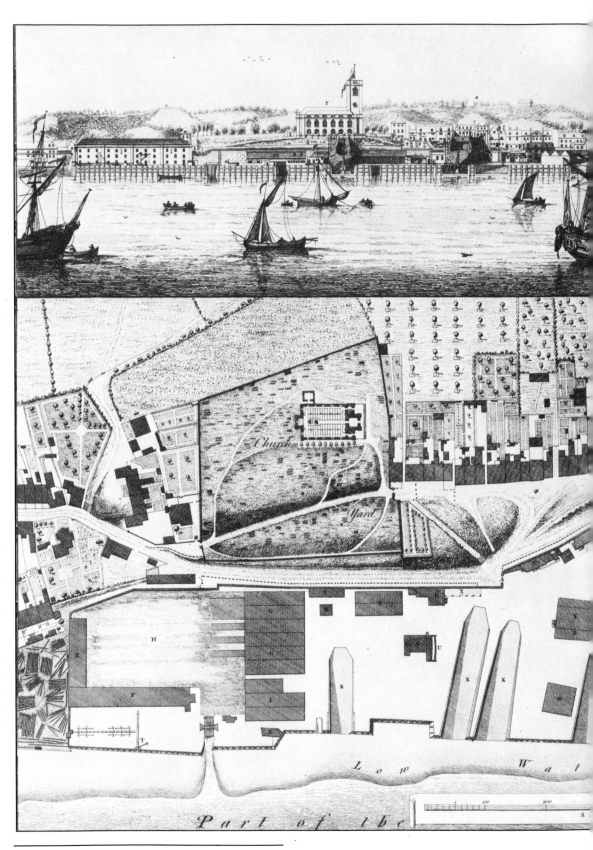

the building of *Royal Sovereign* was not capitalized upon for another 150 years.

Royal Sovereign had an outstanding fighting career. She was outstanding in other respects as well, being extensively decorated with heavy gilded carvings. She was probably the most expensive ship ever built to that date, and must have contained good-quality timbers as she was still in service in 1696 when she was accidentally destroyed by fire.

These were heady times for the small yard at Woolwich. A high proportion of ships of the line were built there despite the limitations of the yard and the narrowness of the river at that point. Of 131 ships of the line in commission in 1774, no less than twenty-one were built at Woolwich (and of course there were others 'in ordinary'). The *Royal George* and *Triumph*, which was really the first of the new order of third rates conceived by Anson, were built there, so the yard retained its innovating role late into the eighteenth century.

There are two specific sources of information that give an outstanding picture of the yard at this time. The first is an engraving made in 1753 by Thomas Milton in which the layout and north elevation is accurately shown to scale (Figure 16). The buildings at the west end of Woolwich can be clearly seen in the background, as well as various vessels in the docks and on the slips. On the river in the foreground is a sloop of war, but more interesting from our point of view is a hulk fitted with a crane, which was clearly used for hoisting masts into place and lifting heavy objects such as guns on board. The second is the detailed scale model of the yard built for George III in 1774 (Figure 17). It is one of a set showing all the royal dockyards in England and was clearly made to satisfy the king's preoccupation with good husbandry and provided the opportunity for an early form of time-and-motion study. It is extremely accurate, showing the arrangement of the yard buildings and even the positions of piles of timber.

With only a narrow strip of flat land by the river, Greenwich Marsh to the west and the town crowding in on the east, Woolwich dockyard was chronically short of space. There was no room to accommodate a ropeyard, a standard ropewalk needing to be at least 400 yards long. The ropeyard which supplied all the cordage for both Woolwich and Deptford, and yards overseas, was located half a mile away.

However, the main drawback of the confined site at Woolwich was the lack of adequate space to store timber. The report of 1774 strongly emphasizes the risks involved in allowing the levels of stored timber to fall below what was considered adequate for maintaining a fleet of serviceable ships. The main danger in yards with restricted storage space was that it was impossible to use timber in rotation. The tendency was for shipwrights simply to take whatever piece of timber came most readily to hand, usually that at the top of the pile. The timber at the bottom of the pile, even if properly seasoned and with air spaces left in between the pieces, was extremely vulnerable to decay, and the rot simply spread to new timber added to the pile.

By careful planning, however, the yard accommodated five building slips and two graving docks, one of which was, in fact, a double dock, capable of taking two vessels, one in front of the other. As can be seen from the plan, it was angled to make best use of the space available. Graving was the term applied to the act of cleaning a vessel's bottom by breaming, i.e. burning off the fouling, and then reapplying tar. The term probably originated from the Old French word *grave* or *grève*, meaning 'shore'. With small vessels this process could be carried out by allowing them to dry out on the shore, but larger vessels, such as ships of the line, had to be heeled over on one side while afloat or docked so that there was no appreciable weight on the bilge of the vessel which could be supported along its whole length.

The essential purpose of the docks was the repair and cleaning of existing vessels. At low water, the gates to the river were opened so that the dock filled as the tide rose. The ship could be floated in when the water was deep enough for the vessel to clear the blocks laid along the bottom of the dock. The vessel was carefully lined and, with the gates to the river closed, the water was pumped out of the dock.* The ship could then sit upright on the blocks, supported along the sides by substantial shores at frequent intervals. When the dock was empty, work could begin on the bottom of the ship. In 1760 this would commonly have consisted of renewing the fir cladding, caulking leaking seams, rudder repairs and a general inspection of the fastenings.

The graving docks were also used for building first and second rate vessels as these were too large to be built on ordinary slips. In the double dock it was possible to have a ship under construction in the top end while using the lower part of the dock for repairing vessels. Large vessels could also be launched simply by flooding the dock until they

*At Woolwich the graving docks emptied as the tide receded. Later graving docks made use of pumps as well, so that the fall in the level of the water could be more easily controlled.

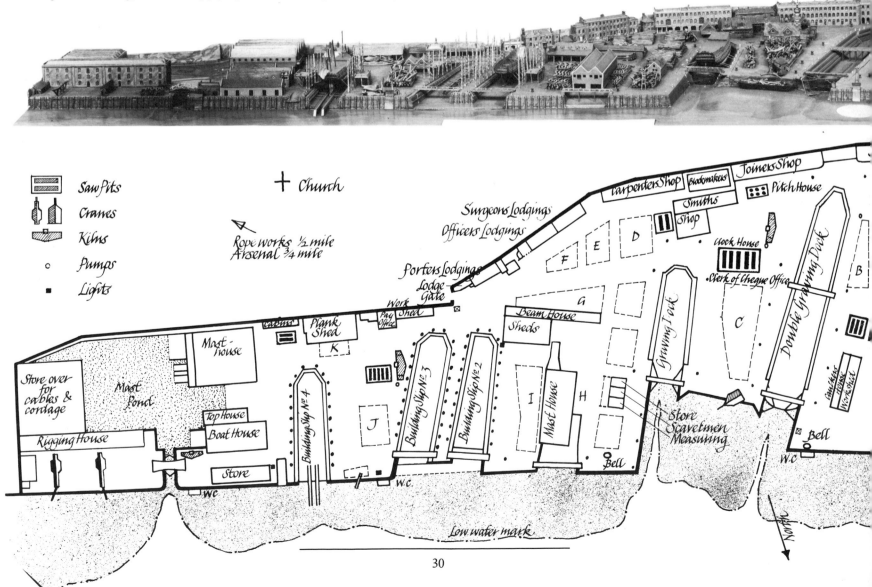

17 Scale model of Woolwich dockyard built for George III in 1774. British Crown Copyright: Science Museum, London. Of ships of the line in commission at this time, twenty-one had been built at Woolwich, according to *The King's Book*

A 540 loads of rough timber
B 60 loads of sided timber
C 180 loads of rough timber
D 180 loads of sided timber
E 110 loads of sided timber
F 66 loads of sided timber
G 310 loads of rough timber
H 60 loads of rough timber
I 180 loads of rough timber
J 216 loads of rough timber
K 20 loads of rough timber

18a and **b** Details from the model of Woolwich dockyard. British Crown Copyright: Science Museum, London

a: Slips nos. 2 and 3, with sawpits in the foreground. Top right is the mast house which was built over a slip. The main dockyard gate is on the extreme left. The hull under construction is that of a sixth rate at framed-up stage.

b: The dry docks. On the left *Mars* is under repair in the single graving dock. On the dock side a house crane unloading timber from a timber barge. Between the two docks is the clock house which contained the offices of the clerk of the cheque. It was built over some sawpits. On the right is the mould loft, with a timber store beneath

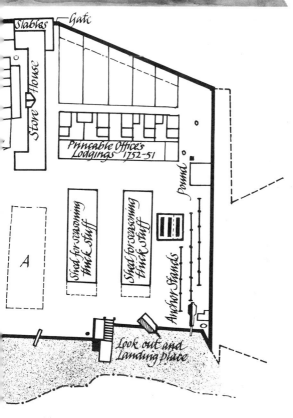

19, 20, 21 The Royal Rope Works, Woolwich, 1700. In 1513 Thomas Allen was commissioned to build a rope house at Woolwich. There was no room for such a large organization in the dockyard itself, so the ropeworks was situated on the east side of the town some 200 yards from the quay at which the hemp and cordage were handled. On a contemporary sketch plan of the yard it is stated that the cables and hemp were carried to and from the wharf on men's shoulders, and that the route was very hilly, with the men having to cross Woolwich High Street as they journeyed to and fro.

It was generally accepted that the best naval ropes came from England in the eighteenth century and the naval ropeyards had a high reputation. Woolwich was large – the spinning sheds were over 100 feet long – and had a considerable output, supplying Deptford and other yards. Large quantities of cordage were handled. In the Christmas quarter, 1759, wharfage, cranage and carrying charges were paid for the handling of some 3600 tons of rope.

For the same quarter the following numbers of men are recorded as having been employed at the works: 133 spinners, of whom four were assistants to the master spinner, who were paid from 14d to 22d per day (the top rate went to the master ropeman, Cuthbert Andrus, who earned £100 a year); nineteen hatchellers, who were paid 17d per day; twelve winders-up at 16d per day; thirteen labourers at 15d per day; and eleven boys at 6d per day. In addition there were twenty-four watchmen who were paid 46s a quarter. The clerk of the ropeworks, Henry Hemson, who was in charge of the administration, was paid £100 a year, with an additional £1 for papers. He was assisted by the ropeyard clerk, Charles Smith, who was paid £40 a year and who also received £3 17s 6d a quarter for inspecting the watchmen and attending the gate in the mornings and during the time of setting the watch in the evenings. A second clerk, John Atkinson, received £30 a year.

The rope was made from imported hemp and came in two basic forms: cable-laid and hawser-laid. Cable-laid rope, which was used primarily for running rigging, consisted of nine strands, three large strands each made up of three smaller strands. Hawser-laid rope, for anchor cables, mooring lines, etc., had three strands each containing a certain number of rope-yards in proportion to the size of rope required.

In the first stage of ropemaking, the hatchellers drew bundles of hemp fibre through a series of steel pins set in a wooden block called a hatchel; several hatchels were used with progressively finer teeth. The fibre, or streaks as it was called at this stage, was then spun into yarn. In Figure 19 the spinners can be seen at work spinning streak fibre into yarn (top left). The spinning wheel served twelve spinners at once, the wheel providing the drive for twelve hooks to which it was connected by a pulley belt, causing them to revolve at high speed. The streak fibre was tied to the hooks and as they revolved so the spinners walked backwards, paying out the streak from round their waists. To stop the yarn from sagging, it was suspended over a series of hooks set in a horizontal rail which ran down the length of the ropewalk. An experienced spinner could spin 1000 feet of even yarn in twelve minutes. The yarn was then wound up on winchels to make sure that it was all the same size.

Next a given number of yarns were tied to each of three hooks, known as whirls, on the table wheel (Figure 19, top right). The more yarns, the bulkier the rope. The table wheel was either powered by a large wheel and pulleys, as shown in Figure 19, or it was cranked by hand with three forelock hooks as shown in Figure 21. This method was presumably used for larger ropes. Later in the century an iron jack was used instead of the table wheel.

The three groups of yarn, or strands, were tied to the three whirls at one end of the ropewalk and to an iron forelock bolt on a sledge at the

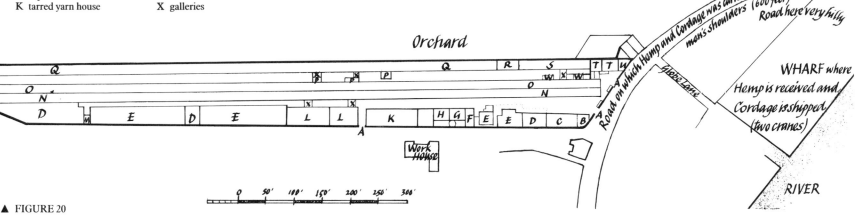

A gateway
B clerk of the ropeyard's office
C cordage house
D master ropemaker's house and gardens
E clerk of ropeyard's house and gardens
F iron loft
G white yarn
H tarring house
I capstan house
K tarred yarn house
L tar cellars
M stables
N laying house } hemp loft
O spinning house } over
P line spinners' sheds
Q new spinning house (two floors)
R parting loft
S hatchell loft on upper floor
T weighing house
U master ropemaker's office
W sheds
X galleries

Orchard

To Dockland → High Street

Road on which Hemp and Cordage was carted and carried on men's shoulders (600 feet)

Road here very hilly

Globe Lane

WHARF where *Hemp is received and Cordage is shipped (two cranes)*

Work House

RIVER

0 50' 100' 150' 200' 250' 300'

▲ FIGURE 20
◀ FIGURE 19
▼ FIGURE 21

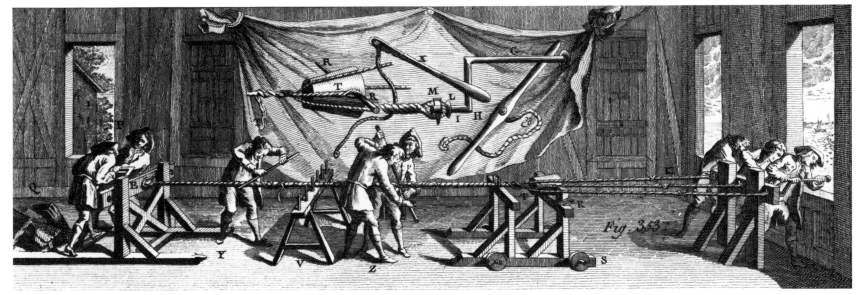

other. The strands were supported by a stake head and pegs along their entire length. They were now ready for winding. First, the layer took his top, a conical wooden block with three grooves, one for each strand, and placed it close to the sledge to stop the strands from getting tangled as the twisting began. The winder then set the whirls spinning. As the strands were spun, so they contracted; once they had shrunk by a quarter of their length, they were twisted as much as possible without kinking.

The winder then continued cranking the whirls and the layer started to walk steadily along the ropewalk with the top. This forced the forelock bolt in the sledge to revolve on its own, forming the rope behind the top as the layer walked towards the table wheel. This process resulted in a medium or soft-laid rope. To make hard-laid rope, the forelock hook on the sledge had to be cranked also (Figure 21), and the layer would walk more slowly. The top was sometimes set on wheels.

The rope was finally pulled to shape with a woolder. Then the ends were removed from the whirls and the forelock hook and whipped with twine.

The rope was now finished.

Before it left the ropeyard much of the rope was treated with tar to preserve it. The tar was heated in large kettles or coppers which could hold between ten and twenty barrelfuls of tar. The rope was drawn through the tar by means of a capstan or crab.

Figure 19 shows 'The Practice of Ropemaking with Tools', from David Steel, *Elements of Mastmaking, Sailmaking, Rigging, etc.*, 1794. Photo: National Maritime Museum, Greenwich. Figure 21 comes from *Encyclopedie Methodique*, 1787. Photo: Science Museum, London

33

floated out. This was a particular advantage on a busy, narrow waterway such as the Thames at Woolwich, although Woolwich Reach was by no means the narrowest and most difficult stretch of water in the upper reaches of the river below London.

It was in the large double dock at Woolwich that *Royal George* was completed in 1756. The story of how she capsized and sank at Spithead in 1782 while repairs were being carried out to an underwater pump inlet is famous in naval annals. Between 800 and 900 people lost their lives, including 358 women and children who were on board prior to the vessel's departure overseas. Her commander, Rear-Admiral Kempenfelt, famous as a pioneer of naval signal communication, went down with the ship, which sank very quickly.* Although never actually proven, the cause of the disaster was thought to have been rot in the main structure amidships to such an extent that the hull collapsed when the ship was heeled to bring the offending pump inlet above water level. Possibly the knees joining the main gun-deck beams to the hull failed, causing the structure around them to collapse. Since *Royal George* took ten years to build, it is not unlikely that parts of the ship were rotten before she was launched.

In Woolwich dockyard we have a compact, but restricted, shipbuilding organization, laid out as well as space would permit. It may not have been ideal, but represents a good standard for the mid-eighteenth century. As can be seen from the engraving, town and dockyard merged into one. Backed by the low hills of Kent, which today are covered by the urban sprawl of southeast London, the town was situated 9 miles from London Bridge on the first stretch of the river with deep water. The houses of the town were only separated from the dockyard wall by the mere width of a street. There were two gates to the yard, with a porter presiding at the main one. The walling of the yard was a simple precaution to safeguard the large amount of valuable stores contained within. The yard employed forty-eight watchmen on a casual basis, most of whom worked during the hours of darkness. Despite this, a great deal of pilfering must have gone on, especially from the river side which must have been particularly difficult to patrol.

With the aid of the model and the plan (Figure 16), it is possible to take a short tour of the yard and see precisely what it contained. Starting at the eastern end, the visitor would first see the mast pond. This all-important feature was linked with the river via

*R.F. Johnson, *Royal George*, C. Knight, 1971.

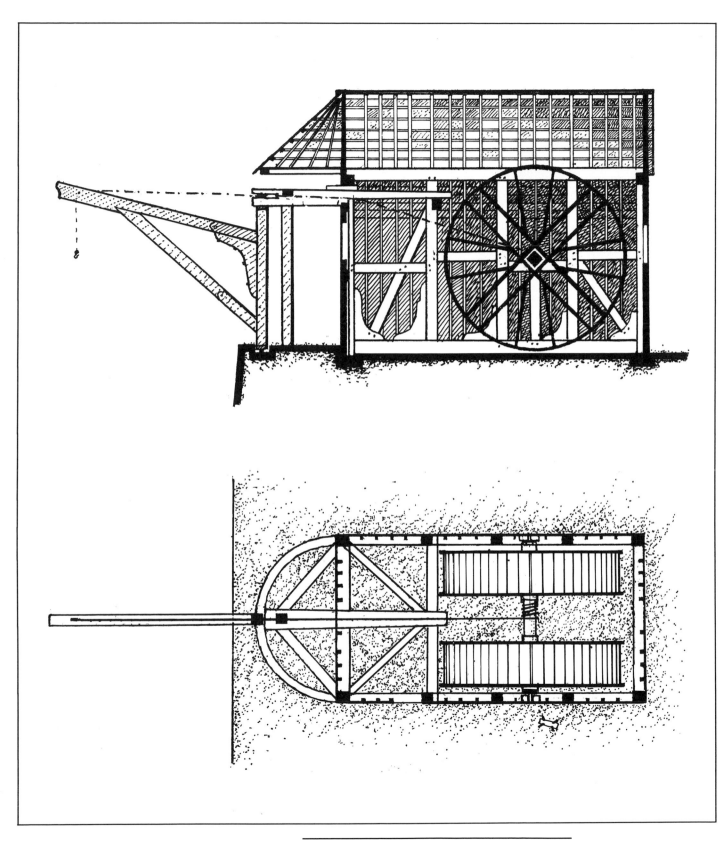

22, 23 The dockyard crane. The oldest wheel cranes were probably used for raising blocks of masonry, roof timbers and bells in building the great medieval cathedrals. A number of wheel cranes survive from the end of the seventeenth and beginning of the eighteenth centuries. These had only one drum and manpower had given way to donkey power – hence the terms donkey wheel and donkey engine.

An excellent example of a dockyard crane can be seen at Harwich. According to Pepys, in March 1666 the Duke of York visited Harwich where he found the yard to be in very bad condition. Orders were given for better equipment to be installed and steps were taken to improve the administration. As a result of his visit, estimates were submitted for a house crane similar to the one in use at Woolwich. Shortly afterwards a crane was erected at Harwich for £392.

No confirmation can be found that a crane with a fixed housing as shown in Figure 23 existed at Woolwich, but it is safe to assume that cranes of the Harwich type were in common use at that period. In the 1774 model (Figure 17) the two cranes at the eastern end of the dockyard are of a crab type; the two to the west are house cranes in which the whole house pivots. A crab crane can be seen in Figure 24.

The crane worked on the treadwheel principle. The operators walked inside the drums, winding the chain round the common axle. This gave an approximate purchase of 16 to 1. Two drums gave a more balanced action. Each drum was 16 feet in diameter and 3 feet 10 inches wide. The jib projected nearly 18 feet and could be swung in an arc of 90° on either side. Curiously, there appears to have been no brake or ratchet. If one of the operators was unfortunate enough to slip over, then the men might well have been spun round as the object they were trying to lift fell

gates which could be opened to allow fresh timber to be floated in or the water to be drained from time to time before it became too stagnant. The mast pond was used for the long-term storage of spars to prevent them from drying out and developing shakes, or long splits which run along the grain of soft woods such as fir if the timber is allowed to dry out too quickly. The poles were marshalled in the pond on delivery, where they were pickled in salt water and mud, then taken to the nearby mast house for drying out as required.

By the pond was the rigging house where the riggers worked, splicing ropes, preparing deadeyes and generally mustering the complicated cordage for rigging new ships and repairing existing ones.

Next, opening directly onto the river, came three building slips, numbered in succession from the east 4, 3 and 2 on the plan. The next slip later served the mast house, which was built over it, as the slip up which the heaviest masts were dragged after being floated round from the mast pond. Over the mast house were the treenail house, where the treenails were mooted and stored, and the armourer's stores.

The yard widened out to the west, and this was where the graving docks were situated. Their entrances were set back from the river. After the double graving dock came slip no. 1 and beyond this

24 A sixth rate on the stocks. Oil painting by John Clevely the Elder. National Maritime Museum, Greenwich. In the eighteenth century some of the permanent staff lived in the dockyard with their families

Building Work at Woolwich between 1751 and 1761*

	Size (length/ beam)	Rate	Guns	Begun	Launched	Tons	Loads of timber	Cost of hull
Falmouth	144/41	4	50	22.8.46	7.12.52	1047	2425	£19,974. 4. 8
Ranger	75/20½	Sloop	8	27.1.52	7.10.52	140	225†	£2381. 3. 3
Dunkirk	153/43	4	60	1.4.46	22.7.54	1246	2562	£20,379. 4. 8
Happy	76/20½	Sloop	8	26.9.53	22.7.54	140	225	£2230. 5. 2
Squirrel	107/29	6	20	19.3.55	23.11.55	404	1086	£7272. 2. 5
Royal George	178/15½	1	100	8.1.46	18.2.56	2047	5756	£54,661. 2. 10
Princess Amelia	165/47½	3	80	15.8.51	7.3.57	1579	3541	£37,562. 2. 8
Boreas	118/34	6	28	21.4.57	29.7.57	587	1086†	£6314. 9. 10
Trent	118/34	6	28	19.5.57	31.10.57	587	1086†	£6929. 1. 11
Rippon	155/42	4	60	23.11.52	20.1.58	1229	2365	£27,486. 6. 1
Mars	165½/46½	3	74	1.5.56	15.3.59	1556	3342	£32,889. 2. 9
Thunderer	166½/47	3	74	17.9.56	19.3.60	1609	3713	£33,044. 7. 2
Blenheim	176/49	2	90	1.5.56	5.7.61	1827	3968	£44,780. 15. 6
Romney	146/40½	4	50	1.10.59	8.7.62	1046	2151	£21,952. 0. 0
Triumph	171½/50	3	74	2.1.58	3.3.64	1825	3028	£31,399. 9. 9
Canada	170/47	3	74	1.7.60	17.9.65	1605	3405	£28,988. 6. 6
Total						18,475	40,825†	£378,240 8s 2d

*Between 1756 and 1760 a further twenty-one vessels were repaired.
†Approximately.

Chronology of the Work Carried out at Woolwich from 1746 to 1765

1765	1764	1763	1762	1761	1760	1759	1758	1757	1756	1755	1754	1753	1752	1751	1750	1749	1748	1747	1746	East
		*Romney** fourth rate 50 guns					*Boreas**		*Woolwich transport**		*Happy**		*Falmouth* fourth rate 50 guns							Slip 4
*Canada** third rate 74 guns			*Thunderer** third rate 74 guns				*Squirrel**		*Dunkirk* fourth rate 60 guns											Slip 3
		*Mermaid**	*Mars** third rate 74 guns						*Ranger*			*Orford* third rate 70 guns								Slip 2
This slip made into a mast house						*Rippon* fourth rate 60 guns				*Dolphin*										Slip/ masthouse
			Tavistock (being made a hulk)					*Essex* (repair)	*Peregrine*											Single graving dock
Queen second rate 90 guns			*Blenheim* second rate 90 guns				*Royal George* first rate 100 guns				*Adventure* (repair)									Double graving dock
Triumph third rate 74 guns			*Trent*		*Princess Amelia* Third rate 80 guns				*Savage*	*Lancaster* (rebuild) 66 guns										Slip 1

← Seven Years' War →

← George III →|← George II → West

*Conjecture.

---

and crooks of oak, most of it in a rough state. A certain amount was sided, i.e. cut on opposite sides. It was in these piles that dry rot grew apace.

For dealing with the rough and semi-finished timber, the yard had twenty-two sawpits, accounting for the forty-four sawyers employed. Conversion of timber into sided timber was part of the yard's work.

In the plank shed, which was more or less centrally sited, the planks were finished before being fitted into place on the hull. This was a very skilled job, especially when planks had to be fitted to a curved part of the vessel.

Clustered against the outer wall of the yard were many of the workshops. These were of a lean-to construction. The smithy was situated within easy reach of the various slips and docks. Nearby was the clock house, any one of its four faces clearly visible from any point in the yard.

One of the most important and largest buildings housed the sail and mould lofts. The sail loft was simply a large open building, on the floor of which the panels for the sails were cut and sewn. The mould loft, which is described in detail in chapter 6, was the brain centre in the construction of any vessel. The accuracy with which the draughts were enlarged determined how closely the shape of a finished vessel corresponded to her model and the original design.

Between 1756 and 1760, while *Thunderer* was being built, the yard was very busy due to the Seven Years' War, with twenty-one vessels being repaired and fitted, surveyed or sold. A letter from the Navy Board to the Admiralty on 18 May 1757 comments that 'no slip or dock at Woolwich is unemployed'. In 1756, starting at the west end, *Princess Amelia*, a third rate, was being finished off on slip no. 1. She was followed by either *Trent* or *Boreas*, neither of which would have taken more than a few months to build. Ten months after *Princess Amelia* was launched, the third rate *Triumph* was begun. In the double graving dock *Royal George* had just been completed and work started on *Blenheim*, a second rate. In the single graving dock *Tavistock*, a fourth rate of 50 guns, was being converted into a hulk. This meant that she was being cut down to deck level to be used for storage or as a floating crane. *Rippon* was being built on the slip that later had the masthouse built over it. In all probability *Mars*, a third rate, was building on slip no. 2, having been started four months earlier than *Thunderer* on slip no. 3. The last slip, no. 4, could have been used for either *Boreas* or *Trent*, and then *Romney*, a fourth rate. *Adventure* was being repaired and fitted at the bottom of the double graving dock while *Royal George* was being built.

---

two large, open-ended sheds for seasoning timber. Here the imported softwood was stacked with spacers between each layer so that the air could circulate freely and the timber, protected from rain and snow, could dry out naturally over a period of time. The results of using unseasoned timber would have been noticed relatively quickly as it changes shape as it dries out. If stacked correctly, with air circulating through the pile, the timber could dry out without any marked distortion.

Great heaps of timber were stored throughout the yard, between the buildings and the ships under construction. No less than seventeen stacks are shown on the model. They consisted of large baulks

The Launching of the 'Adventure', Blackwall Yard. Oil painting by Francis Holman, 1767–84. National Maritime
Museum, Greenwich

5
THE SHIPBUILDERS

Of all the industrial organizations that flourished in the eighteenth century, the dockyard must rank as the most complex, involving no less than twenty-six different trades, either skilled or unskilled. A high degree of management was required to run such an operation, which in many respects can be regarded as one of the forerunners of modern industrialization. Indeed, the first real example of mass production, a workshop for making blocks, was set up in the royal dockyard at Portsmouth at the end of the century.*

Administering the dockyards was the Navy Board, which was responsible for putting into effect the decisions of the Admiralty Board. It consisted of twelve officers, of whom at least seven were master shipwrights. It frequently acted in an advisory capacity to the Admiralty Board on the practical aspects of shipbuilding, victualling and stores.

The commander of each dockyard as a naval base was the port admiral, an admiral of the Navy on shore duty. However, the senior officer responsible for the shipbuilding activities was the resident commissioner, who was appointed by and nominally a member of the Navy Board. He and his subordinates were civilian naval officers, i.e. they were not sea-going, and their various tasks and duties were meticulously laid down by the Navy Office. As we have seen, Woolwich had no resident commissioner at this time, the running of the yard being carried out by seventeen senior officers. These were part of the established staff, that is, permanent staff paid out of what was known as the ordinary vote of funds for the Navy. According to the records, their salaries were paid on a quarterly basis. They were assisted in the enormous amounts of paperwork by sixteen clerks, quaintly referred to in the payrolls as 'instruments to the officers', who were important enough to be regarded as junior officers. The yards also had a number of officers, called 'shipkeepers', responsible

for ships nearing completion or laid up in reserve (described as 'in ordinary') or afloat but without a full crew, usually undergoing repair. All other employees were unestablished, which effectively meant that their numbers fluctuated with the working requirements of the yard. They were paid out of the extraordinary vote of naval funds, which frequently became a matter of great dispute in Parliament, which was only too aware that the Navy could soak up money as a dry sponge absorbs water.

*Blocks and deadeyes were made by hand until the invention, in 1799, of a blockmaking machine by the French-born Sir March Isambard Brunel, father of Isambard Kingdom Brunel. He offered his invention to the British government and, prompted by the vast demand for blocks occasioned by the war against France, the Navy Board uncharacteristically voted for the immediate adoption of the machine. The first ones were installed at Portsmouth where they were a great success. Ten men working the forty-three machines were able to do the work previously done by over a hundred men. One source says that in 1808 they produced 130,000 blocks, previously the output of 110 blockmakers.

Dockyard posts were highly prized positions since they carried good salaries and offered a high degree of security. They also afforded the opportunity to augment one's official income by bribes and perquisites. Many abuses were finally stamped out towards the end of the century, in particular the practice of accepting cash from suppliers for contracts awarded. In any event, the senior ranks of yard officer were paid sufficiently well to make corruption unnecessary, particularly when compared with employees in other industries. So far as security of employment was concerned, the royal dockyards provided a fair degree of permanency because of the naval expansion that took place in the eighteenth century.

On a day-to-day basis, the yard was administered by the clerk of the cheque and by the storekeeper. As his title indicates, the clerk of the cheque was responsible for the finance and for ensuring the smooth functioning of the yard. His job specification was a formidable document which laid down that he must supervise every conceivable aspect of the yard's operations. For this he received £150 per annum, which, supplemented by 'payments from other sources', would have been regarded in eighteenth-century England as adequate for maintaining a respectable middle-class existence. Such a salary was probably equivalent to between £12,000 and £15,000 today, but as there was no income tax at that time and as people's expectations were relatively modest, this particular dockyard officer was probably somewhere near the top of the professional tree.

Working closely with the clerk of the cheque on the adminstrative side was the storekeeper, who was also paid £150 per annum. He carried great responsibility, having charge of a vast range of stores covering everything from timber to provisions. The large amount of paperwork entailed in both these jobs is reflected in the fact that both were paid annually £5 'more for papers' and were allocated five clerks each. In 1759, the senior instrument to the clerk of the cheque received £45 per annum, two were paid £40, and the remaining two £35 and £30 respectively. The storekeeper's instruments were paid at the same rates.

In charge of the building and repair work was the master shipwright, assisted by a number of subordinate officers. In a sense he was the most important man in the yard, looked on with respect by the artificers and exerting a far-reaching influence since he was the chief technician. He was paid £150 a year, and rated a clerk at £45 per annum, £3 more for papers, and two senior assistants, who were each paid £80 per annum, the second doubling as master caulker.

Closely associated with the building and repairs was the clerk to the survey, who was responsible for making surveys of ships coming into the yard for repairs, and for examining prizes to see if they were in a fit state to be taken by the Navy, with or without repair. He was also paid £150 per annum, and had three clerks, paid £45, £40 and £35 per annum respectively.

Finally, among the senior officers paid £150 per annum was the master attendant, who was the harbour master for the yard. He was responsible for all craft belonging to the yard, which comprised boats for transferring men from ship to shore, store ships and hoys for ferrying stores, plus mooring any vessels afloat off the yard, docking or laying up, and for Woolwich transport (barges). His chief assistant was the boatswain, who was responsible for the rigging both for new ships and for those in for repair. The boatswain also checked the anchors and cables of ships in the yard. Rated as a yard officer, he was paid £70 per annum.

Other important officers included the purveyor, whose job it was to ensure that all supplies needed were actually ordered, and the various master craftsmen of the main trades: the master mastmaker, the master boatbuilder, the master joiner, the master house carpenter, the master bricklayer, the master sailmaker, and the master smith, who would have made the anchors and various iron bolts and fittings. A surgeon regularly appears on the pay lists, indicating that work in a dockyard was not without its risks. Paid £100 a year, he was apparently an important member of the yard's establishment.

In every royal dockyard was a measurer, whose function was to ensure that the correct amounts of timber were delivered. A measurer's shed is shown on the plan of Woolwich dockyard (Figure 17). An

Ordinary Officers at Woolwich, 1 January to 31 March 1759	
	Quarterley wage
Clerk of the cheque: James Butler Morn	£37 10s 0d
Storekeeper: Hezekiah Hargood	£37 10s 0d
Master attendant: Walter Taylor	£37 10s 0d
Master shipwright: Isral Pownoll	£37 10s 0d
Clerk to the survey: Ezekial Pomeroy	£37 10s 0d
Master shipwright's assistant: George White	£20 0s 0d
Master caulker and second assistant to master shipwright: James Mooringe	£20 0 0d
Boatswain: Richard Dutton	£17 10s 0d
Purveyor: George Goldsworth	£15 0s 0d
Surgeon: Jeremiah Fitcher	£25 0s 0d
Master mastmaker: Isaac Weeks	£11 11s 0d
Master boatbuilder: Richard Luallett	£11 11s 0d
Master joiner: Andrew Doe	£9 12s 6d
Master house carpenter: Mathew Ellery	£9 12s 6d
Master bricklayer: Martin Smith	£9 12s 6d
Master sailmaker: Joseph Pratt	£11 11s 0d
Master smith: Joseph Rippington	£10 19s 0d
Porter: Hezekiah Woodall	£6 5s 0d
as keeper of the plugs	£2 5s 0d
Rat killer: John Edwards	£1 0s 0d
Keeper of the clock: Simeon Hill	15s 0d

Also on the ordinary pay roll were the clerks or 'instruments to the officers', the nightwatchmen, and the skeleton crews for eleven vessels.

example of how much a man was paid is found in a document relating to Plymouth for the period from 31 December 1783 to 1 January 1785:

To measure and keep account of all English oak timber of every species whatsoever, all Dantzig and Norway timber of every kind and to mark in the contracts for the same. Also work carried on by contracts . . . likeways taskwork performed by House Carpenters, bricklayers and stone masons on jetty heads, slips, wharves, etc.   £50 11s 0d
Other allowances   £10 6s 0d
Servant as shipwright   £91 13s 6d for attending the receipt of all English and foreign timbers, planks, deals, sheathing board, etc.
Measuring, costing and keeping account of all works carried out by contract.

Henry Symonds, master shipwright measurer at the crane (that is, the dockyard crane where the timber was unloaded from the timber barges), was paid 2s 6d per day.

Another member of the ordinary staff of the dockyard was the porter, on duty at the yard gate to check on who came and went. At Woolwich he was also given the title of 'Keeper of the Plugs'. This strange-sounding task was essentially very simple, albeit necessary. All the ships and boats in the yard were fitted with bungs or plugs which had to be removed on the ebb tide to drain the water that had collected in them. This was to save having to pump them out. The keeper simply had to remember to take the plugs out at ebb tide and put them back on the flood. For this important, indeed essential, task he received £10 per annum. The yard also employed forty-seven watchmen, who were paid £2 6s on average for forty-five nights and one and a half days; they normally worked at night.

Also on the ordinary staff were a rat killer, paid £4 a year, and a keeper of the clock, whose duty it was to see that the yard clock, clearly visible on the model of Woolwich, kept good time. At Woolwich the job appears to have been undertaken by the chief instrument to the clerk of the cheque, thus adding to his salary £3 per year.

Most of the figures given above for the number and salaries of officers apply to Woolwich in 1759. Clearly, there would be some variation in other royal dockyards, although the overall picture was probably similar.

The extraordinary employees at Woolwich during the period that *Thunderer* was being built numbered around 1000 men, of whom the largest group was made up of shipwrights – 454 in 1756, falling to 399 in 1760 as the demands of the Seven Years' War were met. The following table is drawn up for these two years only. No compass maker or oar maker is listed, but both these trades were practised at nearby Deptford.

The rates given in the table are averages only, and it is not exactly clear how the wages were worked out. For example, Stephen Barefoot, a shipwright, was paid at a daily rate of 2s 1d. However, for working 74½ days, 10 nights and 135½ tides, his quarterly wage was £13 6s 4d and he was charged lodging of 2s 6d. Foremen appear to have been paid at a slightly higher rate. Bridg Hatchman, foreman shipwright, and John Puckey, foreman afloat, were both paid 3s a day.

In the Christmas quarter, 1756, there are several examples of contract work. For example, a paviour

Extraordinary Staff at Woolwich			
	October 1756	January 1760	Average daily rates
Shipwrights	454	399	2s 1d
Quarterboys	20	12	8d
Caulkers	27	30	2s 1d
Oakum boys	21	11	6d
Joiners	32	29	2s 0d
House carpenters	43	39	1s 10d (or by the task 6s 6¼d, 6s 8d, 7s 0¼d)
Wheelwrights	2	2	2s 0d
Plumbers	1	1	2s 6d
Pitch heaters	1	1	1s 3d
Bricklayers	9	10	1s 10d (or 5s 2d per task)
Bricklayer's labourers	13	13	1s 2d
Sailmakers	26	27	1s 10d
Scavelmen	37	30	1s 3d
Riggers	30	24	1s 6d
Rigger's labourers	17	10	1s 2d
General labourers	195	180	1s 2d
Blockmakers	1	1	2s 1d
Braziers	1	0	2s 6d
Locksmiths	3	3	2s 6d
Teams (1 man, 4 horses)	5	6	6s 8d
Watermen	1	1	2s 0d
Smiths	19 }	55	1s 8d
Hammermen	61 }		
Treenail mooters*	1	0	
Paviour*	1	0	
Masons	0	0	
Coopers	0	0	
Lime burners	0	0	
Armourers	0	0	
Compass makers	0	0	
Sawyers*	44	44	
Oar makers	0	0	

*Paid on a piece rate.

James Morehouse, paved 1868 yards at 2¾d per yard, receiving a total pavement of £21 8s 1d. In all the naval dockyards the areas surrounding docks and slips were paved with flat, square stone slabs, and keeping them in good order was a constant job, but it was obviously more economical to employ men on contract when repairs needed urgent attention.

Treenail mooting was largely a cottage industry paid on a piece work basis. In 1756, treenail mooter, Richard West, working on contract, is recorded as having produced the following:

Treenails of 30 in long	700	@ 1s 9d per 100
27 in long	6300	@ 1s 6d per 100
24 in long	6325	@ 1s 3d per 100
21 in long	4100	@ 1s 1d per 100

Unfortunately the records do not show how quickly he worked, but he was paid a total of £9 0s 2d.

There is evidence that a certain amount of outwork was done by women. In the Christmas quarter, 1759, Elizabeth Blake, a widow, was paid the sum of £27 16s for making lashings and spun yarn. The rate for the job was 2s per hundredweight.

The Shipwright

Of all the trades involved in shipbuilding in the eighteenth century, the shipwright was supreme. Originally the term covered a wider range of work, including mastmaking and boatbuilding, but by the 1750s these had become sufficiently specialized to be considered separate, highly skilled trades. The shipwright proper was responsible for work on the hull and his skills could only be acquired by a long apprenticeship, seven years being the time laid down by the Company of Shipwrights. An apprentice – known as a quarterboy – was indentured to the master shipwright in a yard, and was put to work with an older, more experienced man, thus at the same time giving him a hand with the heavier jobs. He was prevented from leaving the yard until his time was served and he had proved himself competent. He then had the right to call himself a shipwright capable of commanding a daily wage. Only then could he freely offer his skills elsewhere.

Woolwich had one notable shipwright's apprentice between 1771 and 1778, when Samuel Bentham, brother of the philosopher Jeremy Bentham, was indentured to the master shipwright there. Bentham went on to become an important naval architect. As adviser to the Russian Navy, he developed a type of explosive shell, but as a naval architect he is possibly best known for the Arrow class of sloop used by the British Navy in the French and Napoleonic wars.

By the eighteenth century the design aspects of shipbuilding had been taken over by naval architects. This situation was engendered as much by the size and complexity of the ships as by advances in design techniques, which had remained fairly static since the sixteenth century. However, by this time it had been recognized that the design of any ship of notable performance was a matter of applying scientific principles; the basis of naval architecture as a scientific skill, calling for mathematical knowledge and a study of hull shapes and rigs as well as an intimate understanding of the mechanics involved in building a strong hull, had been established.

However, English shipwrights of the eighteenth century flourished, working for the most part in well-ordered surroundings, particularly in the royal dockyards. They were regarded as a strategic body of men, of more importance to the nation than, say, the army or even the crews that manned the ships they so ably built. As early as the reign of Henry VIII, it had become apparent that the wealth and power of the nation lay in its ability to dominate the seas, and that a standing navy was infinitely more crucial than a standing army. Shipwrights already were high in the structure of sixteenth-century society, a position they were determined to maintain, especially in view of the increasing number of merchant ships required as overseas trade grew, particularly with the Far East and North America.

The Company of Shipwrights was instituted in the reign of James I and was to become an exceedingly influential body with the right to view and approve draughts of ships to be built for the king. The Company had a master, two wardens and sixteen assistants. The first master in 1605 was Matthew Baker, followed by Phineas Pett, who was sworn in in 1607. Meetings were held at the King's Head in New Fish Street in the City of London. In 1612 a new charter was approved, incorporating the Ship-wrights of England, with Phineas Pett as master. In April 1638 it was also established by warrant from the Lord High Admiral that carpenters should not be appointed to ships until they had been examined and licensed at Shipwrights' Hall. By 1700 membership of the Company was 1780, rising to 3776 by 1800.

Among its many recommendations and rules, the Company of Shipwrights saw to it that sick pay was given to members unable to work due to illness or injury. Sick pay was laid down as 2s 1d per day for a maximum period of six weeks. The Company even went so far in its enlightenment as to lay down superannuation payments for different classes of shipwrights if they were incapacitated as a result of injury at work or if they had achieved uninterrupted service of thirty years. The sum varied from £20 to £24 per annum.

With the pattern of employment that existed in the eighteenth century, a journeyman shipwright might work for a number of different yards in close proximity in a single year. One of the reasons for the concentration of yards on the Thames, for example, was that they were able to share the available labour and no yard need employ more men than it actually needed. That this is true of the royal dockyards is doubtful. The muster lists show considerable continuity of service each quarter for shipwrights and certain other craftsmen and although there were natural fluctuations between years of peace and war, these yards seem to keep consistently high numbers of men other than the ordinary (permanent) staff. Perhaps this is due in part to the fact that men were

willing to pay for their jobs, in much the same way as suppliers of timber and other stores were willing to pay to get contracts. There is no evidence of this, but it would be consistent with the policy exercised by the officers of the yard in respect to other matters. A berth in a royal dockyard would have been worth having,

compared with taking one's chance on the open market. In the 1750s we know from the rolls that a journeyman shipwright could command 3s per day, to which he could add his right to offcuts of timber up to 3 feet long, and, presumably, any other perks that came his way. This was at a time when a country

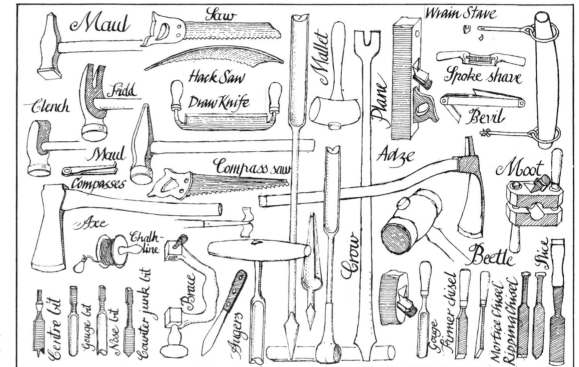

25 The shipwright and his tools. Two different methods of using an adze are shown. Shaping wood with an adze was known as 'dubbing', from the characteristic noise the tool made as it hit the wood

labourer might consider himself fortunate indeed to earn such a sum in a week; more likely he would have to be satisfied with a paltry 1s for the same period.

The highest position a shipwright could attain in the yard was that of master shipwright, whose function was to ensure that the building plans were faithfully executed and that work on the vessel proceeded smoothly. He was effectively in charge of the building and head of the day-by-day work. A master shipwright, if he was diligent and considered suitable, could be invited to become a member of the Navy Board, a position of some influence and importance, with a say in how warships should be designed.

Many shipwrights were also expert wood carvers up to the middle of the eighteenth century, when more elaborate decoration on ships was abandoned. At one time there was a school for wood carvers at Portsmouth. Probably the best-known decorator of ships was the Frenchman Pierre Puget, who ran his own workshop in Toulon in the seventeenth century.

As shipwrighting encompassed so many different skills, it is virtually impossible to describe a standard kit of tools for the trade. However, there are a number of tools common and necessary to any man working on the preparation of timber and the building of the hull. Where he owned his own tools, the shipwright might have made them himself, or bought them made to measure from a skilled toolmaker or blacksmith.

The most popular and best-known tool, still to be seen in use, was the adze. The shipwright's adze had a longer blade than those used in other trades, being roughly 9 inches long, and the handle had a double curvature. In the hands of a really skilled man, the adze was (and is) capable of performing the most delicate operations in shaping and finishing timber. It was equally good on the flat or the round, such as shaping masts and spars. Sharpened to a razor's edge, it could be used to finish the surface of a plank to almost the same standard as that achieved with a joiner's plane.

Here it may be pertinent to comment on the quality of the steel used for tools by the eighteenth-century shipwright. The very method by which it was made – continuous hammering of iron with the addition of pure carbon – ensured that the final product was carefully tempered and free from impurities. The result was a steel which would hold its edge very well, and cutting weapons of the time, made by skilled armourers, were of the highest quality. Indeed, the eighteenth-century shipwright enjoyed tools of a very high standard, better perhaps than the mass-produced tools of later centuries.

Of the other tools used by the shipwright, axes and saws were the next most important. The shipwright's axe was used for rough work, preliminary to the use of the adze. A good shipwright would ensure that his axe was well balanced and fitted his hand. He probably had several axes of varying sizes in his kit. The commonest saw was the handsaw, similar in appearance to the carpenter's handsaw of the present

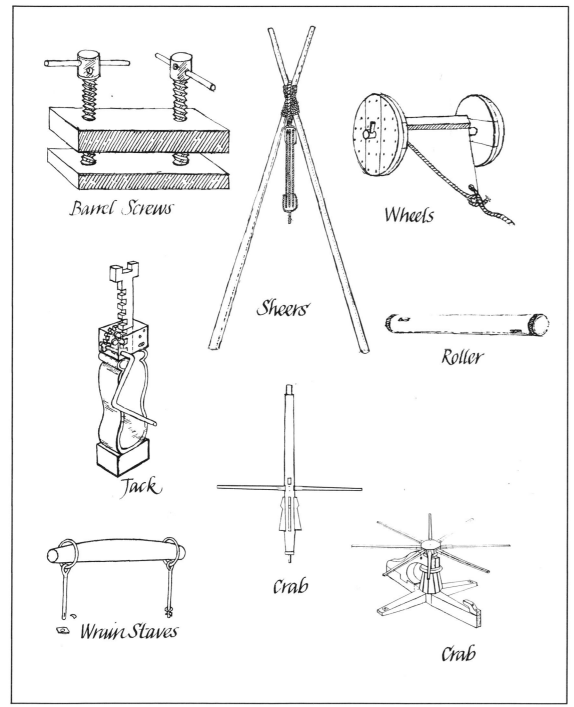

Barrel Screws

Sheers

Wheels

Jack

Roller

Crab

Wrain Staves

Crab

26 The shipwright's engines. Barrel screws were used for forcing heavy timber into place. They were also used as driver screws when launching the vessel (see page 109)

day. The shipwright would also have used pit saws from time to time, especially the narrow rib saw designed for curved work.

Chisels and gouges were essential components of any shipwright's kit. They were mostly of a heavier type than those used by joiners, and many were made with long blades and wide cutting edges. The blades measured up to 3 feet in length; the longest would have been used for cutting and trimming the socket holes in the capstan head.

A ship's maul, which was a long-handled hammer nearly 3 feet in length, must have featured in any set of tools. It had a head weighing anything from 1½ lb to 8 lb and was used for driving spikes, treenails and bolts. There was also a variety of smaller hammers. Other commonly used tools included augers, wooden braces and bits, scrapers, and caulking irons and caulking mallets. For new vessels, caulkers were engaged separately from shipwrights, but every shipwright was capable of performing the all-important function of rendering the seams between the planking watertight. A shipwright might also have a spoke shave, a draw knife and an all-iron splitting-out chisel.

The difficulties facing the eighteenth-century shipwright stemmed from the heaviness of the work, with great baulks of timber to be handled, and the fact that all operations had to be carried out by hand. One example will suffice to give some idea of the painstaking slowness with which his work progressed. To take the bolts which bound together the keelson and the floors, numerous holes had to be drilled through solid timber up to 12 feet thick. A stemhead bolt would involve a hole up to 20 feet long. To drill the holes, a special auger, made from a long iron rod, with a pod at the cutting end, was used. The diameter of such an auger would not have been less than 1½ inches and it would have to pass through solid oak and elm. As soon as the pod was filled with woodshavings, the auger was withdrawn and the pod cleared. It could take two men a week to bore one hole, painstakingly turning the auger with an iron bar or brace. Thus the hole deepened steadily but slowly until it broke through. After the holes were bored they were reamed out with a hot iron to clean and harden them, as well as to provide a certain protection against rot, it being recognized that scorched wood did not rot so easily.

Holes also had to be bored for treenails, some of which were as long as 4 feet. Driving the treenail through the hole required skill and patience so that the wooden peg was not broken in the process. Once home, the treenail's ends were cut off and split and wooden wedges driven in to force the pin to an even tighter fit.

These were typical of the tasks of the eighteenth-century shipwright, requiring skill, patience and time, which the craftsmen of that age still clearly possessed.

The Caulker

The caulker (also spelt *calker* in 1760) was second in importance to the shipwright, receiving only slightly less in pay than the latter, and sometimes even the same. At Woolwich the master caulker was second assistant to the master shipwright, which underlines his superior position. His services were required throughout the entire life of the ship, from the moment the keel was laid until her last repair. On him rested the responsibility for seeing that the ship was watertight, that none of the decks leaked, and that all the seams in the hull were filled.

Figure 27 shows a caulker at work on the gun deck. In practice he would have had an apprentice – an oakum boy – in attendance to keep him well supplied with materials, to roll the oakum, to see that the pitch in the ladle was kept hot and generally to hand him his tools. The oakum consisted of old hemp ropes, untwisted and pulled apart, then rolled, a task performed by the oakum boys, but later a favoured occupation for prisoners in His Majesty's gaols. Also at hand would have been a water engine (fire engine) since the oil and pitch used by the caulker presented a constant fire hazard, as did another of the caulker's jobs, that of breaming the ship's bottom to remove fouling. Caulkers at work breaming a small boat in the yard can be seen in Figure 91.

The verb 'to caulk' possibly derives from the French word *calage*, meaning hemp. Caulking involved driving strands of hemp oakum into the seams of the planks and into the butts where one plank joined another. On the topsides of a large ship, for example, this would entail driving home three strands of oakum one after another. No matter how well the planks fitted together, they were still caulked as the ship's structure would move considerably after she had been at sea for a short time. Caulking could only be satisfactorily accomplished with seasoned timber which would not dry out and cause the oakum to fall out. After the oakum was driven home, it was covered with hot melted pitch or resin to prevent rotting in the water.

Caulkers were expected to complete a set number of feet per day, though they were not actually paid on a piecework rate like the sawyer (see below). The

27 The caulker using a creasing iron on the gun deck and, opposite, his tools

customary allowance or stint for caulking planks from 1½ to 10 inches in thickness is as follows:

Thickness of plank (inches)	Threads of oakum Black	White (untarred)	Hair	Length of seam for one day's work	
1½	1	1	0	43 ft	0 in
2	1	1	0	32	0
3	2	2	1	23	0
4	2	3	1	18	0
5	3	3	2	16	6
6	4	4	2	16	0
7	5	4	2	15	0
8	5	5	2	14	6
9	5	6	3	14	0
10	6	6	3	13	6

These figures were probably based on the average rate at which a caulker could work. Note the use of hair in the seams of planks 3 inches thick and upwards. This was a mixture of goat and cow hair, expensive, but cost was no impediment so far as His Majesty's ships were concerned. It was used below the waterline where bilgewater tended to collect and oakum would have rotted.

The caulker's tools are also shown in Figure 27. The basic tools were a rave for cleaning out the old oakum from the seams, a mallet, the best of which were made of lignum vitae (it was important for the mallet to be a good one as the ring of the mallet on the iron told the caulker when the caulking was well and truly home), caulking irons – sharp ones for the first stage of driving the oakum into the seam in small loops, creasing irons for finally driving the oakum home, specially shaped ones (e.g. the horsing iron) for awkward corners, and reaming irons for opening out seams prior to caulking – a pitch ladle, and an oil box with linseed oil for dipping the irons to keep them from sticking in the seams. The logger heat was heated in a fire and plunged into the ladle to keep the pitch hot. A short scraper would be used for removing the surplus pitch from the seams. A special treenail iron was used for caulking the ends of treenails inside and outside the hull.

For breaming, the caulker needed special tools: a breaming fork for holding bunches of burning faggots against the hull; scrapers, probably made to individual designs for taking off the detritus; and a tar brush and pitch pot for tarring the bottom after breaming.

Sutherland in his *Shipbuilding Unveiled* gives some useful details of materials used by caulkers. Here is his table of requirements for caulking a ship of 1700 tons, close to the size of *Thunderer*, in 1717:

Waterline upwards		
Black oakum	20	hundredweights
White oakum	5	hundredweights
Oyl	18	gallons (trayne oil or linseed oil)
Pitch	6	barrels
Tar	2	pounds
Thrum*	14	pounds
Leather	1	pound
Twine	1	pound
Candles	16	pounds
Buckets	8	
Lashing	2	coils
Deals	30	
Workmanship	£47	

*Thrum was coarse rope yarn used for mops, instead of tar brushes.

Thunderer was completely recaulked on arrival at Gibraltar in May 1760 after her maiden voyage, an indication of the frequency with which this task had to be done.

For graving a 1700-ton ship in 1717, the requirements were as follows:

Waterline downwards		
Rozin	20	hundredweights
Oyl	55	gallons
Brimstone	3	hundredweights
Thrum	25	pounds
Twine	2	pounds
Leather	2	pounds (for renewing the flaps on the scuppers)
Reeds	3200	bundles (for burning off)
Broom	2800	bavins (if no reeds)
Sweeping brooms	9	dozen
Pitch	5	hundredweights
Burning poles	24	
Double buckets	20	
Men	30	(probably one of the most onerous jobs for some of the labourers in the yard)

The resin, oil and brimstone were used as antifouling.

The Sawyer

Although a certain amount of timber was converted in or near the forests, most of the oak and elm was dealt with by the yards. Sawyers retained the right to convert timber by hand as late as the nineteenth century. On the Continent sawmills, driven by wind or water power, or by horse gin, were in common use, but in England the sawyers successfully resisted mechanization.

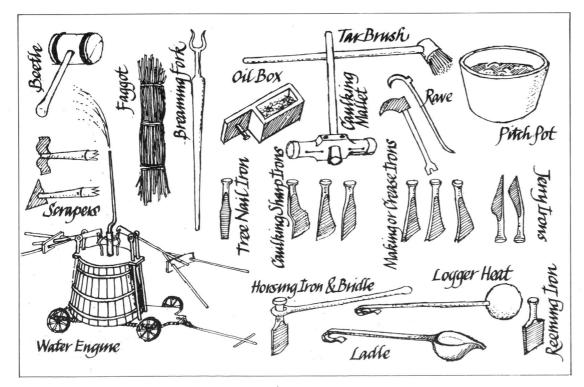

Beetle — Faggot — Breaming fork — Tar Brush — Oil Box — Caulking Mallet — Rave — Pitch Pot — Scrapers — Tree Nail Iron — Caulking Sharp Irons — Making or Crease Irons — Jerry Irons — Water Engine — Horsing Iron & Bridle — Logger Heat — Ladle — Reeming Iron

For converting large pieces of timber sawpits were permanent features of the royal dockyards. They were oblong pits, deep enough for a man to stand upright, and lined with boards (probably elm as it is resistant to rot when wet). Access was by a ladder or set of permanent steps at one end.

Sawyers worked in pairs, the pitman in the pit itself, with the second man, known as the topman, on top. The timber to be cut was laid on baulks, as shown in Figure 28, and held securely in place with timber dogs – D-shaped iron fastenings with a sharp point at each end, rather like large staples. The men worked as a close team, with the topman drawing the saw and following the line of cut, and the pitman acting as the donkey, pushing the saw along so that the sawdust fell in front of him rather than in his eyes. Other sawyers would have been occupied in sawing smaller pieces of rough or sided timber.

For converting timber, sawyers were paid by the 100-foot run, the highest rate – 3s – being for oak, presumably regardless of thickness. Fresh cut or newly seasoned oak is not particularly hard in comparison with the matured wood, but the work must have been heavy nevertheless. Using oak as a common denominator, Sutherland gives a table showing the comparative hardness and density of different kinds of wood used in shipbuilding and the relative rates of 100-foot runs.

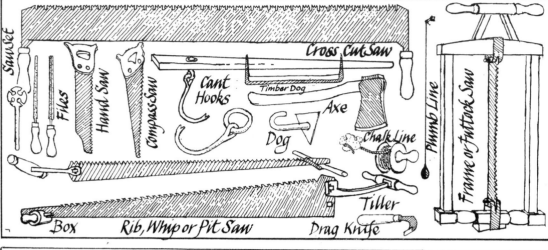

Oak to elm is in weight as 13 to 9
Oak to fir is in weight as 8 to 5
Oak to beech is in weight as 95 to 93
Oak to ash is in weight as 21 to 20

(1 cubic foot of oak weighs on average 56 lb, elm 43 lb, and fir 40 lb)

Rates per 100-foot run:

Oak	3s 0d
Elm	1s 1d
Fir	1s 10d
Beech	2s 11½d
Ash	2s 10½d

The topman, being the more highly skilled of the two, received 1s 8d out of the 3s per 100-foot run for sawing oak, with the pitman receiving 1s 4d, an equitable apportionment of earnings in the ratio of 5 to 4. To give some idea of the rate at which sawyers worked, in the Christmas quarter of 1756, William Ryecroft and John Reading sawed 14,091 feet of elm and fir; and between 26 October and 31 December in the same year, William Perry and William West sawed no less than 15,265 feet of oak and 545 feet of elm, earning between them £23 11s 6d, which does not seem a large amount for such heavy work.

In general, sawyers were responsible for keeping their own saws sharp, but occasionally a man was employed for the purpose, probably when the saws were owned by the yard, or when the yard was very busy and speed was crucial. There is a note in the Woolwich records that a man was employed in the Christmas quarter, 1756, when a large quantity of

28 The sawyer and his tools. Sawpits are thought to have been first used in the middle of the eighteenth century. Before that timber was sawn on trestles using a frame saw

timber, especially oak, was being cut, specifically to whet the two-handed saws used in the pits. He was paid 4½d per saw and sharpened 373 large saws during this period.

The sawyer's tools are shown in Figure 28. The frame saw, with its narrow blade supported by a frame, was ideal for cutting futtocks or any other large, curved pieces. It went out of fashion in the 1750s in England as the quality of steel improved, but continued in use on the Continent for a relatively long time. The cross-cut saw was used for cutting across the grain. The pit saw, which was used for cutting long pieces of timber, had a removable box at the lower end so that the saw could be slipped out through the cut when the timber needed adjusting on the baulks so that the sawing could proceed. The cant hooks were used for canting, or turning, the timber; the dog would have had a rope attached to the hook and was used for hauling pieces of lumber. Other tools included the sawset for bending the saw teeth, files for sharpening, and a drag knife for marking out timber before cutting.

The Smith

The smithy at Woolwich, with its six double-bellow and eight single-bellow furnaces, required the services of sixty or more smiths and hammermen at any one time, an indication of the enormous amount of ironwork needed for building wooden ships. Iron fastenings were used on all parts of the hull outside the main planking and lining, and these had to be manufactured on the spot. They ranged from simple nails and spikes to quite large and complicated ring bolts, all of which were hand-forged. Only the finest wrought iron was used, much imported from Spain and Sweden until the invention of the puddling process by Henry Cort in 1784 opened the way for cheaper, home-produced iron. However, in 1759, when *Thunderer* was being completed, wrought iron was still made by the expensive, labour-intensive method of hammer-welding. Iron billets, square in section, were first hammered into hexagonal profile and then rounded.

There was a basic set of patterns for iron fastenings, and illustrations of these can be found in contemporary nautical dictionaries, for example, Sutherland's *Shipbuilding Unveiled*. The largest bolts were used through the knee of the head and could be up to 20 feet long with a diameter of 1½-2 inches. These were made from bolt staves – long, square rods of iron. On the keel of a 74 not less than 100 bolts, each some 17 feet long, were used, with eight through each keel scarph, more through every frame, with alternate ones being driven through the floors to the keelson. The bolt holes were bored with a fractionally smaller

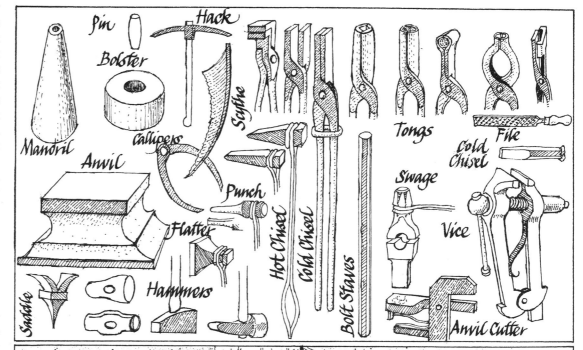

29 Smiths and their tools. The basic forge and anvil are similar to those in use today. Hearth staves, for clearing the fire or removing large cinders, are shown leaning against the wall with some long bolt staves. Also shown are the grindstone and a tub of water for quenching pieces of hot iron. The vice is of a type which can still occasionally be seen today.

For heavy work, such as forging anchors, the smith would use a trip hammer; one version, known as the Hercules, is shown in Figure 32

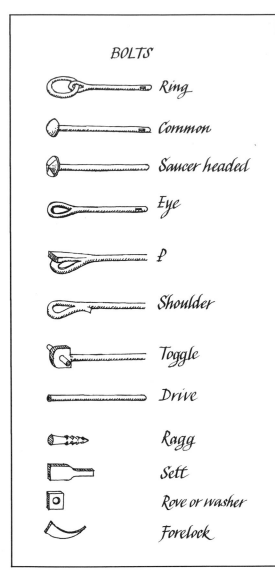

BOLTS

- Ring
- Common
- Saucer headed
- Eye
- P
- Shoulder
- Toggle
- Drive
- Ragg
- Sett
- Rove or washer
- Forelock

30 Various types of iron fastenings

diameter than the bolt they were to carry. Sutherland gives a table of recommended auger sizes for bolts of different diameters, a ½-inch auger being used for a bolt of ¹⁄₃₂ inch diameter.

Until the invention of the thread-cutting lathe by Maudsley,★ which enabled accurate threads to be tapped, bolts were not tightened with nuts, but clenched over a metal washer or square plate. Clenching consisted of simply hammering the bolt end so that it mushroomed out over a washer while the head was held against another hammer. The

whole bolt would swell up and shorten, a process which actually strengthened the metal. The result was a very tight fastening. Clenched bolts were used on all permanent features such as main frames, knees and planking. Another form of fastening was the forelock (its use with wrain staves is shown in Figure 84) for bolting chain plates and eyebolts. The forelock was a bolt with a slot cut near the end into which a wedge was driven home and then bent over. This had the advantage that the forelock could be removed more easily than a clenched bolt. They were later replaced by threaded bolts and nuts.

Other types of bolt included eyebolts to take various tackle hooks on the ship's decks and sides, fender bolts, which were driven into the ship's wales to protect the hull from damage when coming alongside another vessel or docking, and a variety of ring, sett and wrain bolts. One special bolt was the ragg bolt, which had a barbed shank and was designed to hold securely in relatively inaccessible places where clenching was not possible.

Other common fastenings were iron nails and spikes, used, among other things, for attaching deck planks to the deck beams. Where planks butted onto each other bolts were used for extra strength. Sutherland defines spikes simply as the largest size of nails. At this period nails were all forged by hand and great care was taken in tempering the iron to give it a medium degree of softness, thus ensuring that it was not too brittle, otherwise it would break when being driven home. Nails were either sharp pointed or flat pointed, the latter being invariably smaller and shorter than the former.

Later, where copper fastenings were thought essential below the waterline, copper or an alloy of copper, zinc and tin was used. Iron has a serious disadvantage when used with oak which is immersed in water. Even wrought iron, with a relatively high resistance to rust, corrodes, the tannic acid in the oak reacting with the iron to speed this process. The result is slackness in the fastenings, seriously weakening the structure. The reaction between iron and oak is easily recognized by a bluish-black stain which appears around the fastening. However, for the long bolts on the keel there was no alternative to iron, and bolts had frequently to be replaced. By the end of the century a bolt extractor had been invented and is illustrated in Steel's *Naval Architecture*. This powerful machine had large screw threads and withdrew the bolts a few inches at a time. Sometimes bolts became so rusted they could not be withdrawn. In such cases, the shipwright would have to resort to driving a new bolt alongside the original.

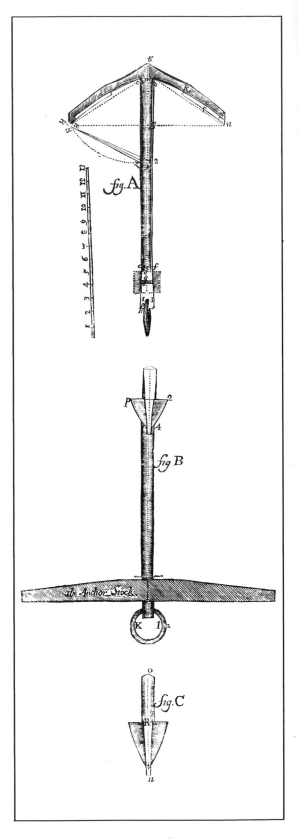

31 Anchors were not forged at Woolwich but outside the yard, being brought up river and stored in the anchor stands to the extreme west of the yard. By the eighteenth century anchors had become standardized in shape, resembling what we would today describe as a fisherman's anchor. The Royal Navy used the angle-crown type shown here until the early nineteenth century. The anchor stock was made of wood, into which nails were driven until no wood could be seen. The shanks were forged from bars of iron, welded together by hammering them while hot. All welding was carried out by this method.

Every vessel had a minimum of three anchors: the sheet, or main, anchor; the bower, or second, anchor; and a small bower anchor. There were also several smaller types which were used for kedging the vessel along in a calm, or for manoeuvring when there was no room to sail.

The anchor illustrated here comes from William Sutherland's *Shipbuilding Unveiled*, 1717. He gives the following dimensions for the main anchor of a 1677-ton ship (*Thunderer* was some 1600 tons):

	ft	in
Shank	18	6
Shank's thickness (max.)		11½
Shank's thickness (min.)		8¹³⁄₂₀
The square	2	11
From end of shank to nut	1	11
Square of nut		2³⁄₁₀
Inner diameter of ring	2	1½
Thickness of ring		4
Hole in shank for ring		4⁶⁄₁₀
Length of crown	1	2
Length of arm	7	0
Breadth of fluke	2	8
Length of fluke	3	9
Thickness of fluke		2⁹⁄₁₀
Square of arm at fluke		7
Length of bill		10½
Rounding of fluke		1¹⁶⁄₁₀₀
Clutching of arm	3	6
Inside meeting	6	6
Outside meeting	6	6
Middle meeting	6	6

Photo: National Maritime Museum, Greenwich

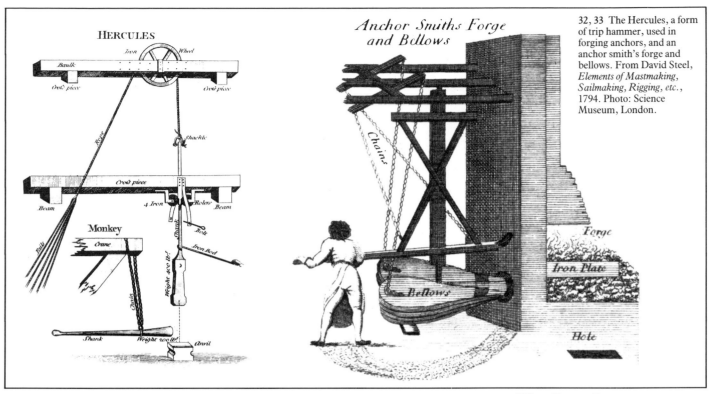

HERCULES

Anchor Smiths Forge and Bellows

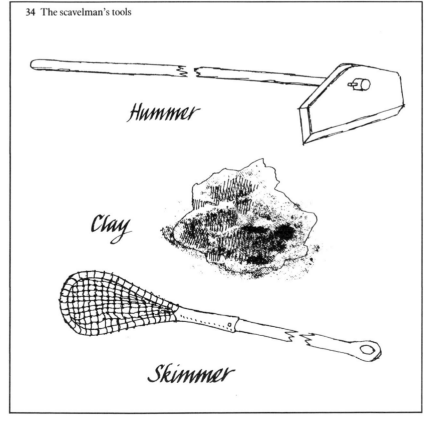

34 The scavelman's tools

Hummer

Clay

Skimmer

The Scavelman

From a treaty dated 30 August 1754 for repair of the mast pond at Woolwich and the provision of new gates, we learn that the scavelman was a labourer whose job it was to keep the docks and slips clear of mud and rubbish. A quotation from the treaty says: 'Scavel work for digging the foundations, driving piles, openings for landtyes and buttresses and backing the wharf with chalk rubbish is estimated at £321 4s 0d.'

The basic tools of the scavelman are shown in Figure 34. With the hummer, which was made of wood, the scavelman raked up the mud and waste from ships' bottoms which had collected in the docks. This task was always performed on the ebb tide so that the detritus would be carried away in suspension as the tide went out. (It was probably then deposited in yards lower down the river, which were engaged on the same task at the same time.) A scavelman using a hummer can be seen in Figure 22. The skimmer was an iron hoop with a net made of rope yarn, and was used for scooping up floating scraps of wood in or near the docks. The scavelman also used a scavel spittar which was a small spade, shod only halfway, for extracting clay and compacted mud. Clay was used for sealing dock gates to prevent water entering once the dock had been emptied.

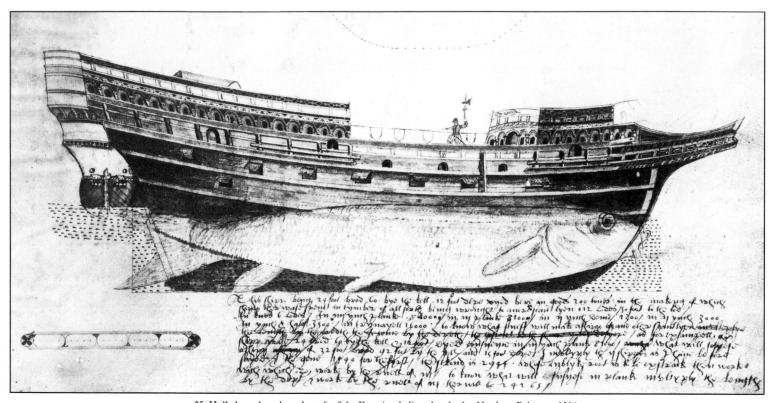

35 Hull shape based on that of a fish. Drawing believed to be by Matthew Baker, *c.* 1586.
Pepys Library, Magdalene College, Cambridge. Photo: Science Museum, London

6
DRAUGHTS, MODELS AND THE MOULD LOFT

The earliest examples of drawings or draughts in ship design come from Venice in the fifteenth century and were used to determine the shape of ships' frames. It is possible that English shipwrights learned their draughting skills from the Italians, for in the sixteenth century Henry VIII brought Italian shipbuilders to England. In 1544, Henry sent master shipwrights James Baker and Peter Pett and three other men 'skillful in ships', according to the order, to Portsmouth to inquire into the state of warships there. Baker and Pett passed their skills and knowledge on to their sons, Matthew Baker and Phineas Pett. The art of draughting and ship design was a closely guarded secret, handed down from father to son. The earliest surviving English draughts (c. 1586), known as 'Fragments of Ancient English Shipwrightry', are attributed to Matthew Baker. They are preserved in the Pepys Library in Magdalene College, Cambridge. To Phineas is attributed the first scale model, built in 1607, which, when presented to James I, so pleased him that he asked Phineas to 'build a great ship in all points like to the same'.

By the eighteenth century the idea of basing the underwater shape of the hull on the lines of a fish, as shown in the drawing by Matthew Baker (Figure 35), had evolved into more scientific considerations of design. Ship designers were aware of Newton's Laws of Motion and performed flotation tests on simple shapes. The earliest tank tests were almost certainly carried out at Karlskrona in Sweden in the first half of the century by Frederick Chapman.

The shape of the seventeenth-century vessels was made up of three, four or more arcs struck from different compass points, using the same geometric principles as in the construction of the four-centred Late Medieval arch. In a list of details for *Sovereign of the Seas*, designed by Phineas Pett in 1635, the length

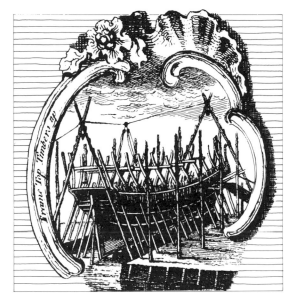

and position of the midship arcs are given. The clearest description of this practice is to be found in 'Rules for Drawing Bends' in *Doctrine of Naval Architecture* (1670) by Anthony Deane. Later the method of drawing arcs from different compass points was replaced by the use of templates – ship's curves – based on circles; they were similar to French curves, although these are based on ellipses. *Thunderer*'s draughts were drawn from arcs struck from different points, but the points were becoming more abstract, and use was made of larger, reverse arcs, which can be seen most clearly at bow and stern (Figure 37).

By the 1750s vessels such as *Triumph* were a compromise between the earlier shape and the need to use less timber and more iron. *Triumph*'s body was more angular than *Thunderer*'s, and closer to French ships in shape. Though *Triumph* heralded a new era in ship design, it is perhaps preferable to look upon

her as marking the end of the rotund elegance of vessels such as the all-wooden *Thunderer*, which epitomizes the essence of Georgian design. This kind of hull shape continued only in smaller vessels like the 64s and the Diana and Minerva class frigates, in which size and quantities of timber were not so critical.

In his book of 1769, William Falconer had this to say about certain design characteristics:

Shipwrights differ extremely in determining the station of the midship frame, some placing it at the middle of the ship's length, and others further forward. They who place it before the middle allege that, if a ship is full forward, she has opened a column of water and that means forcing the ship forward, besides having more power on the rudder, in proportion to its distance from the centre of gravity. This also comes nearer the form of fishes which should seem the most advantageous for driving the fluid.... It is also necessary to remember the sheer of the wales and to give them a proper 'hanging', because the beauty and stateliness of a ship depend greatly upon their figure and curve, which, if properly drawn, will make her appear airy and graceful on the water. We now come to consider the upper-works, and all that is above the water, called the *dead-work*; and here the ship must be narrower so that all the weight lying above the load waterline will thereby be brought nearer the middle of the breadth. Above water, we must be careful not to narrow her too much, as there must be sufficient room left on the upper deck for the guns to recoil. The security of the masts should likewise be remembered, which requires sufficient breadth to spread the shrouds. A deficiency of this sort may indeed be in the breadth of the channels.

To build a ship, three principal draughts were needed (see Figure 39). They were set out on one large piece of paper to a scale of 1 to 48, so that a quarter of an inch on the draught represents 1 foot full size. This scale was used until quite recently, but the scale of 1 to 12 has now been adopted with computerized drawings.

The first of the three draughts shows the *sheer* or *profile*. It shows the line of the sheer and the curve of the deck to match this, and the rise of the floors, which are based on the segments of the circle. In addition to the *table of dimensions* (also called the *table of offsets* or *scantlings*), the sheer plan also shows the keel, stem and stern, as well as the positions of the frames, called *stations*. It also shows the heights, or *station lines*, and spacings for gun ports, rails and so on. In other words, it is a complete view of the hull from the side.

The *half-breadth plan* shows the curve of the waterlines (which appear as straight lines on the sheer plan), the *sirmarks* (diagonals) and the rise of the floors. The station lines are straight, as they are on the sheer plan. This is a view of half the breadth of the ship seen from above or below.

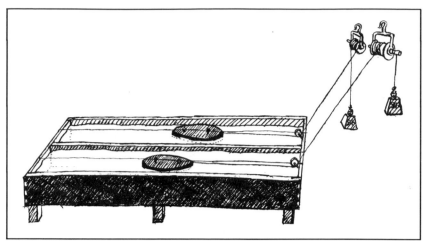

36 Early flotation test to compare different hull shapes. Equal weights, suspended over pulleys, were attached to two model hulls. The first hull to reach the end of the tank was deemed to be the better design.

38 Contemporary model of *Thunderer/Hercules*. National Maritime Museum, Greenwich ▶

37 Draughts of *Thunderer*, designed by Sir Thomas Slade, 1756. National Maritime Museum, Greenwich. Compare the draughts of *Hero* (Figure 4) and *Hercules* (Figure 5)

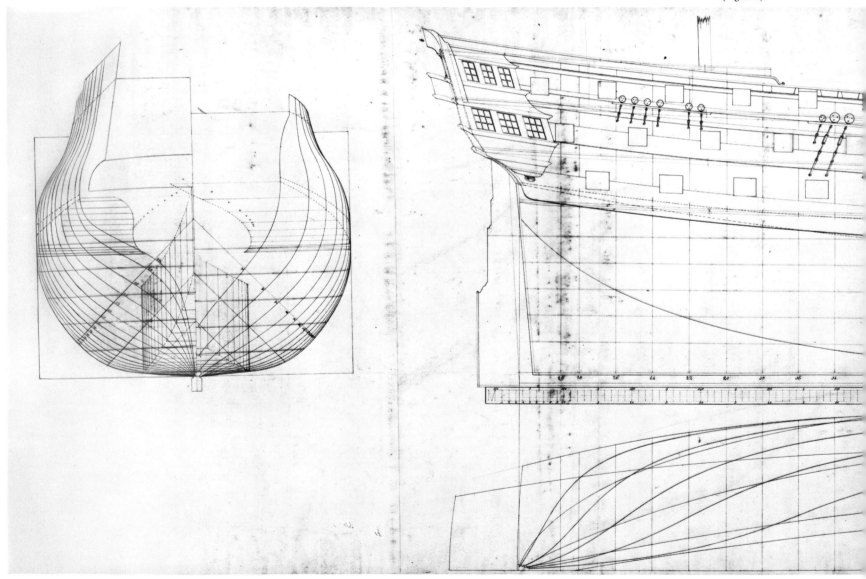

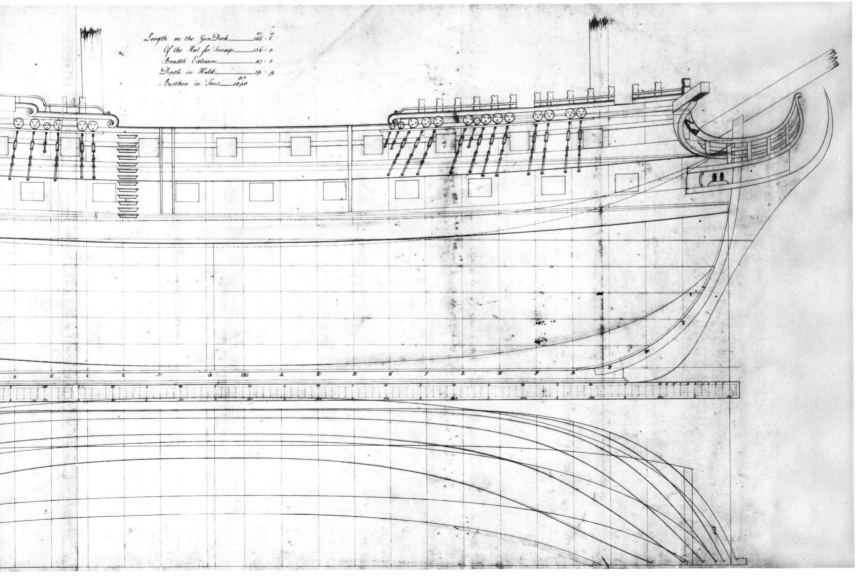

Length on the Gun Deck ____
Of the Keel for Tonage ____
Breadth Extream ____
Depth in Hold ____
Burthen in Tons ____

The *body plan* shows the hull in section. On the right-hand side of the drawing the reader is looking at the bows from aft; on the left-hand side the stern can be seen from forward. The plan shows the curve of the station lines, while the sirmarks and waterlines appear straight.

The draughts were not drawn in strict order of sheer, half-breadth and body plan. Rather, they were built up by cross-referring from one plan to another, starting with relatively few basic dimensions. The test of a good drawing is that a line which is straight in two of the draughts appears as a fair curve on the third. For example, the station lines are straight on the profile and half-breadth plan and curved on the body plan.

Once the draughts were complete they were sent to the yard which then constructed a model of the vessel which was sent to the Navy Board for approval. This was, perhaps, a way of ensuring that the particular yard understood the draughts of a new vessel (or type of vessel) and also any fundamental changes in construction incorporated in the design, before large sums of money for building work were committed. If the Navy Board approved and the Admiralty Board also agreed, the yard was then commissioned to undertake the building.

Figure 38 shows the model of *Thunderer/Hercules* before it was rigged. Builder's models were never rigged at the time they were made, there being standard rigs for each rate.

Models were made in a variety of forms. Sometimes one or both sides were left unplanked or only partially planked, thus exposing the frames (see Figure 75). This enabled the master shipwrights to see inside the vessel to examine the proposed construction method. Also, a model might show details not included on the draughts by combining information on the draughts with the table of dimensions. Some models were made to be lifted apart at the line of the gun deck. Such examples are relatively rare, however, and were usually only made when some new method of construction was being proposed, as in the *Bellona* model (see Figure 86) which has anchor-stock waling, a more rigid form of planking (see chapter 7). The commonest form of

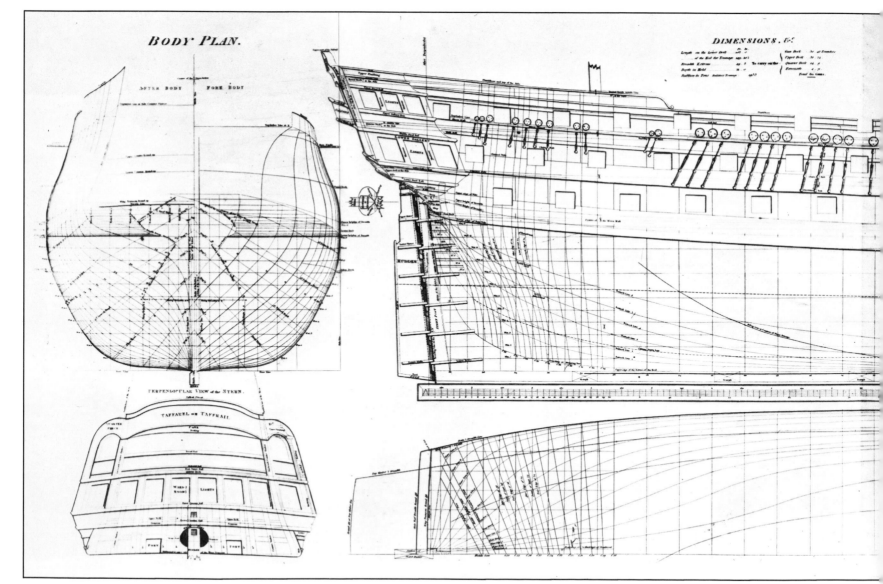

BODY PLAN.

DIMENSIONS. &c.

model is that of the *Thunderer/Hercules* type, illustrating a class or rate fully planked except for parts of the upper decks, where the deck beams, carlings, knees, etc., are exposed.

There appears to be no model of *Hero*, although hers was clearly the master draught for all three vessels and perhaps others, including *Bellona*. It is possible that the original model has been lost, or that the model which is attributed to *Thunderer/Hercules* is actually that of *Hero*; the three vessels were virtually identical. Also it is unclear where this particular model was made and by whom. It was probably built at one of three yards – Plymouth, Woolwich or Deptford – by an experienced shipwright, helped by an indentured apprentice.

Model making was a highly skilled craft in the eighteenth century. Some yards had special workshops where model makers were trained. Nor were models produced only in royal dockyards. A yard like Buckler's Hard in Hampshire, where several large ships were built for the Navy, certainly undertook such work. There were also private firms of model makers who produced models from draughts. Figure 40 shows a trade card of one private modeller who worked in Southwark.

These models are so beautiful that one can only marvel at the skill and accuracy with which they were made. Constructed entirely in boxwood, they have survived two hundred years and more. Their value at the time they were made is exemplified by the story of

Samuel Pepys during the Fire of London in 1666. Having decided to move his household possessions by lighter to below the Tower of London for safety, Pepys then went to the Navy Office and collected his important papers and also his ship models. In the following year, when the Dutch attacked the Medway, Commissioner Phineas Pett's first thought was for the safety of his models, though on this occasion, fearing an invasion of the country, Pepys put more effort into getting his annual salary of £400 paid.

There is a fine collection of builder's models in the National Maritime Museum at Greenwich, spanning over two hundred years of wooden ship construction. From them and from contemporary paintings it is

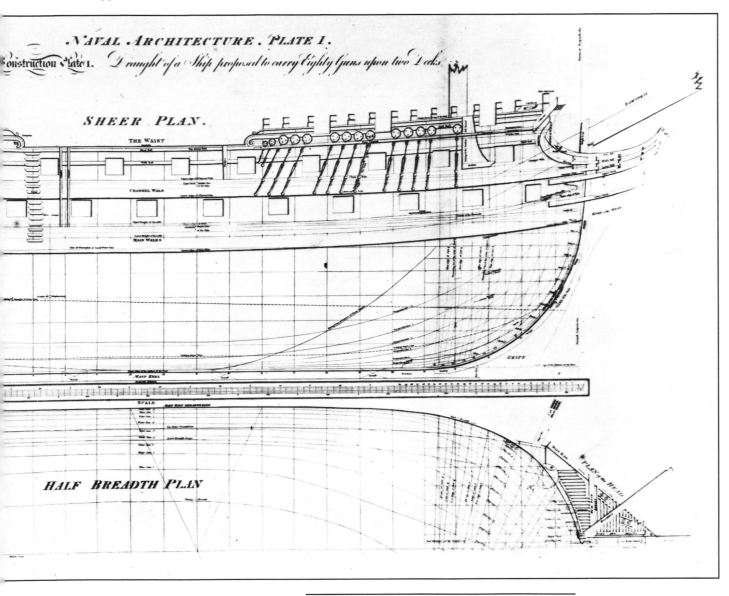

NAVAL ARCHITECTURE. PLATE I.
Construction Plate 1. Draught of a Ship proposed to carry Eighty Guns upon two Decks.

SHEER PLAN.

THE WAIST

CHANNEL WALK

MAIN WALE

HALF BREADTH PLAN

39 Labelled draughts from David Steel, *Naval Architecture*, 1805. Photo: Science Museum, London. These drawings contain more information than normal shipyard draughts and provide an excellent introduction to the vocabulary used to describe different parts of a ship. The design is closer in shape to *Triumph* and later 74s than to *Thunderer* and reflects the influence of French ships

possible to see precisely what the original ships looked like.

The design of merchant ships was not so advanced as that of naval ships. One of the most famous of all types of merchant ship, the East Indiaman, in the shape of the Blackwall frigate, was derived directly from naval frigate designs.

Once the draughts and model had been approved, details of the draughts had to be reproduced full size so that the *moulds* – light wooden templates from which the individual pieces such as the frames and the stem- and sternposts were cut – could be made (see Figures 46 and 47). This operation was carried out in the mould loft, which was a large spacious room with extensive windows in the ceiling to give good light directly from above. At Woolwich the mould loft was above the sail lofts and the wood store for sided timber. The building overlooked the double dock in the very centre of the yard. Being on the first floor, the loft was dry and also beyond the reach of prying eyes, so that the loftsman's secrets remained safe.

First, measurements were taken from the draughts and entered in a small book so that the draughts themselves need not be left on the floor and damaged.

The dimensions were then 'laid off' or 'laid down' to full size on the mould loft floor, which was made from planed deals laid diagonally and covered with black plaster known as gesso, which is made from gypsum and becomes quite hard when dry. The loftsman, who wore canvas shoes or went barefoot so as not to damage the floor, drew the dimensions in chalk, taking care not to erase any lines as he worked.

Drawing the dimensions to full size enabled the accuracy of the draughts to be checked by the method of fair curves and straight lines described earlier. A

40 Trade card of an eighteenth-century ship's model maker. Photo: Science Museum, London

line which appeared fair on the draught, which was, after all, only $\frac{1}{48}$th full size, might need adjustment when scaled up to full size.

The drawings on the mould loft floor were made in the order and manner in which they appeared on the draughts. As mould lofts were seldom long enough to permit laying down the dimensions of a large vessel in full length, parts of the plans were drawn overlapping each other. The loftsman used a chalk line for long straight lines and ash battens held in place with small nails or pins to mark fair curves. Battens were also used to join the arcs of the body plan. The arcs themselves were drawn with *sweeps*, large wooden compasses which held chalk in one end. Other tools in the loftsman's bag were a bevel, a folding ruler, dividers for transferring measurements, small compasses holding chalk, and a large set square.

The moulds themselves were made from dry seasoned deals, planed all round. At Woolwich the deal yard was conveniently situated just behind the mould loft. The timber was first cut by the sawyers to its sided thickness, the sidings usually being given in the table of dimensions. The shipwrights would then cut the sided timber to the shape of the mould, including any bevels (see Figure 9).

7

THE BUILDING I

Building a large wooden ship, perhaps the most complicated structure of its time, was a systematic, carefully planned process. The eighteenth-century shipwright was bound by standards for building that allowed him little room for error. In this chapter our account is largely based on the following contemporary sources, although where they contradict one another on various methods and on the order of building, we describe what seem the most practicable procedures:

William Sutherland, *The Shipwright's Assistant*, 1711: floor timbers, deadwood, half timbers, keelson, foot-hooks

William Sutherland, *England's Glory; or Shipbuilding Unveiled*, 1717: deadwood, floor timbers, foot-hooks, keelson

T. R. Blankley, *Naval Expositor*, 1750: dead rising (or deadwoods), floor timbers, half timbers, hawse pieces, top timbers

William Falconer, *An Universal Dictionary of the Marine*, 1769: deadwood, floor timbers, keelson, futtocks, cant timbers, hawse pieces, top timbers, etc.

David Steel, *The Elements and Practice of Naval Architecture*, 1805: hawse pieces, stern half timbers, floor timbers, futtocks, keelson

In these books it is also possible to trace the development of the shipwright's language; for example, foot-hook–futtock, clinch–clench, flower–floor, etc.

We have also used Mungo Murray, *References and Explanations of Four Prints Exhibiting the Different Views of a Sixty-Gun Ship*, 1768. Murray, who was a shipwright at Deptford and then a ship's carpenter on HMS *Weymouth*, does not give an order of building, but provides information on certain technical points

not found in any other source. His book is referred to in the text as *The Sixty-Gun Ship*.

The order of building we have followed is mainly based on Blankley and Falconer, who were writing at roughly the time when *Thunderer* was being built. Blankley's book, which is an illustrated dictionary, was considered an important work when it appeared in 1750. Lord Anson regarded it highly enough to give a copy to one of his best friends, and this may be seen on display in the National Maritime Museum at Greenwich. Falconer's *Dictionary* is the most readable account of shipbuilding and nautical language of

the day, easy to follow and succinct. It is possible that Falconer derived his idea for a dictionary from Blankley; some of the illustrations are identical. In addition to these works, we have also drawn fairly extensively on David Steel's *Naval Architecture*, which is a fascinating summary of eighteenth-century shipbuilding practice, containing perhaps the most complete and detailed account of the subject. He includes a comprehensive table of dimensions for all rates, and was regarded in his day as providing the definitive textbook on the subject.

Blankley and Falconer differ from Steel in two practices. First, they suggest that the floors and cross chocks only should be fitted before the keelson is put in; Steel, however, recommends that floors, cross chocks and frames should be positioned before the keelson, which means that the keelson would have to be manoeuvred into place between the frames rather than simply lifted over the ends of the floors. Second, Falconer advises that the keel bolts should be clenched from the top, implying that they were driven upwards from beneath the keel. This would have necessitated digging a hole several feet deep in the slip under each bolt. Moreover, driving bolts home was a time-consuming and strenuous process, taking perhaps several days for each bolt (see page 44). Steel recommends driving bolts from the top and clenching on the bottom. By the time Steel was writing, the introduction of copper and bronze bolts and the invention of the bolt-drawing machine* in the 1780s made the operation of withdrawing bolts when they needed renewing much easier, although to cut off a clenched head and drive the bolt down, as implied by Falconer's advice, would have been relatively simple. It is unlikely that *Thunderer*'s

---

*Steel includes an illustration of the bolt extractor in his article on shipbuilding in the third edition of the *Encyclopaedia Britannica* in 1793.

aftermost keel bolt, which was 13 feet long, could not have been clenched other than on the bottom. Even her midship bolt was 5 feet long.

In the royal dockyards ships were built either on slips or in graving docks, the latter almost invariably reserved for first and second rates to facilitate launching. *Thunderer* – a third rate – was built on a slip. In the case of ships built in docks, standards were not required due to the depth of the dock, which also made it easier for shipwrights to move large pieces of timber into position from the dockside.

Both slips and docks were carefully built so that they were capable of taking the weight of large vessels. They were lined with piling and brickwork or wooden shuttering, which was probably backed by rubble. The floor of the slip was paved or prepared from compacted gravel, as was the surrounding ground, with groundways – large pieces of timber – let into the floor at 5-foot intervals. These were held in place by stakes and served as the foundation for large blocks of hard, knotty stuff (oak), 16 inches thick and between 2 and 3 feet wide. Upon these were placed splitting blocks which were made from clear-grained timber with no knots. This was to ensure that the blocks could be cleaved out cleanly when the false keel was put on and the ship ready to launch. Occasionally, instead of splitting blocks, the method preferred by the Navy, a block with two wedges was used. This method was less secure, but allowed for any adjustments. Also it was easier to remove the wedges than to split out the blocks. Each set of blocks was nogged together with treenails; in the latter method, however, the wedges were left free. The declivity of the blocks on the slip was ⅝ inch in 1 foot, giving an adequate slope for launching.

All vessels were subject to hogging, which is the tendency for the ends of a ship to sag due partly to the weight of the fore- and aftercastles or superstructures. Once a ship was badly hogged, there was no remedy. To prevent this tendency, a rocker – or slight curve, rather like the rocker of a rocking chair – was built into the keel as the keel blocks were laid. The curve of the rocker was not great, being approximately 1 inch in 50 feet.

The next stage was to lay the elm *keel*, which was made from seven baulks, each approximately 26 feet long. Amidships the keel was 1 foot 6 inches square. The length of each piece was calculated to allow sufficient timber at each end for the scarphs and coaks. Each scarph was 4 feet 6 inches long, with one coak towards the lip and another halfway along the scarph. The coaks, which were from 1 inch to 1¼

inches thick (see Figure 65), locked the scarphs firmly into place. The scarph joints, which can be seen in Figure 45, were in the vertical plane so that they could withstand stress better.

The shipwrights and sawyers would ensure that the keel pieces were straight and square and fitted together well enough to satisfy the master shipwright that the workmanship was good. The pieces were then taken apart and a ¼-inch chamfer taken out of each scarph to allow for caulking. It was also common at this stage to trim out the rabbet in the keel which took the garboard strakes, leaving about 2 feet of rabbet from the ends of each scarph to be cut in after the keel was bolted up.

The keel was then placed piece by piece on the blocks. Tarred flannel, or sometimes tar and hair, was laid between the scarphs, which were then bolted together with eight 1⅛-inch bolts. The upper bolts were set just below the rabbet and the lower bolts about 4 inches from the lower edge.

41 The order of building for a first rate. From T. R. Blankley, *Naval Expositor*, 1750. Photo: National Maritime Museum, Greenwich

42 The dissection of the body of a first-rate man-of-war. From an engraving by Joseph Nutting, showing George St Lo, Commander in Chief Medway and at Nore, 1712–14. Photo: National Maritime Museum, Greenwich

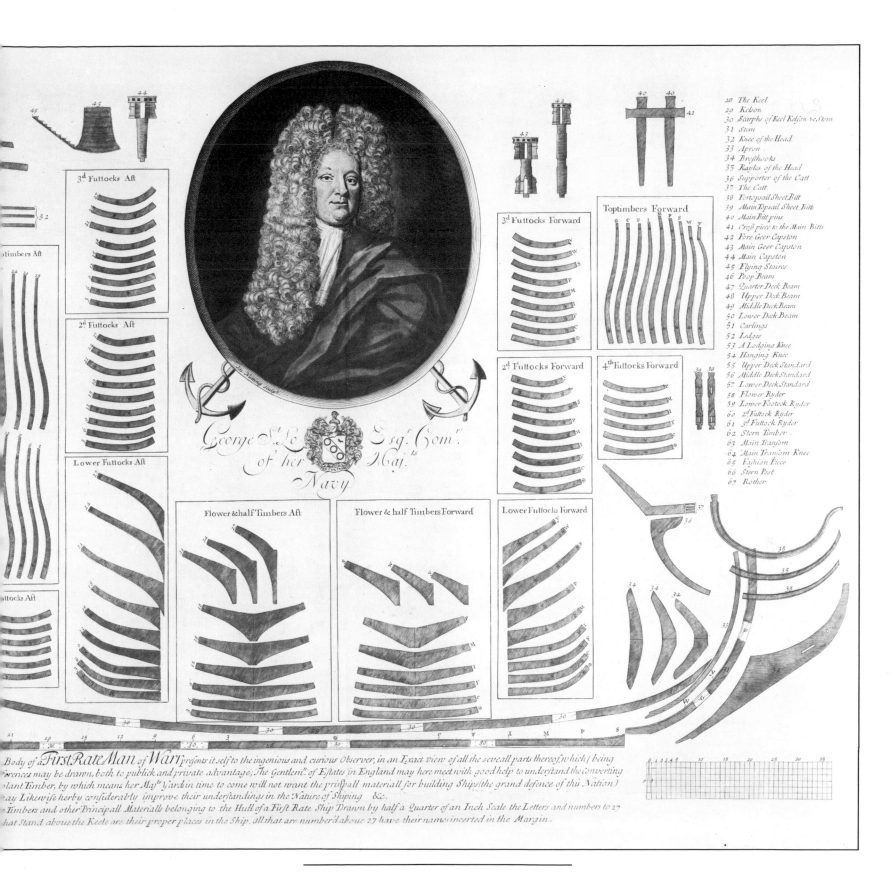

3^d Futtocks Aft

2^d Futtocks Aft

Lower Futtocks Aft

Toptimbers Aft

Flower & half Timbers Aft

3^d Futtocks Forward

2^d Futtocks Forward

4th Futtocks Forward

Toptimbers Forward

Flower & half Timbers Forward

Lower Futtocks Forward

George S^t Lo Esqr Com^r
of her May^{ts}
Navy

28 The Keel
29 Kelson
30 Scarphs of Keel Kelson & Stem
31 Stem
32 Knee of the Head
33 Apron
34 Bresthooks
35 Rayles of the Head
36 Supporter of the Catt
37 The Catt
38 Fore topsail Sheet Bitt
39 Main Topsail Sheet Bitts
40 Main Bitt pins
41 Cross piece to the Main Bitts
42 Fore Geer Capston
43 Main Geer Capston
44 Main Capston
45 Flying Staires
46 Poop Beam
47 Quarter Deck Beam
48 Upper Deck Beam
49 Middle Deck Beam
50 Lower Deck Beam
51 Carlings
52 Ledges
53 A Lodging Knee
54 Hanging Knee
55 Upper Deck Standard
56 Middle Deck Standard
57 Lower Deck Standard
58 Flower Ryder
59 Lower Footeck Ryder
60 2^d Futtock Ryder
61 3^d Futtock Ryder
62 Stern Timber
63 Main Transom
64 Main Transom Knee
65 Fashion Piece
66 Stern Post
67 Rother

... Body of a First Rate Man of Warr, presents it self to the ingenious and curious Observer, in an Exact view of all the severall parts thereof, which (being ... ferences may be drawn, both to publick and private advantage; The Gentlemⁿ. of Estates in England may here meet with good help to understand the converting ... plant Timber, by which means her May^{ts} Yards in time to come will not want the principall materiall for building Ships (the grand defence of this Nation) ... ay Likewise herby considerably improve their understandings in the Nature of Shiping &c.

... Timbers and other Principall Materialls belonging to the Hull of a First Rate Ship Drawn by half a Quarter of an Inch Scale the Letters and numbers to 27 ... hat stand aboue the Keele are their proper places in the Ship. all that are number'd aboue 27 have their names inserted in the Margin.

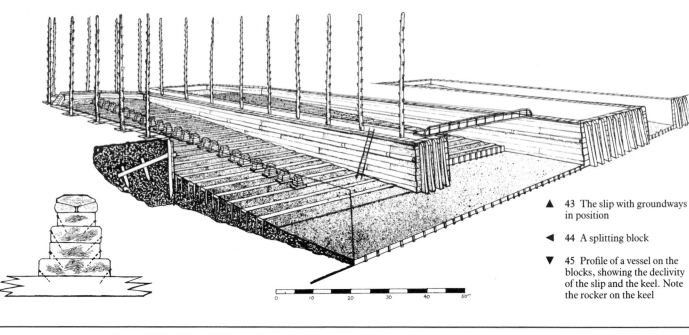

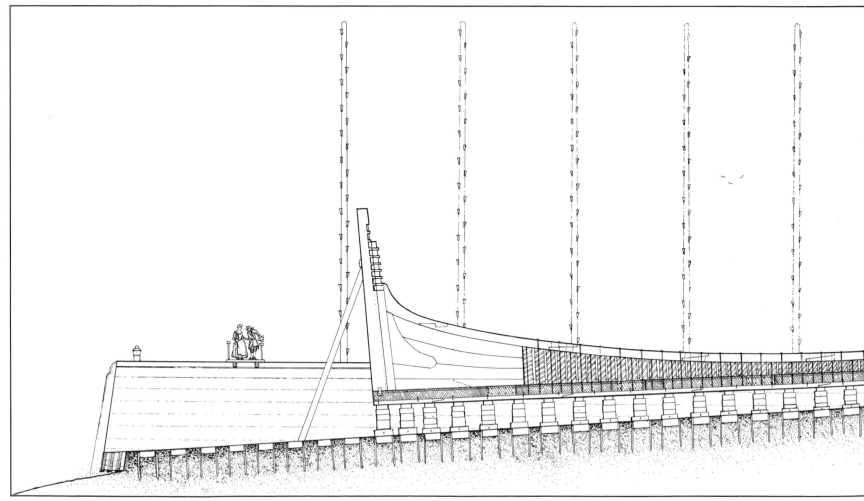

▲ 43 The slip with groundways in position

◄ 44 A splitting block

▼ 45 Profile of a vessel on the blocks, showing the declivity of the slip and the keel. Note the rocker on the keel

46 The stem and apron. ▶
A: The dimensions marked out on the mould loft floor (the diagonal lines represent the floorboards); B: the batten moulds made to these dimensions for the individual pieces; C: the timbers cut to shape from the moulds

47 The sternpost. A: The ▶▶ batten mould; B: the profile of the sternpost and inner post; C: the sternpost and inner post viewed from inboard. Note the slots for the transoms and the tenons for the mortice in the keel ◀

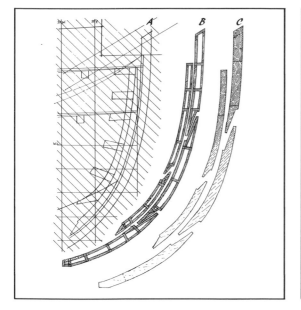

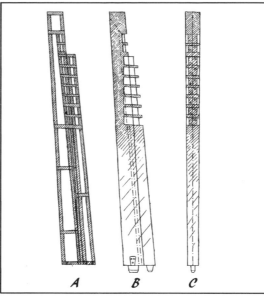

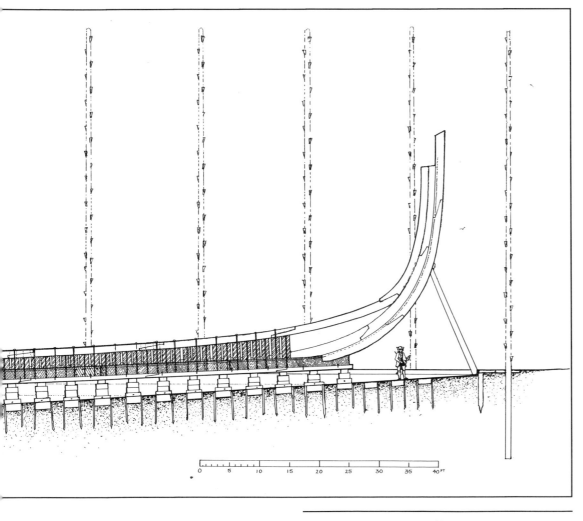

We have already noted that Falconer and Steel were of different opinions on the method of driving bolts home. We assume in *Thunderer*'s case that the bolts were driven from above and clenched beneath the keel, as advised by Steel. He also recommends that every bolt should be clenched over a plate or ring of 'full size' let into the wood. Any spaces were to be caulked as soon as the plate was recessed, and the final clench was to be covered with a lead tingle.

The keel was laid fair and straight along the blocks by eye. To keep it in position it was nogged with treenails driven diagonally from the sides of the keel into the blocks. Sometimes the keel was actually let into the splitting blocks to a depth of 1½ inches to ensure that it did not move. Then the seams along the upper sides of the scarphs were caulked and a ¾-inch oak batten, with tarred flannel under it, was let in flush over the joint of each scarph.

When the keel was truly placed and securely fastened, the shipwright set off the exact length of 150 feet fore and aft, the measurement being taken from where the lower part of the keel ceases to be straight at the bow, called by shipwrights the 'touch'.

The first timbers to be raised on the keel were the *stem* and *apron*, the piece of timber immediately behind the lower part of the stem (Figure 46). The timber for the stem was first sawn and trimmed to its sided thickness as given in the table of dimensions. Then the moulded side was marked out from the mould (B in Figure 46), any relevant information was marked on, plus a line square to the keel as a guide for setting up. Then the moulded side was cut out.

The table of dimensions laid down that the stem was to consist of no more than three pieces of best quality oak. These were scarphed together with tables or hooked coaks in the scarphs. The scarphs were the same type as those used on the keel, but were positioned horizontally. Each scarph was 4 feet long with 5-inch lips. The scarph at the lower end of the stem where it joined the keel was called a boxing scarph. This was, in effect, a table or hooked-coak scarph, similar to those used on the keel, but set at an angle of 45° (see Figures 48 and 50).

The apron was made of two pieces of timber, sawn and trimmed in the same way as the stem. It was fayed (faired or fitted) to the after side (inside) of the stem. The stem scarphs were then firmly bolted through stem and apron, each with eight 1⅛-inch clenched bolts. Tarred flannel was laid in the scarphs prior to bolting. Care had to be taken to see that none of the bolts interfered with the rabbet in which the plank ends finished. This was chopped in after the stem had been assembled.

The stem and apron were then hauled to the slip on a 'pair of wheels', probably by a team of four horses. The foot of the stem was lifted into position above the boxing scarph by means of a large tackle attached to a pair of sheerlegs. The fall of the tackle passed through a single block at the foot of one of the sheerlegs, and from there to a crab, a kind of mobile capstan (see Figure 51). Another large tackle was then attached higher up the stem. Two smaller tackles were fastened to the foot of the stem and to the top corners of the slip to prevent the stem from slipping too far aft. An additional pair of tackles was taken from the head of the stem to the first two standards on either side of the slip. The greater part of the weight was taken by the sheerlegs, but the head of the stem was raised by the two tackles attached to the standards. Once the stem reached a certain height, these tackles simply acted as guys, with practically all the weight being taken by the two massive tackles attached to the sheerlegs. The stempost of a 74 stood approximately 40 feet above the base of the slip and it required no mean skill and effort to hoist it into place without accident. Once it was judged square to the keel and at the right angle of inclination, it was well shored up and nogged to the shores. The boxing scarph, joining the stem to the keel, was caulked and bolted in the same way as the keel scarphs, with eight 1⅛-inch bolts.

After the stem, the next item to be raised on the keel was the *stern assembly*. First, the sternpost, inner post and transoms had to be cut out and fastened into place while the assembly was still on the ground.

The *sternpost* was one of the most important large timbers in the ship, for it carried the rudder and had to withstand extraordinary strains at sea. The timber was therefore very carefully selected and only the finest quality oak was used. For obvious reasons it had to be a single piece 30 feet long, sawn into square bulk to the given dimensions, then trimmed. This was done by laying it fore side up and scoring a centre line on the forward face. The sidings were then measured from this centre line (C in Figure 47). After the timber had been trimmed to these dimensions, the mould was applied which gave the shape of the moulded side in the fore–after direction, i.e. parallel with the keel. The rabbet and length from head to heel were also marked, as well as the stations for the transoms and harpins, and the rake of the sternpost.

The sternpost was jointed to the keel with a tenon which engaged a mortice in the keel. When the heel of the sternpost was trimmed, allowance was made for the tenon to be cut equal to one third the depth of the keel. The thickness of the tenon was one third the

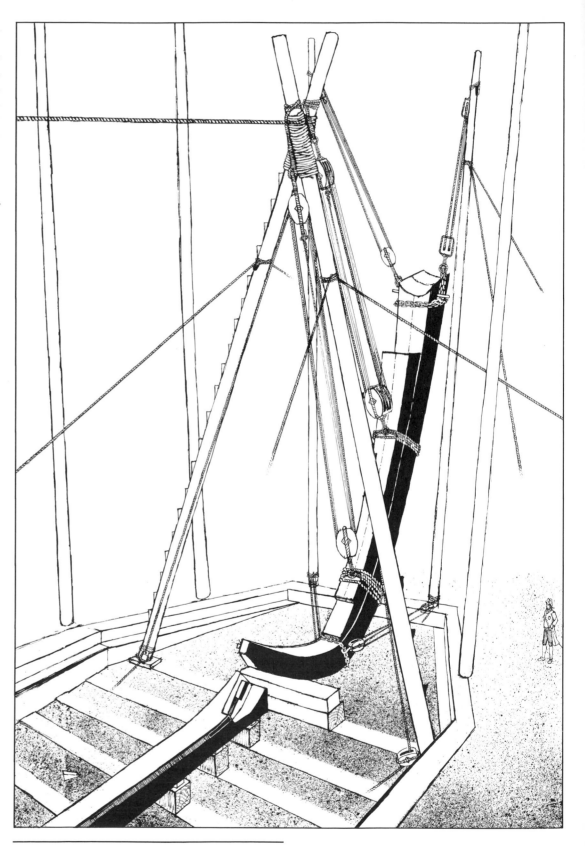

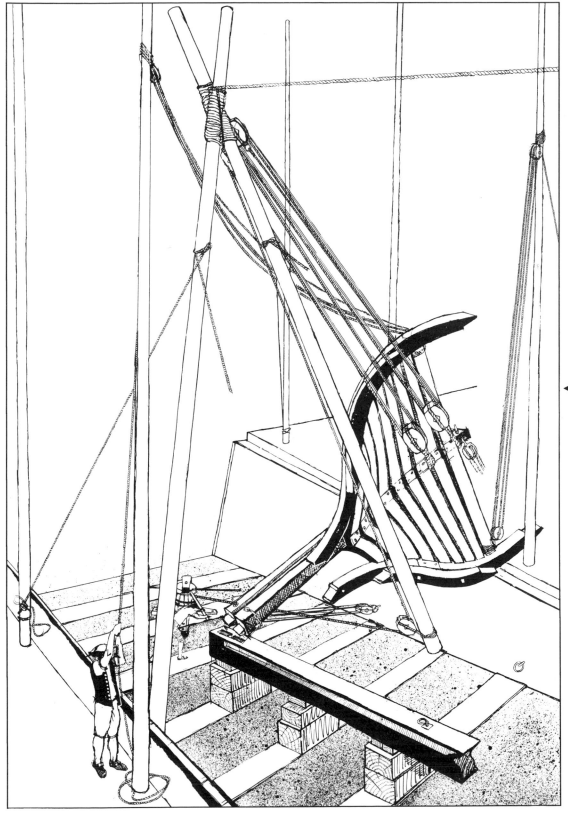

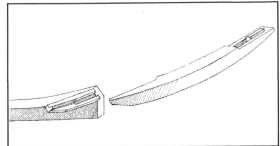

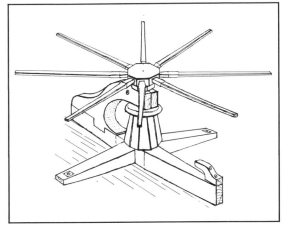

◀ **48, 49** Raising the stem and apron and the stern assembly by means of sheerlegs

50 (top) A boxing scarph, used for joining the stem to the keel

51 (above) A crab capstan. This was a portable capstan that could be fixed in position wherever it was needed

width of the keel, and its fore–aft dimension was double its thickness.

Next the rabbet for the ends of the hull planks was cut, a 4-inch V-shaped groove to take the 4-inch bottom planks. It was specified that the rabbet should have not less than 1 foot of timber between it and the after end of the sternpost. At the lower, or keel, end it had to have a standing bevel of ½ inch on the after edge.

The fore side of the post was then ready to be moulded to the shape of the body on each side of the centre line and trimmed to the depth of the rabbet. The fore and aft taper of the post could then be cut, as well as the taper from the head to the keel. When the post had been trimmed, an iron staple was driven into the top of the head to prevent the end grains from flying (springing or splitting) when the timber dried out.

Occasionally, if the timber available was not sufficiently large in the fore–aft direction, a false post was fitted between the sternpost and the inner post.

However, this was known to be a source of potential weakness and was avoided where possible, especially in larger craft, although ironically that is just where it was most likely to have been needed.

Next the *inner post*, which may be regarded as the counterpart of the apron, was sawn according to the dimensions table. It was then trimmed to a taper of 1 foot 11 inches fore and aft at the head to 1 foot 4 inches fore and aft at the keel. Fayed against the fore side of the sternpost (or the false post if one was fitted), the inner post had its head let into the underside of the deck transom to a depth of 1 inch. The inner post was fastened to the sternpost with tree nails or 1-inch bolts in the spaces between the transoms. A tenon was cut into the heel of the inner post in the same manner as in the sternpost.

The next pieces to be cut and fitted to the stern assembly were the *transoms*, which provided the lateral structure and reinforcement for the stern assembly. Starting at the head of the sternpost, they consisted of the post wing transom, the filling transom, the deck transom, and six more, numbered 1 to 6 from the top. The wing transom was approximately 28 feet above the rabbet on the keel and was 34 feet long on the aft face. Its sided thickness was 1 foot 1 inch. The moulded shape tapered from 2 feet at the centre to 1 foot 6 inches at the ends. Transoms 1–6 were 11 inch sided and they diminished in length and moulding from top to bottom. Each transom was sawn to its siding, whether rounded upwards or straight, then cut to the mould and trimmed to the bevels. They were fastened to the sternpost and inner post by two 1½-inch bolts. Thus the whole stern assembly was held more or less rigidly together.

Steel comments:

Transoms require much trouble and expense to shift them and the quality of timber ought, therefore, to be the best, quite free from any defect whatever. Transoms are to be trimmed with the utmost exactness and then let on to the stern post and inner post, with scores on each side of one inch deep or more, observing great precision as to letting them down, horning and positioning. The ends, when cut, are left long enough to tenon and face onto the fashion pieces one inch and a half.

The *fashion pieces*, which provided the foundation for the stern structure, were the next timbers to be assembled. They were of complicated shape, curving outwards and backwards, and were constructed from several pieces of naturally curved futtocks in the same way as the frames (see below). Once assembled, they were joined onto the ends of the transom timbers.

Then the complete stern assembly was raised into position as shown in Figure 49. Apart from the two

treble blocks on the sheerlegs, a further treble block was attached to the stern frame between the deck and filling transoms. Another treble block was fitted just above the wing transom, and the fall taken to the after block on the sheers. When the assembly was hoisted into place, this block and tackle had to be vertical above the sternpost; 3½-inch ropes were used for this purpose. Another double tackle led forward from just above the wing transom at the sternpost, enabling the men to control the fore–aft movement of the assembly as it was raised. This tackle used 4½-inch ropes. A double tackle, known as a horning tackle, was attached to each of the outer ends of the wing transom and led to standards on the sides of the slip. These were used to 'horn' or square the framework. Guys to steady the sheers were led fore and aft and attached to the feet of convenient standards. Since these were vital in ensuring that the sheers remained steady, it was recommended that 7-inch hawsers should be used.

Great care was taken to ensure that the sternpost, like the stem, was placed true and perpendicular on the keel and not winding in any direction. This was done by drawing a middle line on both the sternpost and the keel. Care also had to be taken that the tenons were not damaged before entering the mortices in the keel. All transoms had to be level, particularly the wing transom, above which the superstructure of the aft end of the vessel would be constructed. Once the assembly was in position, it was supported by shores (placed on to timber foundations called shoals, which were firmly nogged to the groundways). Until the deadwoods were fitted, it was held in place by a chain fastened to the keel and by guys to standards and to the sides of the slip.

The *deadwoods* or rising woods were the next timbers to be fitted. Fore and aft the deadwoods

provided a solid foundation for the half timbers and the plank ends where the hull narrowed as it tapered away to the stem- and sternposts; they can also be thought of as massive knees binding stem- and sternposts firmly to the keel. The lowest deadwood was elm; the rest close-grained oak in various thicknesses, trimmed, tabled together and fayed onto the upper side of the keel. (The deadwood moulds are shown in Figures 55 and 56.) One piece ran the entire length of the keel, like a hog. It was 8 inches thick and 1 foot 9 inches wide so that it overhung the keel by about 2 inches on each side. The scarphs in this piece 'gave shift' to the scarphs in the keel, i.e. they were staggered, and were fastened with treenails. Below the stepping for the frames fore and aft, the deadwoods were trimmed to continue the shape of the body of the ship. The deadwood above the stepping inside the vessel was built up high enough for the underside of the keelson to be fayed onto it (see Figure 45). The scarphs were staggered with those of the keel and with each other.

Some of the deadwood bolts were stepped in size halfway along their length, which made it easier to drive them through a hole ¹⁄₁₆th of an inch smaller in diameter, and also resulted in a tighter fit. The bolt through the after deadwood was positioned 9 inches from the end of the keel, and the next bolt aft was driven through the heel of the sternpost so that it bound the end of the vessel securely.

The *floor timbers* now had to be introduced. These were placed across the keel and formed the base for the ship's timbers and frames. *Thunderer* had forty-eight floor timbers of best quality oak. They were about 1 foot 4 inches square, with a maximum length amidships of 25 feet 6 inches, and were fastened in place with 1½-inch bolts. Great care had to be taken when crossing the floor timbers that the rabbet in the

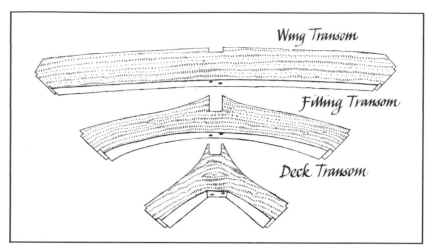

52 The transoms. These were fitted to the sternpost before it was raised on the keel

53, 54 The stem and the stern assembly in position (to scale) ▶

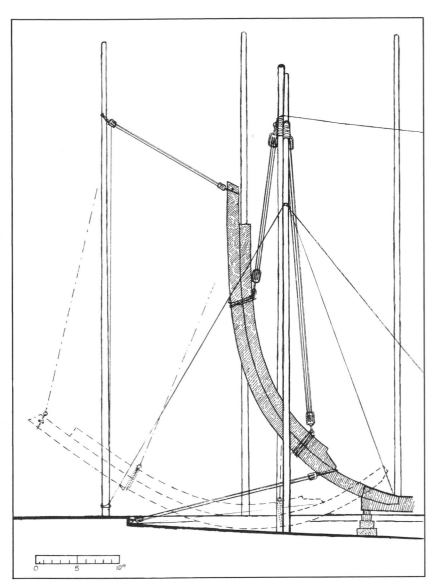

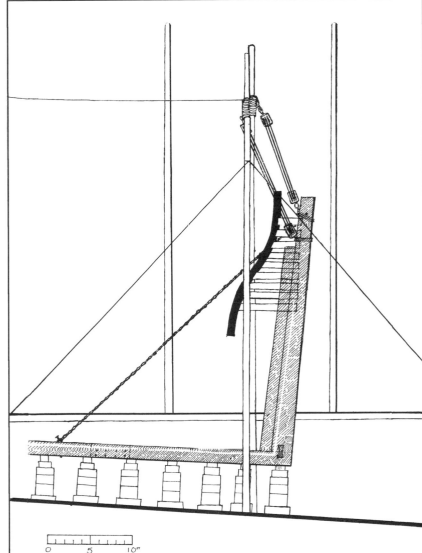

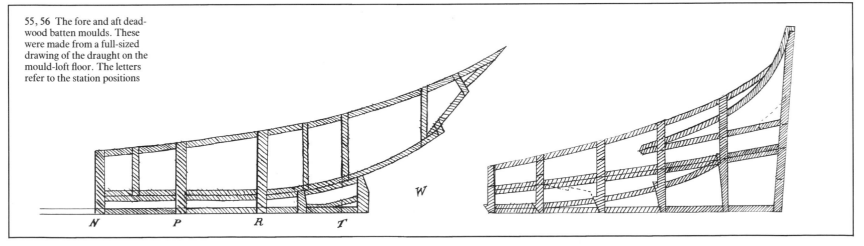

55, 56 The fore and aft deadwood batten moulds. These
were made from a full-sized
drawing of the draught on the
mould-loft floor. The letters
refer to the station positions

W

N   P   R   T

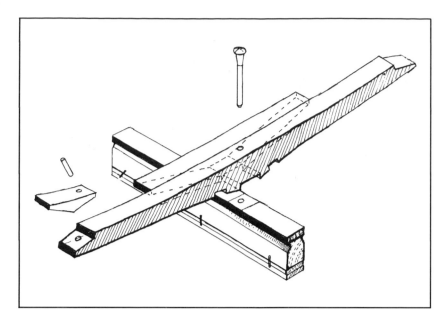

keel was not damaged. The midship floor was set in place first, then the floor timbers fore and aft. It is likely that at this stage only every other floor timber was set on its station line, having been cut to shape from the mould, and that the remaining floor timbers were spiled (see below) from these as they were fitted. The floor timbers had cross chocks attached to their sides before they were put in place (Figure 57).

Commonly, the next floors to be put in were the *rising floors*, which, as the name suggests, were the floors which began to rise at either end of the hull from the level floors of the middle section, and which came before the half timbers (see Figure 58). The rising floors, particularly those close to the after part of the vessel, were difficult to cut from a single piece of timber because of their acute angle. Instead, they were made of three or four pieces of straight-grained timber, thus strengthening them, and were called *made floors* (Figure 59). Once trimmed, the rising floors were crossed in their respective stations, let into the deadwood, set level, and horned, or squared, to the middle line.

At this stage the shipwrights fitted four *ribbands* – strong, pliable battens of fir – nailing one on each side of the vessel halfway between the floor heads and the keel, and another on each side at the floor heads. The position of the lower batten was called the *lower sirmark*, and the upper one the *floor sirmark*. Sirmarks were points marked on the moulds where bevelling was to be applied, and they ocurred at several levels – lower sirmark, floor sirmark, breadth sirmark, etc. The ribbands held the floors in place and acted as guides to make sure that they were all fair, one with

57 A floor with cross chock being fitted on the keel. 'The cross Chocks . . . are fitted across the Keel, upon the two opposite Futtocks, and may be considered as another Floor-timber, and by this means be stronger than if the Futtocks carried their full thickness to the Keel, for then the whole length of the floor will be one bed of timber' (Mungo Murray, *The Sixty-Gun Ship*, 1768)

58 Floor timbers. From the ▶ bow: half timber, rising floor, midship floor, rising floor, half timber aft

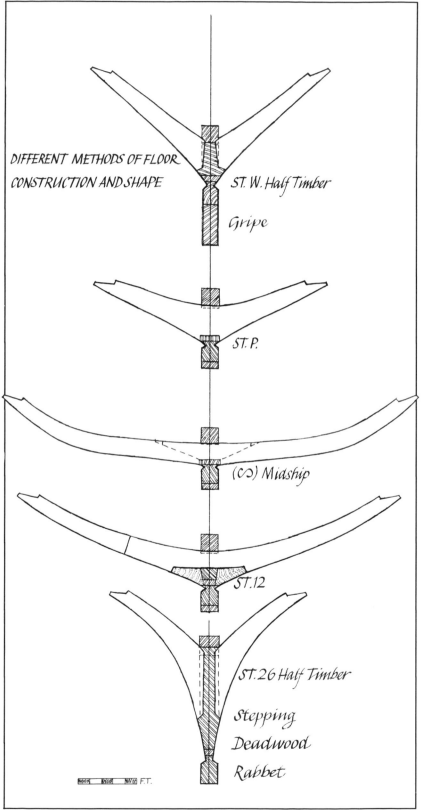

DIFFERENT METHODS OF FLOOR CONSTRUCTION AND SHAPE

ST. W. Half Timber

Gripe

ST. P.

(C0) Midship

ST. 12

ST. 26 Half Timber

Stepping

Deadwood

Rabbet

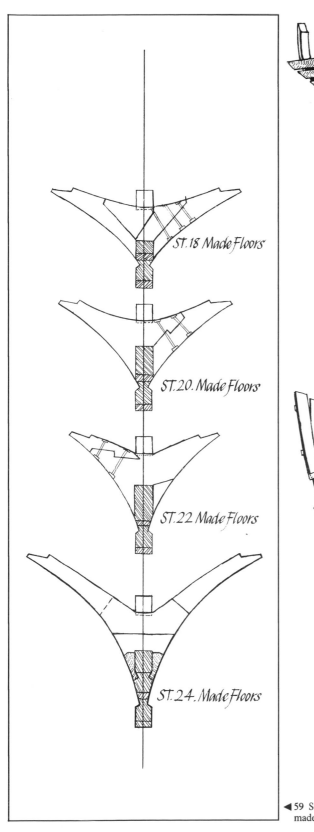

ST.18 Made Floors

ST.20. Made Floors

ST.22 Made Floors

ST.24. Made Floors

◀ 59 Some examples of made (rising) floors

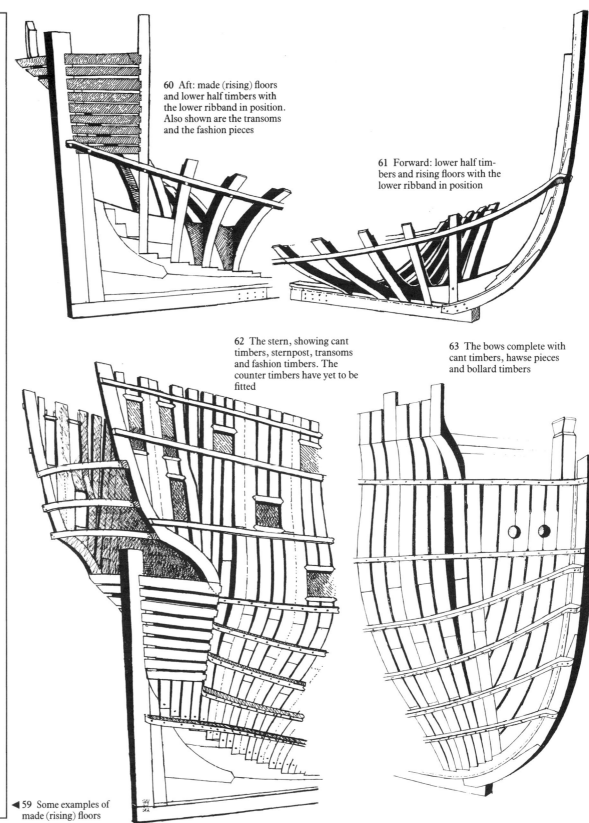

60 Aft: made (rising) floors and lower half timbers with the lower ribband in position. Also shown are the transoms and the fashion pieces

61 Forward: lower half timbers and rising floors with the lower ribband in position

62 The stern, showing cant timbers, sternpost, transoms and fashion timbers. The counter timbers have yet to be fitted

63 The bows complete with cant timbers, hawse pieces and bollard timbers

another. It was very important at this stage to make sure that the floors were exactly level and square with the keel, as this structure, once completed, was the backbone on which the rest of the ship was built. After any minor trimming and adjustment that might be necessary, the floors were then bolted into place and shores placed under the ribbands from the groundways on the slip floor. These pieces of timber had to be very substantial as they would, in due course, take the whole weight of the vessel. They were capped with nails at the head, and nogged with treenails at the heel.

Only then were the remaining floors put in. These were probably spiled (cut to shape) to fit the ribbands from the floors already in place. They were not bolted to the keel, but were temporarily fastened by a spike or treenail to prevent them riding up. They were only finally fastened once the keelson was in place, so the temporary fastenings had to be placed so that they would be clear of the keelson bolts. Another, better, method of fastening them was to drive an eyebolt through a hole in the middle of the floor and forelock it under the keel (see page 48). This bolt could be pulled out later. Temporary fastening of the floors was only really necessary when the practice of putting the keelson in after the frames had been fitted was adopted later in the century (see page 57).

The next timbers to be put in were the *cant frames*. These in fact were half timbers, inserted between the rising floors and the fashion timbers aft, and between the rising floors and the hawse pieces (see below) forward to the stem. The cant frames did not cross over the keel and deadwoods, but were notched into their sides, hence the description *half timbers*. They were called cant timbers because they were said to cant (i.e. slope) at an angle to the centre line of the ship. The notches into which they were fitted were called the *stepping* because as the cant frames were fitted fore and aft they 'stepped up' the deadwoods.

The next main piece to be fitted was the *keelson*, but before this operation the gaps between the floor timbers and cross chocks were filled with pieces of well-seasoned oak cut to the width of the keelson and driven down tightly to the keel, with the grain athwartships.

The keelson itself was the counterpart of the keel on the inside of the ship. It was made in six pieces joined with 5-foot 6-inch scarphs which lay in the

64 *Thunderer* on slip no. 3 at floored-up stage with ribbands in position and supported by shores. To the left is the payhouse, then five sawpits under one roof with a kiln for steaming planks and a pump; in the foreground on the left a timber cart is being unloaded by means of sheerlegs

opposite plane to those in the keel, i.e. they were horizontal rather than vertical. Care was taken to see that these scarphs were staggered with those in the keel and that none fell immediately under where a mast would stand. The timber for the keelson came from the sawyers straight and square, so it needed to be fitted to the inner, concave, shape of the vessel. The shipwright would first place the keelson in position, then measure the largest gap, that between the keelson and the midship floor, with dividers. He would next mark this distance along the whole length of the keelson measuring from the top of each floor, and then trim the keelson to these marks. This simple way of *spiling* one piece of shaped timber to another is one of the most important methods of fitting curved shapes in shipbuilding. Once fitted, the keelson was bolted through the alternate floor timbers – those not already bolted to the keel – with 1½-inch diameter bolts. It was considered good practice to carry the keelson as far forward and aft as possible as it acted as a strengthening backbone to the ship. Amidships, it had a square dimension of 1 foot 5 inches.

After fitting the keelson, the shipwright turned his attention to reinforcing the bow and stern. In the bow he fitted a *stemson*, or inner stem, which was a curved oak timber which covered the scarph in the apron and thereby reinforced it. In effect, it was a continuation of the keelson, into which it was scarphed. In larger ships, such as *Thunderer*, it was usually made in two pieces scarphed together as naturally curved timber of this dimension would have been difficult to obtain. Whereas the apron was taken up to the top of the stem, the stemson stopped about halfway up, faying into the apron.

At the stern it was necessary to fit the *sternson knee*, which was cut from a naturally curved oak crook. It was trimmed and fayed against the inner sternpost, the transoms and the upper side of the deadwood, and was scarphed into the after end of the keelson with a hooked scarph. It was then bolted through the sternpost, transoms, deadwood and keel. Thus, the sternson knee became an important extension of the keelson and a major support for the sternpost.

Confusion can easily arise when studying ship-building practice in the eighteenth century from the indiscriminate use of the terms 'frames' and 'timbers'. Strictly speaking, 'timbers' refers to the main ribs of the skeleton of the vessel as it is built up on the keel prior to planking up. For the sake of clarity, we use the term 'frames' for these timbers, and 'filling frames' to describe the timbers which were inserted in the spaces between the frames.

The *frames*, which were made from the moulds, were fitted on the station lines, effectively becoming extensions of the floors, which were by now firmly bolted into place. Had the sides of the vessel sloped outwards in a simple V-shape, it would have been possible for shipwrights to use single, long pieces of oak for each frame. However, eighteenth-century ships were well rounded in shape; therefore it was necessary to make each frame from several pieces of compass oak joined together. For extra strength, each frame was made in two segments, the pieces of one segment arranged so that their joints came in the middle of the pieces of the adjoining segment. The middle section of each frame was called the *futtock*, but confusingly the term was also applied to the pieces which made up this section, and to the frame itself. The uppermost pieces of each frame were known as the *top timbers*, each frame having one short and one long top timber (see Figure 66). The futtocks tapered at each end, that is, at the head and the heel, like a scarph, and were joined by butt chocks, 3 or 4 inches thick in the middle, which were scored into the futtocks and treenailed. The lower, second, third and fourth futtocks and top timbers were bolted together with 1⅛-inch bolts, care being taken to see that no bolts were driven where gun ports or port sills would come.

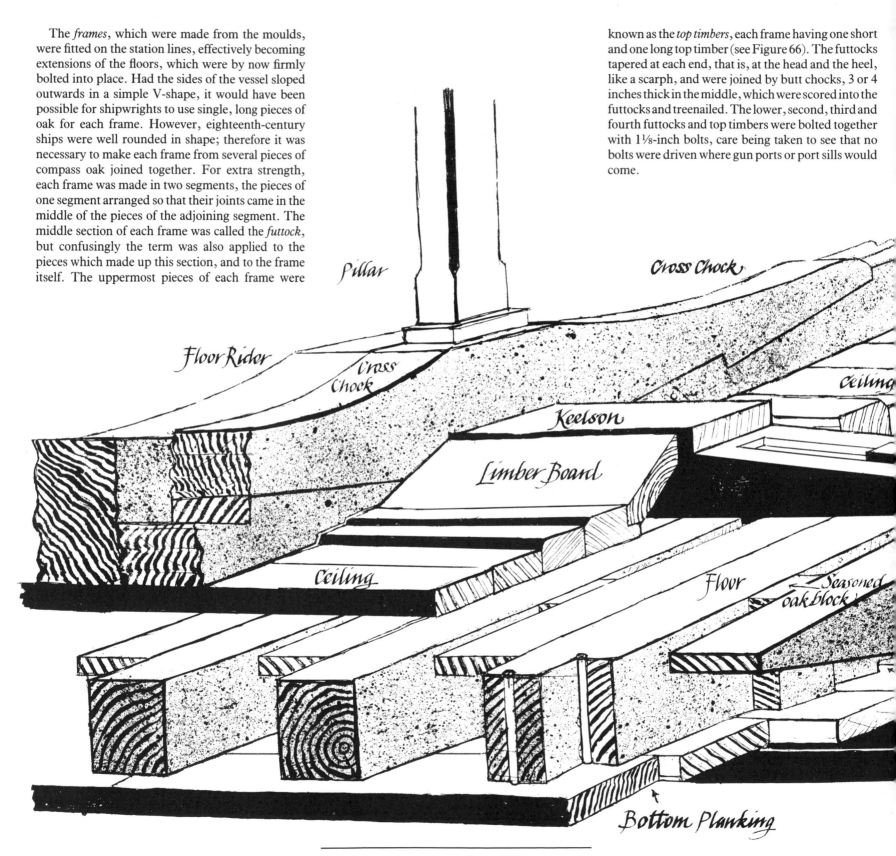

Pillar

Cross Chock

Floor Rider

Cross Chock

Ceiling

Keelson

Limber Board

Ceiling

Floor

Seasoned oak block

Bottom Planking

65 Detailed cutaway of the foundation of the ship (to scale)

66 The midship frame. The frames were made of two adjoining segments for strength, the one side containing the first and third futtocks and the other the second and fourth futtocks which overlapped their neighbours. 'Timbers in a ship, are the same as ribs in the animal or human body, and serve to support the sides, the planks being all fastened to them. . . . The heel of the first Futtock comes to the Keel, and the middle of it alongside the Floor-head; the heel of the second Futtock rests on the Floor-head, and the middle of it alongside the head of the first Futtock; the heel of the third Futtock rests on the head of the first, and the middle of it against the head of the second; and if there be a fourth Futtock; its heel must rest on the head of the second: if there be no more than three Futtocks, the heel of the Top-timber must rest on the head of the second Futtock' (Mungo Murray, *The Sixty-Gun Ship*, 1768)

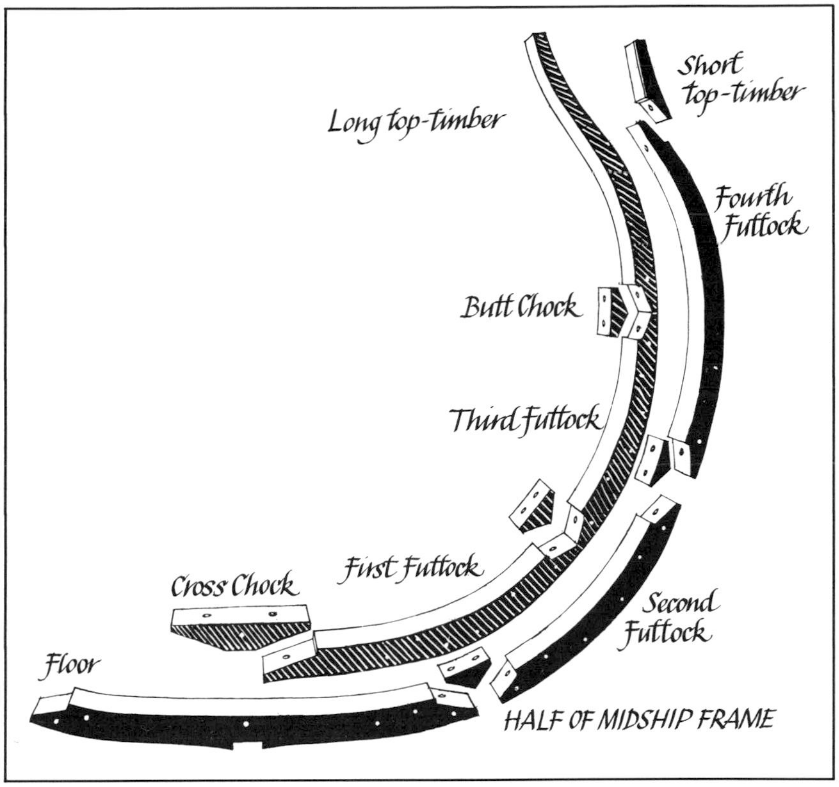

Short top-timber

Long top-timber

Fourth Futtock

Butt Chock

Third Futtock

First Futtock

Cross Chock

Second Futtock

Floor

HALF OF MIDSHIP FRAME

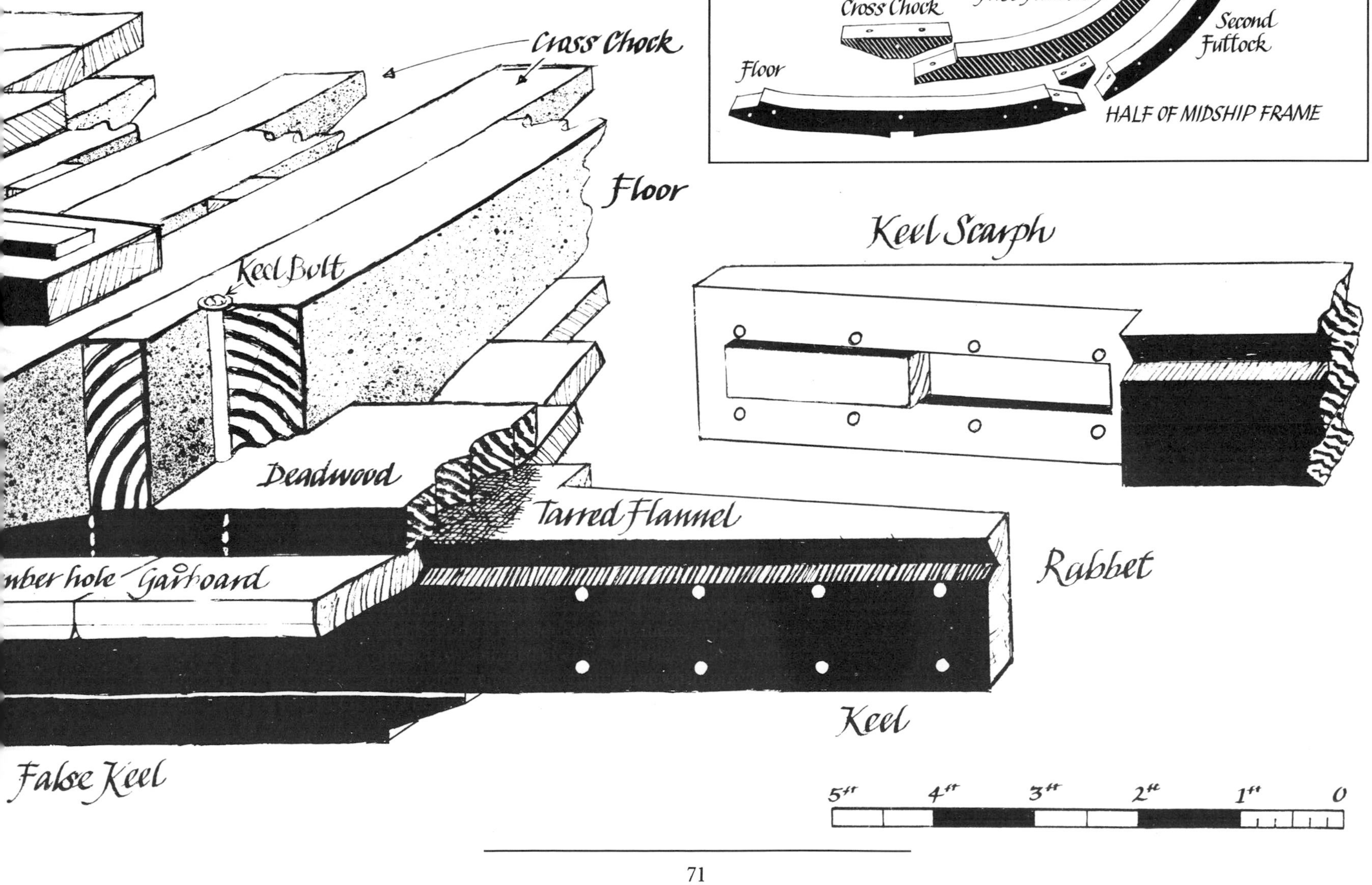

Cross Chock

Floor

Keel Bolt

Deadwood

Keel Scarph

Tarred Flannel

Rabbet

Timber hole Garboard

Keel

False Keel

5ᶠᵗ 4ᶠᵗ 3ᶠᵗ 2ᶠᵗ 1ᶠᵗ 0

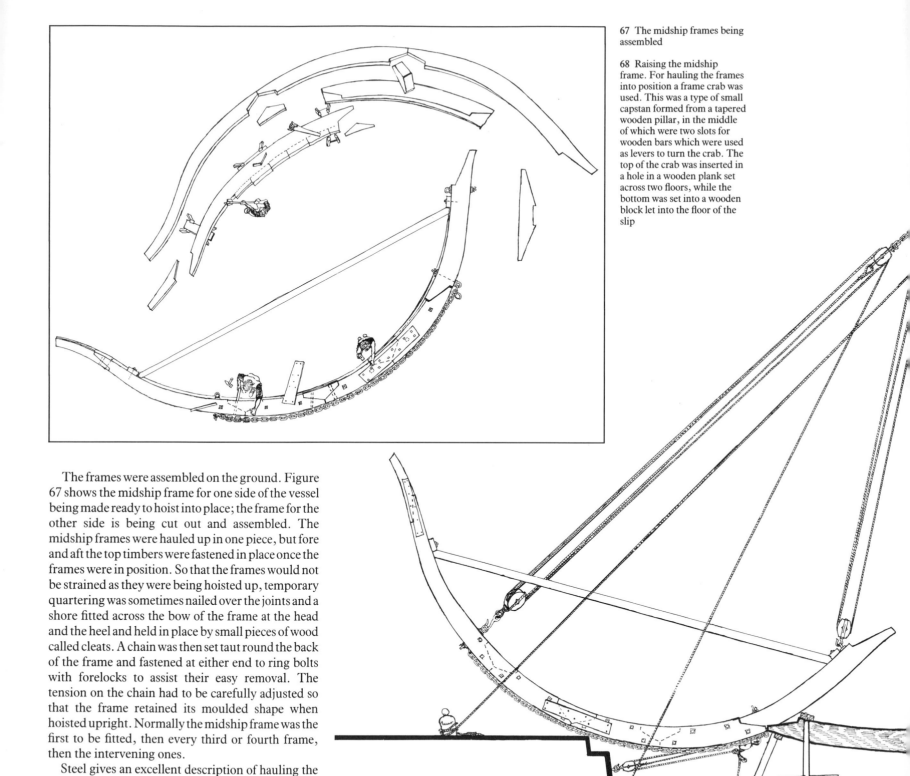

67 The midship frames being assembled

68 Raising the midship frame. For hauling the frames into position a frame crab was used. This was a type of small capstan formed from a tapered wooden pillar, in the middle of which were two slots for wooden bars which were used as levers to turn the crab. The top of the crab was inserted in a hole in a wooden plank set across two floors, while the bottom was set into a wooden block let into the floor of the slip

The frames were assembled on the ground. Figure 67 shows the midship frame for one side of the vessel being made ready to hoist into place; the frame for the other side is being cut out and assembled. The midship frames were hauled up in one piece, but fore and aft the top timbers were fastened in place once the frames were in position. So that the frames would not be strained as they were being hoisted up, temporary quartering was sometimes nailed over the joints and a shore fitted across the bow of the frame at the head and the heel and held in place by small pieces of wood called cleats. A chain was then set taut round the back of the frame and fastened at either end to ring bolts with forelocks to assist their easy removal. The tension on the chain had to be carefully adjusted so that the frame retained its moulded shape when hoisted upright. Normally the midship frame was the first to be fitted, then every third or fourth frame, then the intervening ones.

Steel gives an excellent description of hauling the frames into place:

The frames are raised into their places by tackles, which are lashed to the sheers, or travel upon a ridge rope. One tackle is applied to the heel of the frame to lighten it off the ribbon

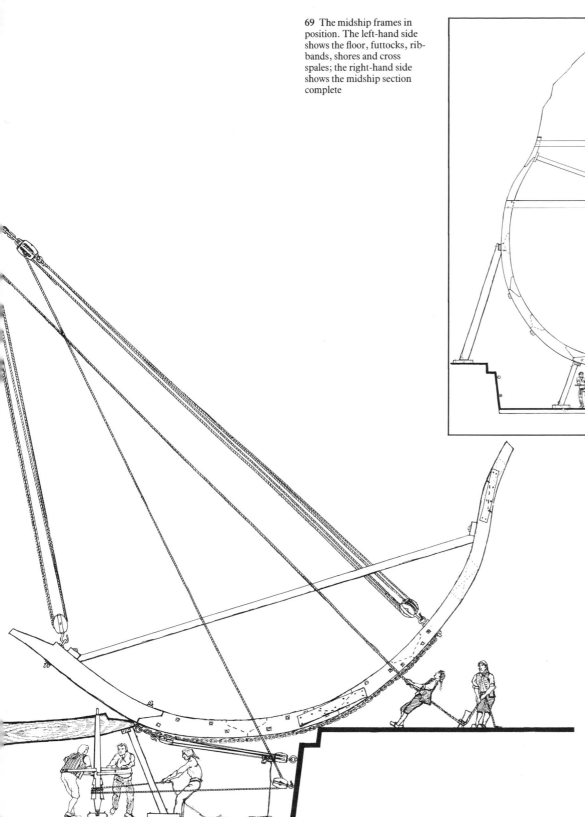

69 The midship frames in position. The left-hand side shows the floor, futtocks, ribbands, shores and cross spales; the right-hand side shows the midship section complete

and one or two near the main breadth, and another to the heel, to prevent it going too far into the ship. Some cant the frame and heave up the heel by one of the breadth tackles, landing it on the ribband; and then to prevent it going too far into the ship, they bore a hole and thrust in an eyebolt, which stops it against the ribband. The frames are shored and cross-spaled* either in the ports or at the main-breadth. Upon the cross-spales is marked the middle line and the breadth of the ship at the place of spaling to which the outside of the frame must exactly conform. Before the cross-spales can be nailed in the joint, the breadth must be squared in. Observe that, when the frames are cross-spaled in the ports, they need not be cut at the ends but may remain till the ship is planked and the beams in and knee'd. The only objection to spaling in the ports is that it is thought by some to be too high.

Cross chocks for joining each pair of frames to the keelson were introduced in 1710. Before that the pairs of frames simply met in a butt joint over the keelson. The use of cross chocks made the joint much stronger, the smaller frame chock replacing the short grain on the inside of the compass timber. In theory, there should be no short grain in compass timber, but in practice it was unlikely that the natural curve of the crook would correspond exactly to the required shape.

*Cross spales can be seen in Figure 69.

73

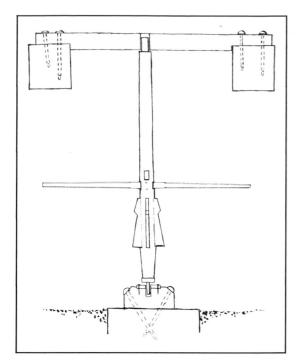

70 A frame crab. 'By this machine so simple in its construction may be hove up the frame timbers' (David Steel, *Naval Architecture*, 1805)

71 Overall view of the first frames going up. One of the most useful 'machines' to be found in any dockyard was the sheers. A pair of sheers consisted of two roughly trimmed masts which were erected across the slip for hoisting ship's frames and other large pieces such as the stem and the stern assembly into position. The masts were lashed together at their upper ends from which tackles were suspended. They were kept upright by guys which ran forward and aft from their head, and the heels were firmly lashed to prevent them spreading or were wedged against the sides of the slip.

The masts were 66 feet long with a spread of 46 feet. The tackles consisted of two treble blocks with the sheaves brass coaked. One block was lashed so that it was fixed to the after part of the sheers and the other to the fore side. The falls were 8-inch ropes, replaced before they became old and never allowed to deteriorate to the point where they became dangerous

Once the frames were in, the *filling frames* were positioned between them. These were not futtocked, but were single all the way up. Nor were they cut from moulds, but were spiled from the frames and the ribbands once they were in place, in the same way as the alternate floors.

At this point the hull was well on the way to taking shape. The gaps between the frames were relatively small and, as the vessel was being planked inside and out, some were made into ventilation shafts so that fresh air could circulate through the bilges.

The foremost timbers of the ship were the *hawse pieces* – a form of cant timber – the lower ends of which rested on the cant frames. They ran roughly parallel to the stem, their upper ends terminating in the lower part of the beak head. *Hawse holes*, to take the ship's cables, were cut in them. The hawse pieces were trimmed to fay to the *bollard timbers*, which were strong reinforcements inside the bow, capable of taking the strain on the cables when the vessel was at anchor. They projected above the hawse pieces and the bowsprit passed between them. The bollard timbers were joined by coaks or tabled to the stem and apron, and were bolted right through where practicable.

The hawse pieces and bollard timbers can be seen in Figures 74 and 76. Figure 76 shows the basic construction from the bow prior to planking. In Figure 77 the ship in the same stage of construction is seen from the stern, showing cant frames, sternpost, fashion pieces, transoms and the gun ports, which

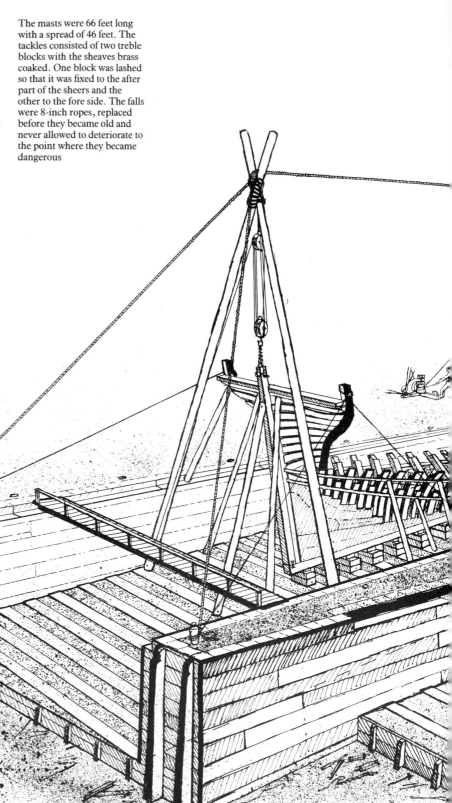

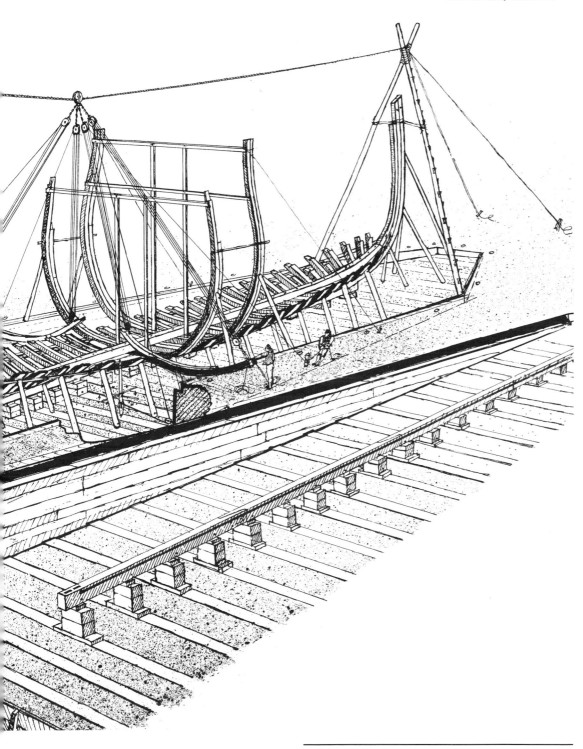

had sills top and bottom, and were spaced so that none of them came abreast any of the main timbers.

Figure 80 is another view from the stern of the vessel ready for planking up. At this stage the *counter timbers* are in place. These are the uprights between the wing transom and the quarter deck. Lower and upper counter timbers curved outwards aft, thus carrying the after cabin way beyond the sternpost and rudder (see Figure 79). Also shown are the vertical filling pieces below transom number 6.

Sometimes, if a vessel was not immediately needed by the Admiralty, it was left to season at this stage. This may be the explanation for the length of time taken to build *Thunderer*.

Once the whole framework of the ship was assembled and securely fastened, the next major stage was to plank the hull. This procedure was sometimes referred to by shipwrights as 'laying on the skin'. The ship was planked both inside and out, the inside planking being called *footwaling* or *ceiling*, possibly a corruption of sealing, as the inside planks did indeed seal the inside of the vessel from the bilges and the frames.

The first parts of the planking to be applied were the *wales*. These were the most substantial runs of planking on the outside of the hull and served to stiffen the vessel, counteracting the effects of hogging and giving the ship the characteristic curved lines when viewed from abeam. The *main wale*, which consisted of 8-inch-thick oak planks, or 'strakes', was placed at the level of the gun deck and just underneath the gun ports, thus reinforcing this crucial, and widest, part of the ship. It also served as a fender when the vessel was coming alongside. The upper deck was similarly strengthened by the *channel (chain) wale*, which was also of oak, but less substantial than the main wale, being only 6–6½ inches thick. The channel wale, as its name suggests,

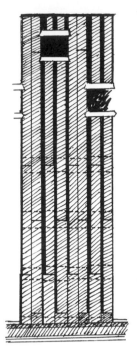

73 Frames and filling frames

74 The hull with frames and filling frames in place. At the bow can be seen the bollard timbers on either side of the stem. At this stage all the ribbands and harpins are in place

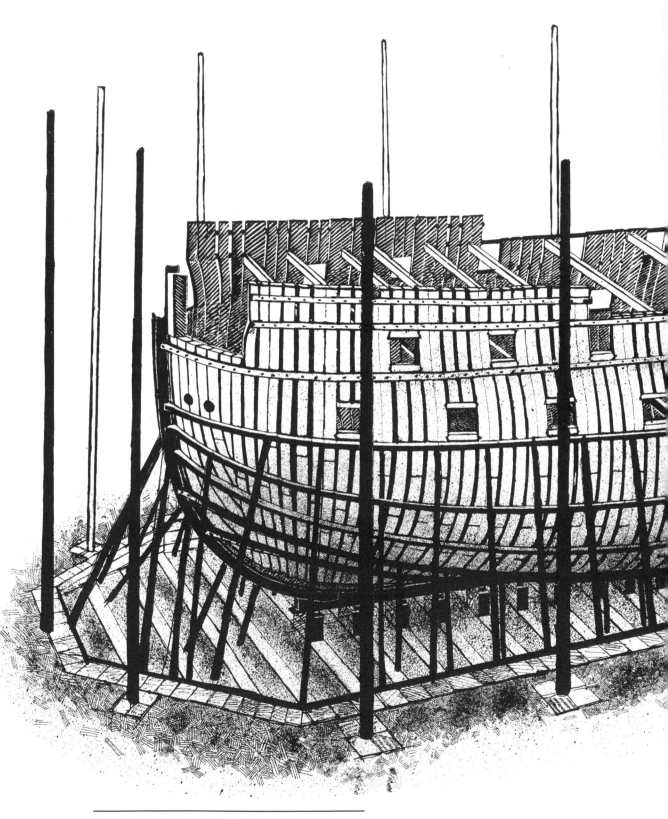

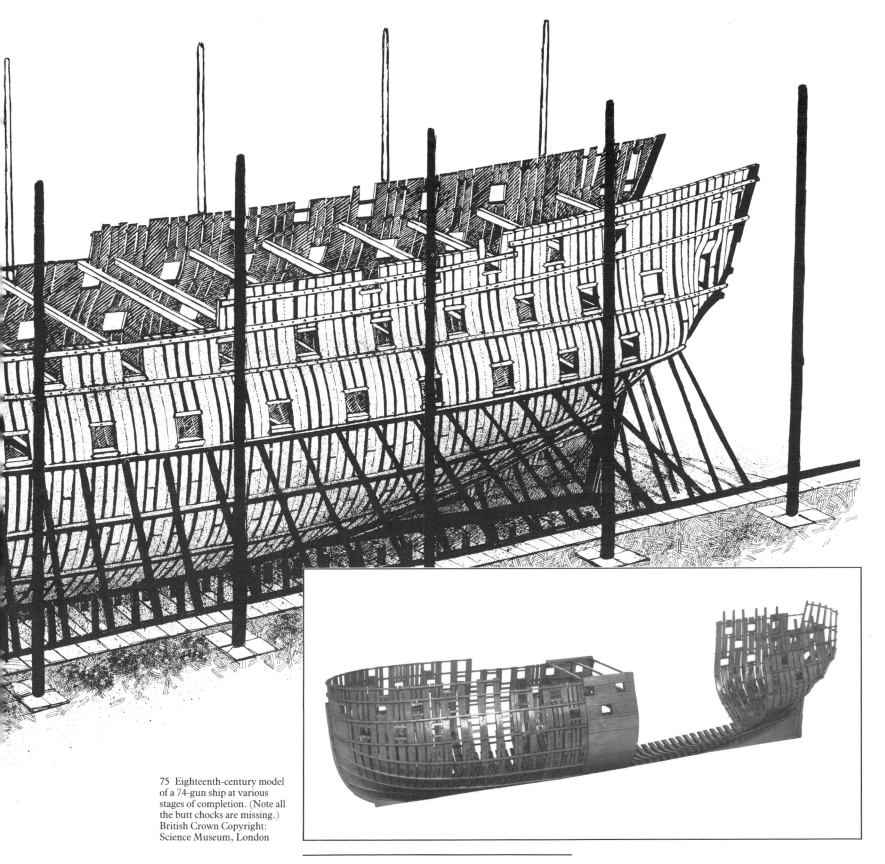

75 Eighteenth-century model of a 74-gun ship at various stages of completion. (Note all the butt chocks are missing.) British Crown Copyright: Science Museum, London

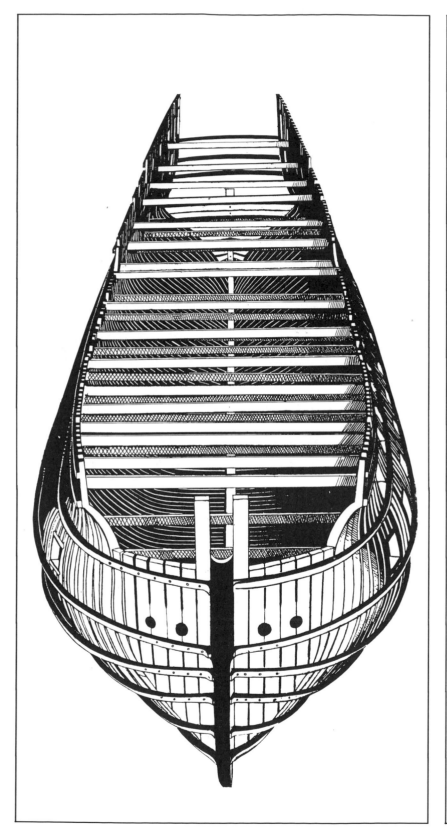

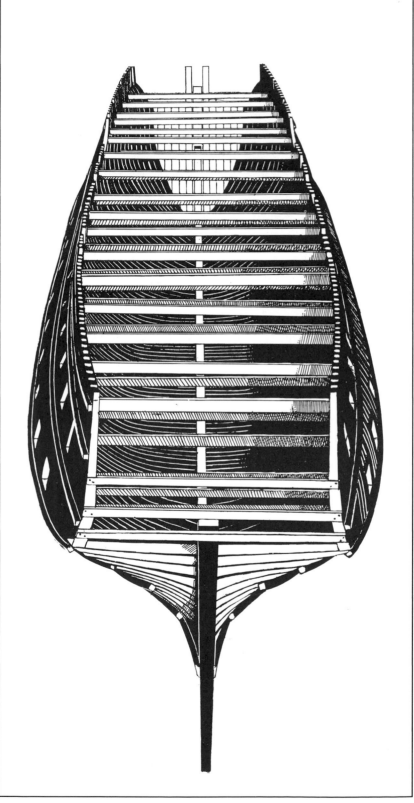

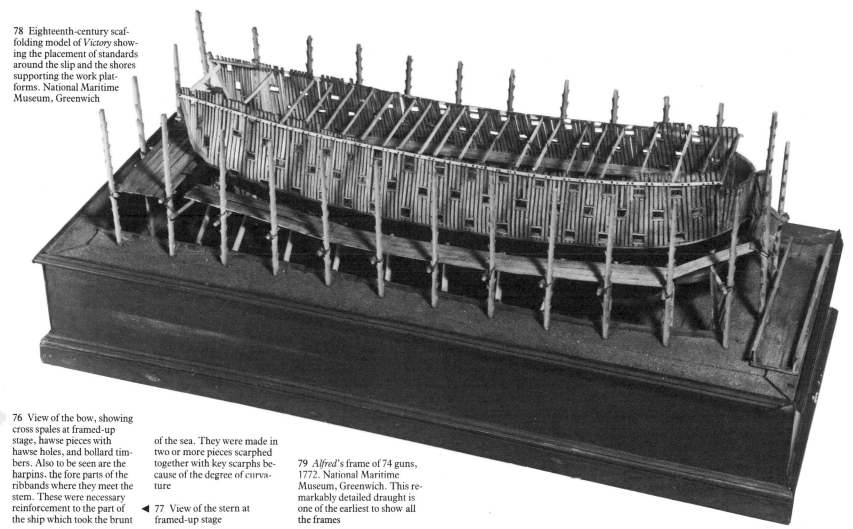

78 Eighteenth-century scaffolding model of *Victory* showing the placement of standards around the slip and the shores supporting the work platforms. National Maritime Museum, Greenwich

76 View of the bow, showing cross spales at framed-up stage, hawse pieces with hawse holes, and bollard timbers. Also to be seen are the harpins, the fore parts of the ribbands where they meet the stem. These were necessary reinforcement to the part of the ship which took the brunt of the sea. They were made in two or more pieces scarphed together with key scarphs because of the degree of curvature

◄ 77 View of the stern at framed-up stage

79 *Alfred*'s frame of 74 guns, 1772. National Maritime Museum, Greenwich. This remarkably detailed draught is one of the earliest to show all the frames

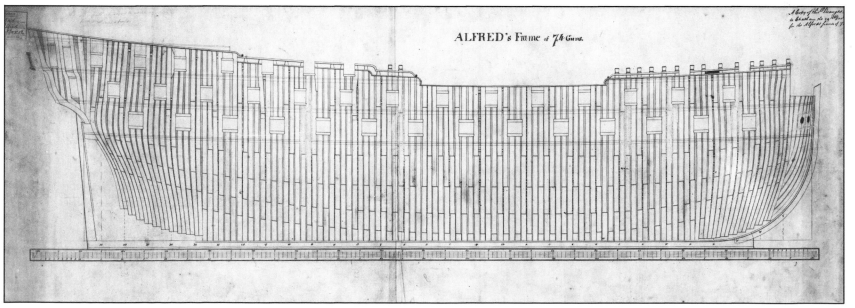

ALFRED's Frame of 74 Guns.

carried the chain plates for the shrouds holding the masts. Both wales can be seen on the model of *Bellona* (Figure 86).

This model is particularly interesting because it shows that an innovation in the way the main wales were planked had been introduced by 1760. This method, known as anchor-stock waling, is shown in detail in Figure 87. In Figure 88 the conventional method of straight-edged planking can be seen. The anchor-stock method was clearly intended to counteract any tendency to hogging, but would have been more costly because of the amount of wood wasted in trimming each plank. Moreover, the shipwright must have found it more time-consuming to fit the planks edge to edge using the anchor-stock method. For these reasons, the straight-edged method was probably the one most commonly used.

When fitting strakes, the planks had to fit the shape of the hull, which curved in two directions. A good analogy can be seen when one peels a segment of an orange so that the peel comes off in a single strip from top to bottom. The edges of the strip have a bevel while the peel curves along its length and is convex on the outside and concave on the inside. Each plank had to be cut so that it fitted snugly against its neighbour along its length and by its depth. A skilled shipwright could cut planks so that the joints between them were barely visible and watertight. Nevertheless, all such joints were caulked for extra tightness.

The strakes were first marked out on the ship's side (see Figure 85), using a batten to get a fair line. The butts (plank ends) were staggered so that no two butts were adjacent, and were always fastened to the main frames, never to the filling frames. In consequence, the length of the planks varied considerably, from being very short between the gun ports to pieces over 30 feet long. There was no standard width for planks; it depended on the lumber available.

For marking out the individual planks from sided timber, the shipwright used a *rule staff* or *spiling board* and a *bevel board*. (These are shown in Figure 81.) Starting with the bottom strake of the main wale, the shipwright tacked a long batten to the ship's side where the plank was to go. This was the rule staff, a thin board about a quarter of an inch thick, some 4 inches wide and about 30 feet long. It was sometimes made of several pieces of wood with pads across the butts. It could easily be bent round the ship's side, but care was taken to ensure that it was only curved in one plane – fore and aft. Then, using a *spiling stick* – a small rule – the length, width and shape of the plank were marked on the staff. As many spilings as necessary were taken, usually at 3-foot intervals along the top and bottom edges of where the plank was going to fit. These were shown by lines scored on the frames, or were spiled from the edge of the adjacent plank already in place on the ship's side. An experienced shipwright could cut a plank from the previous plank's spiling board so that it fitted into place with the minimum of trimming.

Next, the angle of the plank edge to the hull was measured at 3-foot intervals; these points were called the *bevelling spots* and the angles were marked on the

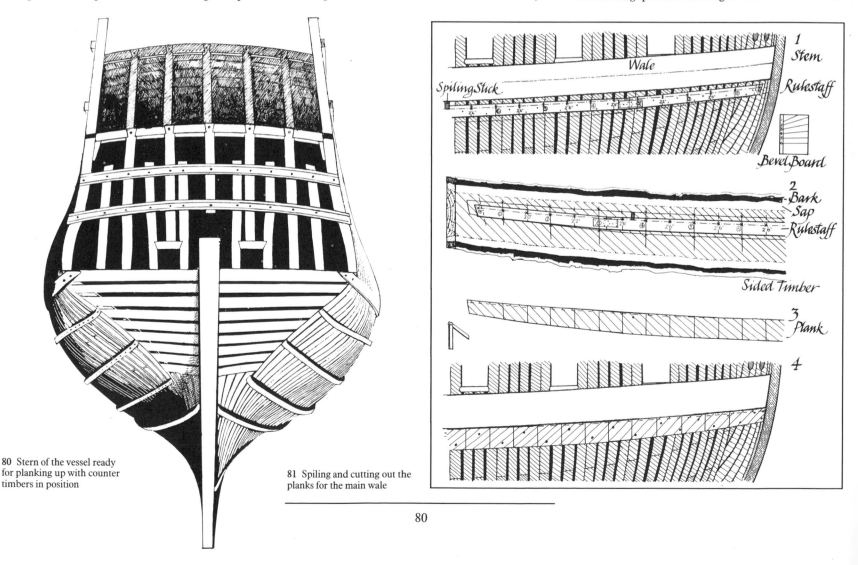

80 Stern of the vessel ready for planking up with counter timbers in position

81 Spiling and cutting out the planks for the main wale

bevel board, from which they could be transferred to the plank to be cut out.

The shipwright now had all the necessary measurements for the shape of the inner face of a strake marked on the outer face of his rule staff. He then had to transfer the marks to the other side of the staff, taking a great deal of care in the process as the plank had to fit first time. He applied the rule staff to a suitable piece of timber, the strake having to be cut clear of the sapwood to the correct length and curvature. The markings were transferred to the timber in reverse order to that in which they had been taken from the ship's side and were joined by a line drawn along the edge of a flexible batten. The plank was cut out with square edges, then bevelled on the top edge, using the bevel board to give the correct angle at any point. Caulking chamfers were put on all edges.

If there was a lot of turn on the side of the vessel, the plank might have to be hollowed out to fit. In that case, the plank selected would have to be thicker than

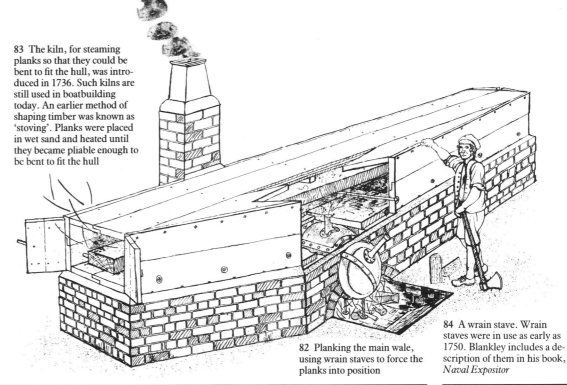

83 The kiln, for steaming planks so that they could be bent to fit the hull, was introduced in 1736. Such kilns are still used in boatbuilding today. An earlier method of shaping timber was known as 'stoving'. Planks were placed in wet sand and heated until they became pliable enough to be bent to fit the hull

82 Planking the main wale, using wrain staves to force the planks into position

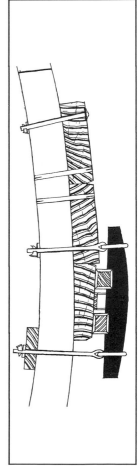

84 A wrain stave. Wrain staves were in use as early as 1750. Blankley includes a description of them in his book, *Naval Expositor*

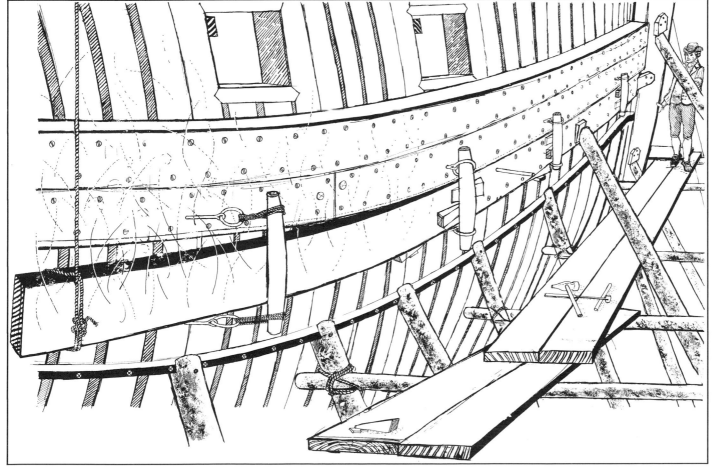

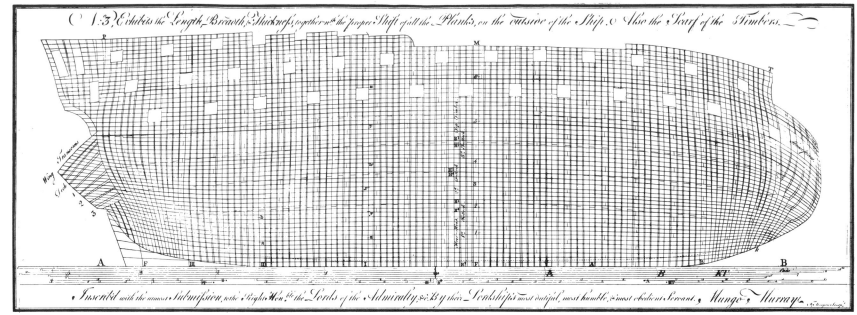

85a and b The length and proper shift of all the planks, both outside and inside. From Mungo Murray, *The Sixty-Gun Ship*, 1768, Plates 3 and 4. Photo: National Maritime Museum, Greenwich. The 'proper shift' refers to the positioning of the butts of the planks so that they are staggered from course to course.

'Though No. III. [i.e. Figure 85a] exhibits the length of all the planks in the outside of the ship, yet it is not to be expected that the strakes, if cut as in the plate, would fay to one another's edges on the model; for if all the planks on the ship's bottom, after being fayed to one another, were taken off and laid flat on the ground, every shipwright knows very well their edges would not come together; for which reason they are obliged to spile for them, that is, they take a rule staff, which is a thin board of about one-eighth of an inch thick, four inches broad, and 20 or 30 feet long; this will bend about any part

86 Contemporary model of *Bellona* showing details of construction including anchor-stock waling and conventional framing. National Maritime Museum, Greenwich

N.4 Exhibits the Length, Breadth & Thickness, together with the proper Shift of all the Planks in the inside of the Ship. Also the Hight of the Beams and Decks.

Inscribed with the utmost Submission, to the Right Honble the Lords of the Admiralty &c. By their Lordship's most dutiful, most humble, & most obedient Servant, Mungo Murray.

of the ship, and so they bring it round carefully, without penning, and then they see how much it wants of faying to the edge of the other plank that is fastened on the ship, which they mark, at conven-ient distances from one another, on the staff, and from thence they transfer them to the plank, on which they lay the rule-staff, after taking off the spilings.

'For this reason, I intend, if I meet with success in this undertaking to publish a plate, exhibiting the form of all the planks, as if they were actually taken off by spilings' (Mungo Murray, *The Sixty-Gun Ship*, 1768)

those amidships where the curve of the hull was at its smallest.

Oak planks of the size of those used on a large ship could not be fastened into place round the curve of the hull without some special treatment to render them pliable. This applied especially to the thicker planks of the wales. So, having been trimmed and cleaned up, they were steamed in a kiln. This was a long wooden chest or trunk, made from deals which were neatly tongued and grooved, set on a brickwork base. It was roughly 3–4 feet square and from 40 to 60 feet in length, with a door at each end, and was held together by bolts. Steam from a copper or iron boiler housed in the base was allowed to circulate freely round any timbers placed in the kiln. Occasionally

two boilers were used to ensure a sufficient supply of steam.

A plank would be steamed for one hour for every inch of thickness with an extra hour for luck – or, in any event, until it was pliable. A piece of wale, for example, would be steamed for eight or nine hours. Green oak was particularly amenable to this treatment, and it was claimed that a 1-inch-thick piece of oak could be made pliable enough to be bent round a 1-inch radius.

Wearing gloves, or with their hands protected by rags, the shipwrights would carry the hot planks to the ship's side and haul them up on ropes tied to the cross spales. Once the plank was hanging in approximately the correct position, *wrain staves* were

used to force it into place, starting at the bows forward and the stern aft. (The ends of the planks which fitted into the rabbets in the stem- and sternposts were called 'whoodings', which has been corrupted to 'hood ends'.) Wrain staves were made from thick billets of ash, tapered at both ends, which fitted into rings on the wrain bolts. The bolts were taken through adjacent strakes or timbers and forelocked on the inside of the vessel. The length of the bolts varied, but it was sometimes necessary to extend them with short lengths of rope. Sometimes these would break, with the result that the plank would spring out, sweeping men from the scaffolding.

Considerable force could be exerted using wrain staves. They were essentially very simple but

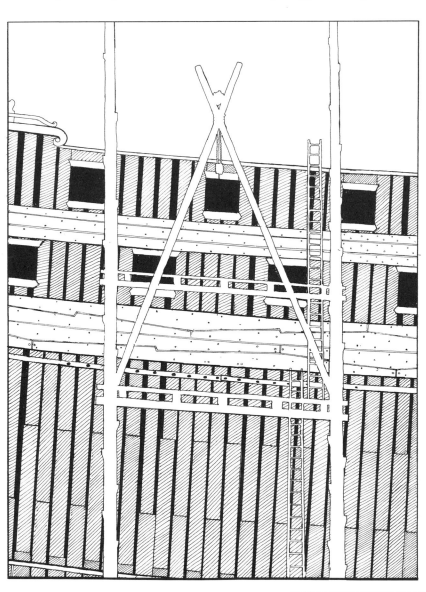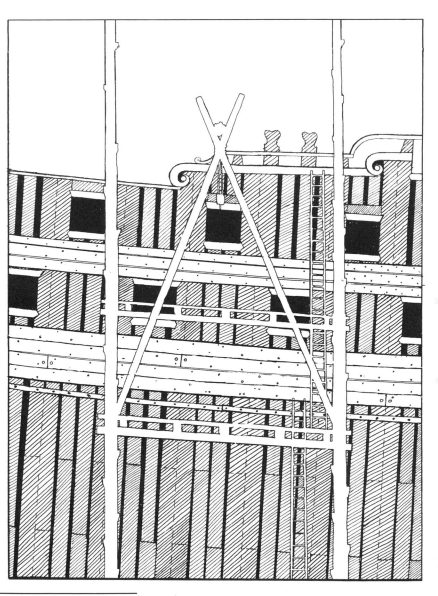

effective forerunners of modern clamps. To force a plank fully home, wedges were driven beneath the ash bars of the staves. Then the plank was fastened, with 1-inch bolts at each end and with two treenails to each frame, working in the same direction as the wrain staves. The staves were left in position until the planks had cooled to save straining the new fastenings, only a minimum of which were used until the inner planking was finished.

Once the three or four strakes of the main wale and the three strakes of the channel wale were in place, the rest of the planking on the outside of the hull was fitted. The hull planking was usually 4-inch thick oak, fastened with treenails 1¾ inches in diameter and with 1-inch bolts driven through the frame behind

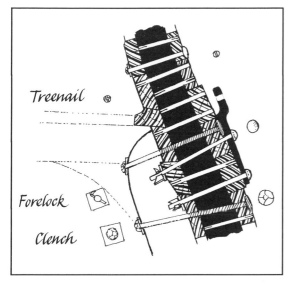

Treenail

Forelock

Clench

87 The main wale planked anchor-stock fashion with conventional planking on the channel wale. In this example the vessel is built without main frames

88 Conventional planking of the main wale and conventional framing

89 Fastenings used on the channel wale

90 The inside and outside planking amidships

each butt and clenched over a ring on the inside. Up to eight gangs of men would be engaged on planking, working up and down from the wales, with another gang working from the garboards upwards. The two garboard strakes on either side of the keel were the last to be fitted, usually not until the upper deck was on, so that rain water could drain away and not collect to stagnate in the bilges. This also enabled air to circulate throughout the hull and, in the case of ships being built on slips, meant that they would not start to float on spring tides.

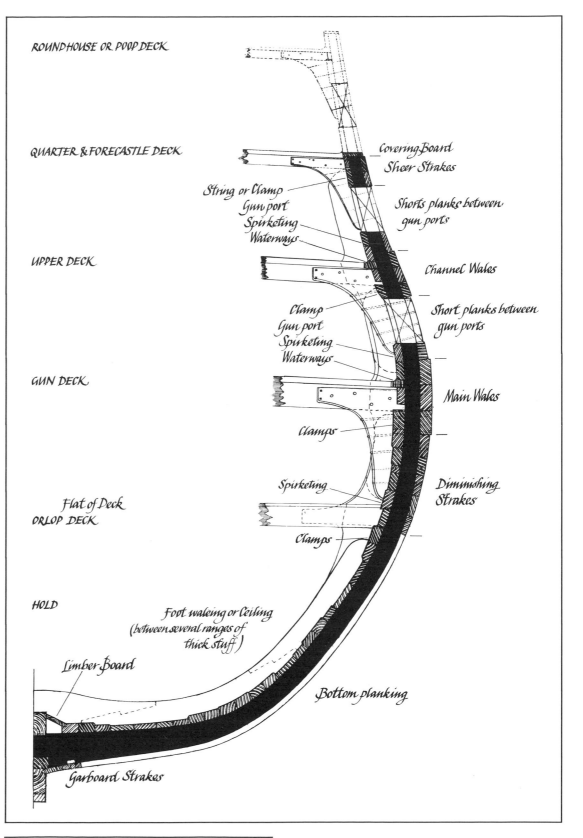

ROUNDHOUSE OR POOP DECK

QUARTER & FORECASTLE DECK

Covering Board
Sheer Strakes

String or Clamp
Gun port
Spirketing
Waterways

Shorts planks between gun ports

UPPER DECK

Channel Wales

Clamp
Gun port
Spirketing
Waterways

Short planks between gun ports

GUN DECK

Main Wales

Clamps

Spirketing

Diminishing Strakes

Flat of Deck
ORLOP DECK

Clamps

HOLD

Foot waleing or Ceiling
(between several ranges of
thick stuff)

Limber Board

Bottom planking

Garboard Strakes

Possibly while the vessel was being planked on the outside, work proceeded on the ceiling on the inside. Here the order was from the bottom up, with the deck beams being fitted at the same time. The wood for the ceiling was oak. Fitting the inside planking presented a slightly more difficult problem than fitting the outer strakes: due to the concave hull inside the vessel, the planks had to be pushed into place in the middle of their length, rather than be pulled into a convex curve as the outer planking, and this required more force to be exerted. For this purpose, the planks were shored from the opposite side of the vessel; wrain staves were used as well. The ends of the planks tended to creep in as the planks were pushed home, which meant that each plank had to be knocked along from one end or the other so that its butt fitted tightly against that of the adjacent plank.

The principal run of thick timber was the two strakes next to the limbers (see below), and these were the first to be fitted. They were followed by the lower footwaling and thickstuff, then the orlop-deck clamps, the orlop deck beams, spirketing, the gun-deck clamps, the gun-deck beams, waterways, spirketing, the run of planks between the gun ports, the upper-deck clamps, the upper-deck beams, the forecastle and quarterdeck clamps, and finally the forecastle and quarterdeck beams. The details of inside and outside planking are shown in Figure 90.

On the inside of the vessel, next to the keelson, ran the *limbers*. These were channels through which the bilge water could drain to the pump wells. They were covered with a limber board to prevent them from becoming choked with rubbish. The limber boards were placed at an angle to permit large quantities of water to drain over the floors and could be removed so that the limbers could be cleared if they became blocked. Next came two 8-inch-thick planks which were known as the *limber strakes*. These were fastened about a foot from either side of the keelson, and helped to secure the heels of the first futtocks under the cross chocks. They were, therefore, subjected to heavy strains. Then came a run of 4-inch ceiling, followed by another run of thickstuff which was made up of five or six strakes of 7- to 8-inch thick, each over 12 inches wide. This spanned the joint at the head of the floor timber and the heel of the second futtock. As this was the turn of the bilge, one of the most acute curves in the hull, where, if the vessel ran aground, its whole weight would bear, the thickstuff was necessary reinforcement to the frame chocks. There was a third run of thickstuff, consisting of two strakes, spanning the joint of the first futtock head and the heel of the third futtock.

After another run of ceiling came the first of the clamps, the *orlop-deck clamp*. These were, in fact, beam shelves or inner wales, upon which the ends of the beams rested. They not only took the weight of the beams and the decks, but considerably strengthened the ship fore and aft. The run of the clamps were the means by which the decks took on the sheer line of the vessel. The orlop-deck clamps were made of two strakes, the upper one 7 inches thick, the lower 6 inches thick, and 1 foot 3 inches and 1 foot 1 inch

91 The ship fully planked. At the top right of the picture are beams under construction, next to the beam house. In the foreground men are loading barrels into a lighter and a timber raft is being towed by a skiff. To the left of the slip, men are busy breaming a boat's bottom

wide respectively. All other clamps were similarly massive. (French ships at this time did not have orlop clamps; the beams rested on the ceiling. This was possibly to save weight.) As the orlop-deck clamps were fitted, so were the orlop-deck beams.

Above the orlop deck was another strake of thickstuff known as *spirketing*, a run of slightly thinner strakes, and then the *gun-deck clamps*. These were even more massive than those of the orlop deck, often extending to four strakes, as they had to support the greatest weight in the ship, the heaviest guns.

Above the gun-deck beams were fitted the *waterways*, long timbers which faired the deck into the sides of the ship so that any water taken on board could easily run away into the scuppers. As can be seen in Figure 90, the waterways were rounded so that no water or rubbish could lodge in them. The *scuppers* were lead pipes leading from the waterways to the outside of the hull. They had leather flaps over their outer ends to prevent water coming back up them. Above the waterways came another run of spirketing which coincided with the lower edges of the gun ports.

The clamps for the upper-deck beams were usually bearded (tapered in a downward direction) from half their depth to less than 1 inch thick on the under side, except amidships. A semicircle was cut into them over each gun port to house the muzzles of the guns (see Figure 96). Above the upper-deck beams came further waterways and spirketing, then another line of gun ports over which there was another set of clamps for the quarterdeck and the forecastle beams. These clamps, lighter than the others, were known as *string*.

Turning now to the outside of the vessel, Figure 90 shows the *garboard strakes*, which were made of elm, then the 4-inch oak bottom planking extending round the turn of the bilge until it coincided with the orlop-deck beams on the inside of the hull. The next run of planking was known as *diminishing strakes* and these were fitted so that there was no abrupt transition from the 4-inch bottom planks to the 8-inch main wale. Then came the main wale itself, followed by lines of short planks between the gun ports, the channel wale, further runs of short planks between the second line of gun ports, and finally the *sheer strake*. Along the top of the vessel's sides, closing in the spaces between the frames, was fitted the *covering board*. The spaces between the frames which were used as air vents had traps constructed over them to keep any water out.

When fully planked, the ship was phenomenally strong. The double skin of oak planking, in places no less than 16 inches thick, plus the frames, which were so closely spaced as to be almost solid, made the sides 26 inches at their thickest point, protecting the ship from enemy cannon fire and rendering it virtually indestructible even from a direct hit. Such ships were certainly not easy to sink. Far greater were the risks of fire or explosion in a magazine, or dismasting. A ship thus crippled would be easy prey to a boarding party, eager for their share of the prize money.

'Britannia' Entering Portsmouth Harbour. Oil painting by G. Chambers. National Maritime Museum, Greenwich

8
THE BUILDING II

While the hull was being planked, the deck beams were being assembled as these were fitted in the ship as soon as the appropriate clamps were in place. Structurally the beams served to bind the sides of the vessel together and to support the decks which, in the case of warships, had to carry a great deal of heavy equipment. In a 74 the beams were distributed as follows:

Deck	No. of beams	Camber amidships
Orlop	20	2½ inches
Gun	26	6 inches
Upper	27	8 inches
Forecastle	12	8 inches
Quarter	29	8½ inches
Poop	18	9 inches

The density of beams was highest for the quarter deck and the poop. These beams were of smaller dimension than the others to reduce the weight above the centre of gravity; hence, the smaller guns were housed on these decks. The fact that the hull was narrower at these points than at gun-deck level also permitted the use of smaller beams. An additional benefit was the better headroom thus provided for the officers who were quartered on the upper deck and the quarter deck. The longest beams were those of the gun deck. They were placed according to the position of the gun ports, with one beam beneath each port, and thus beneath each gun, and one between each port.

All the beams arched in the middle, giving the decks a pronounced camber. The purpose of this was threefold: to give structural strength; to allow any water shipped in heavy weather to drain quickly to the waterways; and to reduce the travel of the guns when they recoiled after being fired. The camber curve was the arc of a circle and ranged from 2½

inches at the lowest deck – the orlop – to 9 inches at the topmost deck – the poop.

In large ships the beams were made up of two, three or even four pieces which, when properly scarphed together, were said to be stronger than a single piece of timber. Beams made in two pieces had a scarph at roughly one third the length of the beam; with three pieces the middle section and the arms were each nearly half the length of the beam, the middle section being scarphed to take the arms on either side. Beams of four pieces had two identical middle sections, the arms and the middle sections each being three sevenths the length of the beam. The length of the scarphs was about one and a half times the depth or moulding of the beam. Tabling later became common. The tables were divided in the middle of the depth and where wood was taken from the upper piece it was left in the lower (see Figure 93). The only problem with this type of scarphing was

that, should the decks leak, the scarphs were liable to hold water and eventually rot. All the scarphs were well dried out by burning reeds or shavings on them. They were then payed with tar before being bolted together at 18-inch intervals. The ends of the scarphs were fastened with two small bolts or iron nails.

The beams were cut to fit the exact span of the hull from clamp to clamp. They were lowered into place on the clamps, into which they were let. To protect the beam ends, where water could collect, as much as possible from rot, the heart wood was bored out with a 1½-inch auger and a red-hot bolt thrust in, left to cool and then removed.

Knees were used to secure the beams to the sides of the ship, hence the Navy's vast demand for grown oak crooks; until iron knees were introduced later in the century there was simply no substitute for naturally curved wood. Indeed, it was the dearth of crooks that encouraged shipwrights to look for alternatives. A combination of iron and wood was tried by some English yards, while on the Continent experiments were carried out with made knees in which straight pieces of wood were lapped together at the crown with a chock fitted into the throat in much the same way as with made floors.

Two sets of knees were used at each end of the beams. These were known as *hanging* and *lodging knees*. Hanging knees were placed vertically, with a 6-foot arm running down the inside of the hull and an arm 4 feet 6 inches long running along the beam. Lodging knees were set horizontally, level with the top of the beam and parallel to the deck, the side arm filling the space between the beam ends against the inside of the hull. The arm on the beam itself was 5 feet long. The orlop-deck beams did not have hanging knees, but were attached by *standards* – in effect, inverted hanging knees – which ran up the ship's sides from the top of the beam.

92 Marking out a small deck beam. The camber on the beam is made up of parts of a circle

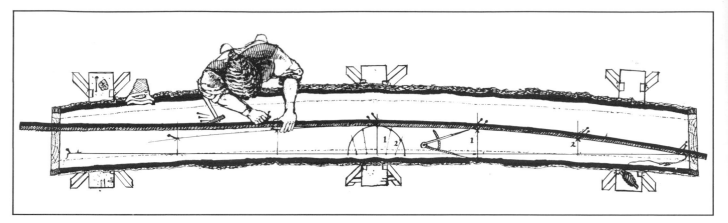

93 Beam scarphs. The top three diagrams show scarphs for beams in two, three and four sections. The bottom diagram shows a table scarph

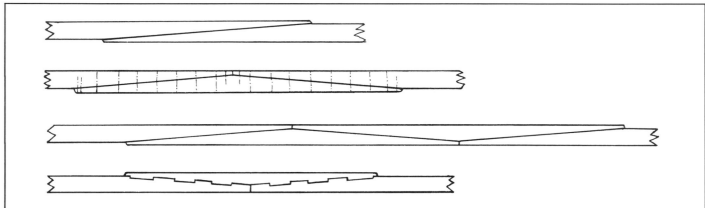

95 Top: dagger, hanging and ▶ cast knees; bottom: lodging knees

94 Spiling a lodging knee

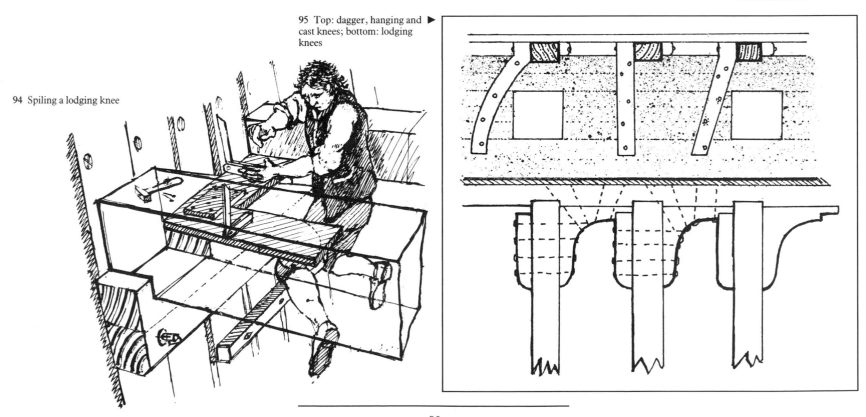

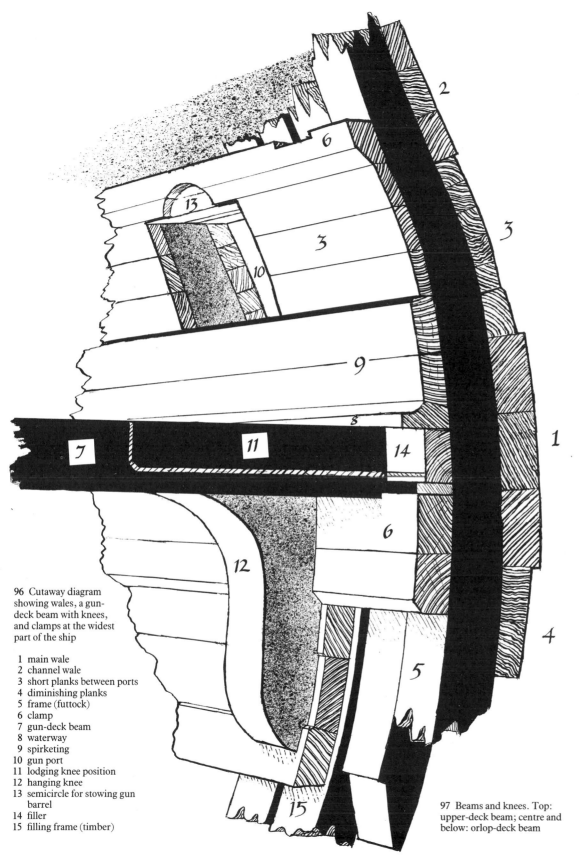

96 Cutaway diagram showing wales, a gun-deck beam with knees, and clamps at the widest part of the ship

1 main wale
2 channel wale
3 short planks between ports
4 diminishing planks
5 frame (futtock)
6 clamp
7 gun-deck beam
8 waterway
9 spirketing
10 gun port
11 lodging knee position
12 hanging knee
13 semicircle for stowing gun barrel
14 filler
15 filling frame (timber)

In shaping knees it was vital that as little wood as possible was taken out of the throat of the crook as this was its strongest point. The knees were attached by bolts driven from the outside of the hull and clenched over countersunk washers.

Knees were used as reinforcement at other points inside the hull (see Figure 98). At the lower part of the bow and stern, *crutches* – four forward and three aft on either side – were attached to the keelson. They ran horizontally. In the stern three *sleepers* were fitted from the ceiling to the transoms on either side. These were bolted to the deck transom and to the lower transoms of the stern assembly. (Transoms below the wing transom had filling inserted between them, but the sleepers were not attached to this.) In the bow there were two large *breasthooks*, which were chocked where they crossed the apron. Just below the hawse holes ran a *hawsehook*, similar to the breasthooks but shorter and slightly less substantial.

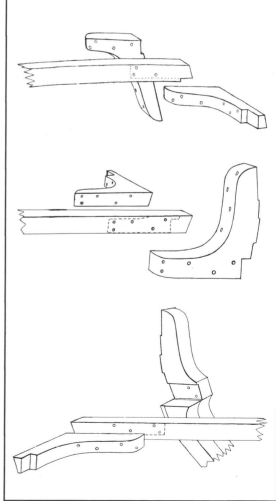

97 Beams and knees. Top: upper-deck beam; centre and below: orlop-deck beam

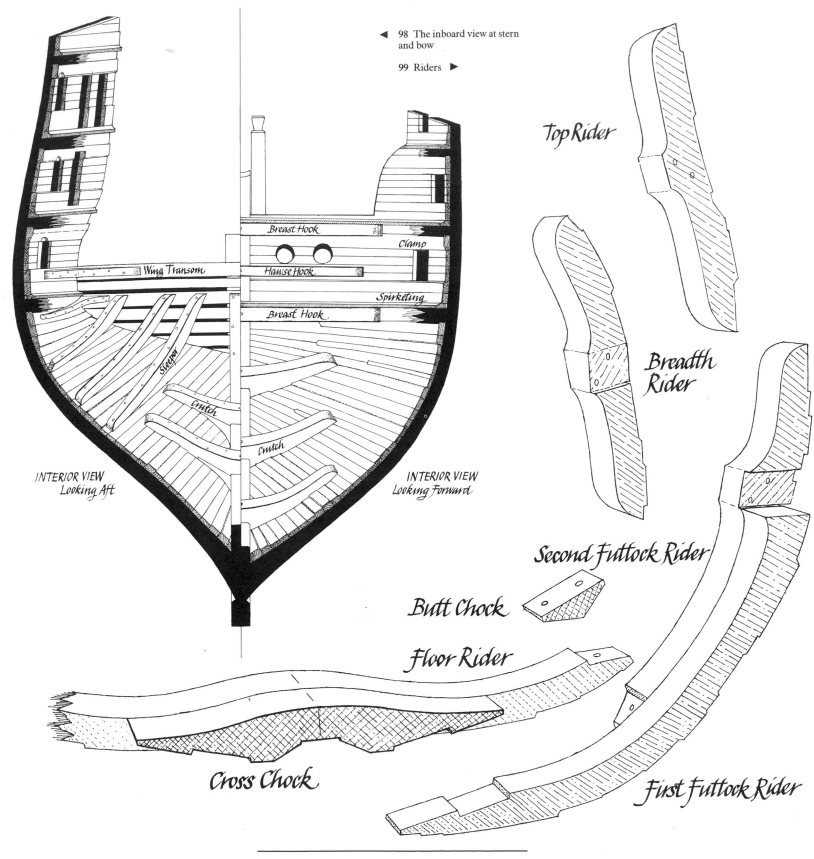

98 The inboard view at stern and bow

99 Riders ▶

Breast Hook

Clamp

Wing Transom

Hawse Hook

Spirketing

Breast Hook

Sleeper

Crutch

Crutch

INTERIOR VIEW
Looking Aft

INTERIOR VIEW
Looking Forward

Top Rider

Breadth Rider

Second Futtock Rider

Butt Chock

Floor Rider

First Futtock Rider

Cross Chock

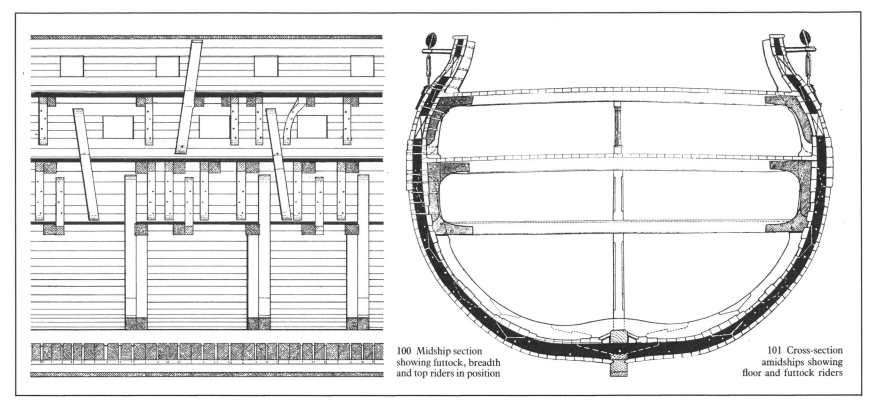

100 Midship section showing futtock, breadth and top riders in position

101 Cross-section amidships showing floor and futtock riders

The interior of the hull itself was further reinforced by *riders* (see Figures 99–101). These were basically interior ribs or frames. Some were set against the ceiling and corresponded with some of the main frames; others were simply scored down at intervals on the keelson. The number varied from ship to ship, but generally a first rate had five *floor riders*, and eight *futtock riders* (i.e. on the main frames), thirteen *breadth riders* and thirteen *top riders* on either side; a 74 had four floor riders, with six futtock riders, twelve breadth riders and twelve top riders on either side. The floor riders were reinforced by cross chocks and were scarphed to the futtock riders which ran up to just below the orlop deck. According to Murray, the futtock riders 'are scored about an inch, or an inch and a half into the Orlop Beams' (*The Sixty-Gun Ship*, 1768). Higher up were the breadth riders and the top riders, some of which were inclined at a slight angle, presumably to clear the knees but also to give strength in two directions, the beginning of cross-bracing.★ The breadth riders extended from just above the orlop deck to just below the upper deck, and had the gun-deck beam let into them. The top riders ran from just above the gun deck to just below

★The use of cross-bracing was introduced by Sir Robert Seppings, Surveyor of the Navy, 1813–32.

the rail amidships or the forecastle forward or the quarterdeck aft, and had the upper-deck beams let into them. The riders were about 12 inches square.

Before the decks were laid, the *bitts*, *capstans* and *steps* for the masts had to be fitted. The main bitts were the *riding bitts*, a massive framework consisting of substantial pieces of oak and situated forward of the anchor capstan, to which the anchor cables were made fast. Consequently, they had to be capable of taking great strain; they were rather like a giant cleat in function, the cable simply being wound round them and let out gradually or held as required. Warships usually had two sets of bitts, and if both were used at the same time, the cable was said to be double-bitted. The uprights of the bitts were approximately 1 foot 5 inches square at the head, tapering to 1 foot 2 inches. They rested on the ceiling and were scored into the orlop-deck and the gun-deck beams, to which they were fastened with two 1½-inch bolts through each joint. The cross pieces were 1 foot 5 inches by 1 foot 3 inches, and were let into each pair of uprights to a depth of 2½ inches. Each cross piece was faced with a 6-inch piece of elm, a very hard-wearing timber. Two pieces of decking, 7 inches thick, were laid from the after pair of bitts to the forward ones, and from the fore bitts to the beam before the foremast. These pieces of decking were

almost certainly oak, and were let 1½ inches into the beams, to which they were bolted, as well as to the carlins (see below), with 1½-inch bolts. The knees reinforcing the bitts were called *spurs* or *standards*, and were bedded into the decking with hair or tarred flannel.

Fore and aft *jeer*, *jear* or *gear bitts* were also fitted before the fore- and mizzen masts. These were used for tying off halyards.

All English 74s were fitted with two *capstans* (or *capsterns* as the word was spelled in the mid-eighteenth century), each the same size, situated at either end of the ship (see Figure 102). Forward, just behind the forecastle and the riding bitts, was the *main capstan*. This was primarily used for heaving up the anchor or kedging the vessel along in a calm or when coming into dock. The second capstan, known as the *jeer* or *gear capstan*, was placed underneath the quarter deck between the mizzen and main masts. Its main purpose was for raising or lowering the upper yards – all yards, that is, except the main yard on each mast – which were known as *gear*. It was also used for handling warps. Both capstans would have been used for lifting heavy weights such as guns, stores and spars.

It was reckoned that a capstan barrel should be five times the diameter of the largest hawser carried on the ship. On a 74, each capstan had two barrels, one on the upper deck and one on the gun deck for manoeuvring the guns. (In some warships, only the main capstan had two barrels until the end of the century.) The barrels were massively constructed, each being cut from solid oak, and were shaped like truncated cones. They had ten or twelve faces, ten being considered the most effective; pieces of oak, called *whelps*, were let into alternate faces to ensure a good grip on the ropes.

The tops of the capstan barrels were made of elm. Round their perimeters was a line of rectangular slots to take the capstan bars, long ash poles, which were pushed by the sailors to turn the capstan. The slots and bars were individually numbered so that the bars could be made to fit their respective slots exactly. Each bar was kept in place by a small iron bolt which acted as a retaining pin, being passed through a hole in the capstan top and through the bar.

Each capstan was mounted on a huge wooden spindle which passed through the upper deck and

103 A pair of riding bitts. 'Bitts are bolted to the gun and orlop deck beams, their lower ends stepping in the foot-waling, two pairs of them, besides there are others upon the upper deck which are fixed by the main and fore masts and are called the topsail sheet and jeer bitts' (T. R. Blankley, *Naval Expositor*, 1750)

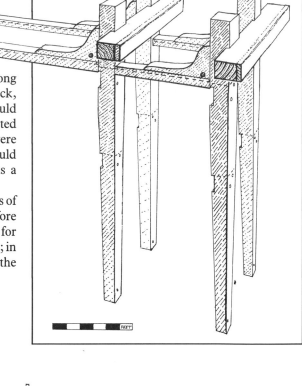

was supported on the gun-deck beams by a strong framework. Where it passed through the upper deck, strong partners were fitted. So that the capstan would not recoil under strain, the lower barrel was fitted with a number of strong iron pawls which were hinged where they joined the barrel so that they could be dropped into a special track which acted as a ratchet and was let into the gun deck.

The *steps* for the masts were simply large blocks of wood with mortices cut in them. The steps for the fore and main masts rested on the keelson, while that for the mizzen mast was usually set on the lower deck; in *Thunderer*'s case, however, it was also placed on the keelson (see Figure 102).

102 Profile of a 74 in cross-section, showing positions of bitts, rollers, capstans, galley stove and steps for the masts

1 hold
2 palleting
3 orlop deck
4 gun deck
5 upper deck
6 quarter deck
7 poop deck
8 forecastle deck
9 waist
10 beak
11 gripe
12 figurehead
13 stern lanterns

A bowsprit
B fore mast
C fore jeer bitts
D filling room
E light room
F bitts
G galley stove
H belfry
I jeer capstan
J rollers and main jeer bitts
K shot lockers
L pump shafts
M main mast
N main jeer capstan
O wheel
P mizzen mast
Q light (aft)
R tiller
S rudder
T powder
U manger

V cable tiers
W box binnacle (two compasses)
X water casks (packed in shingle ballast)
Y salted meat
Z 'spirituous liquor'

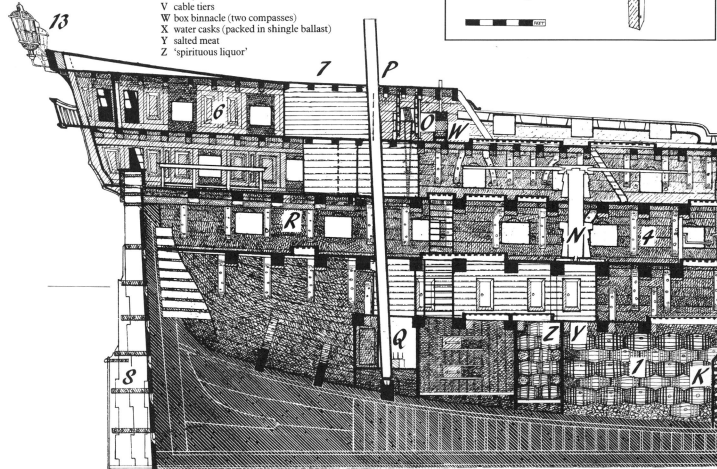

104 'Main Jear Capstan of an Eighty Gun Ship', from John Knowles, *The Elements and Practice of Naval Architecture*, 1822, Plate 7. Photo: National Maritime Museum, Greenwich. The top capstan barrel could turn independently or with the lower drum. Although this is a later design, little has changed from the type used on *Thunderer* (see Figure 42)

105 Galley stove for a 20-gun ship, 1745. British Crown Copyright: Science Museum, London. The galley was situated on the upper deck beneath the forecastle (see Figure 102). Cast-iron stoves were an innovation at this time; previously they had been built of brick

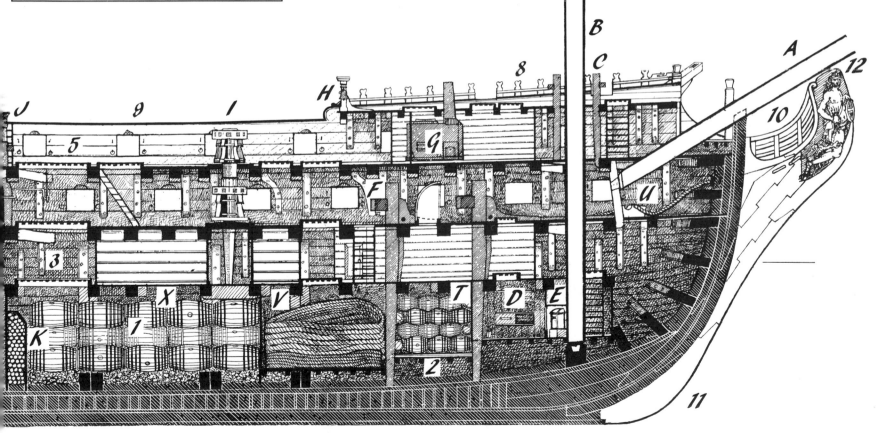

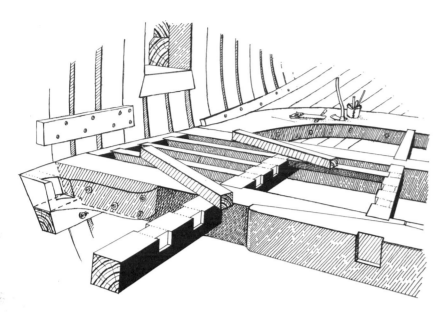

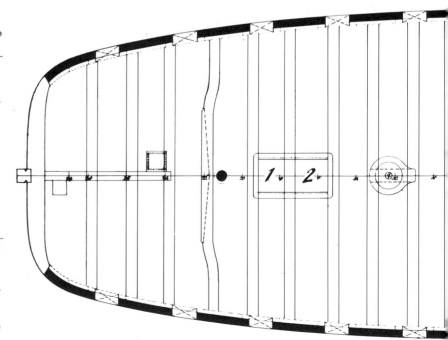

106 Ledges and carlins aft on the gun deck

Figure 107 *Key to diagram*

Hold

1 light room
2 lockers for filled cartridges
3 filling room
4 shot lockers
5 passage to powder room
6 powder room
7 light room

Orlop deck

A steward's room
B purser's cabin
C slop room
D mariners' clothing
E fish-room hatch
F 'spirituous liquor'
G dispensary
H doctor's cabin
I captain's storeroom
J lieutenants' storeroom
K after hatch
L well
M main hatch
N sail rooms
O fore hatch
P block room
Q boatswain's storeroom
R sail room
S passage to light room
T passage to powder room
U gunners' storeroom
V carpenter's storeroom
W pitch and tar room

As additional reinforcement for the decks, *carlins* or intermediate beams, were let into the main beams. The carlins ran fore and aft, and between them athwartships ran *ledges* or joists (Figure 106; see also Figure 147).* The beams were also supported by pillars, which ran in two lines down the centre of the ship. These were normally turned.

The decks were planked with Danzig deal, best-quality Baltic pine up to 3 inches thick, planed and chamfered for caulking. The exception was the outer five or six planks of the gun deck and the upper deck, which were of English oak to withstand the wear and tear imposed by the guns and the gun-carriage wheels. (The quarter deck was made of Prussian deal, with the two outer planks of English oak.) The planks were fastened to the beams, carlins and ledges with iron nails, their butt ends coinciding with the deck beams, but staggered in the same way as the hull planks. Countersunk bolts were used to fix the butts. The longest deals available were used, usually 40 feet or more, and a certain amount of shaping was necessary to make them conform to the curve of the ship's sides.

The upper deck was the first to be planked, thus allowing work to proceed on the interior of the hull without interruption from inclement weather. Openings were left in the decks for the hatches and for the masts and pumps. Where there were large hatches, beam spurs were fitted since the beams could not be carried across the full width of the ship (these can be

*French ships of the period were deficient in this respect. Nor did they have the orlop deck divided into compartments (see Figure 107). In both cases the intention was to save weight and expense.

107–10 *Thunderer's* deck plans. These were virtually standard for a 74 of this period. National Maritime Museum, Greenwich.

The orlop deck and hold (Figure 107) was where the bulk of the stores, victuals and cables were kept. The hold was the only space available for the huge coils of heavy cable. Every ship had to have at least three cables, each 120 fathoms in length, and a ship the size of a 74 had cable up to 18 or 20 inches in circumference, the largest size manufactured at this period. There would also be spare anchor cables, as well as lighter ones called stream cables for mooring alongside or in sheltered conditions. In really exposed conditions a ship might need to lie to four anchors, so the amount of rope that had to be stored was phenomenal. In addition, all spare standing rigging was housed in the hold.

Also in the hold, right forward, was the light room. This contained a specially protected lantern which was kept constantly alight from which the slow tapers for firing the guns were lit. The light room was separated from the rest of the hold by a bulkhead, and access was gained by a passageway through a hatch in the orlop deck.

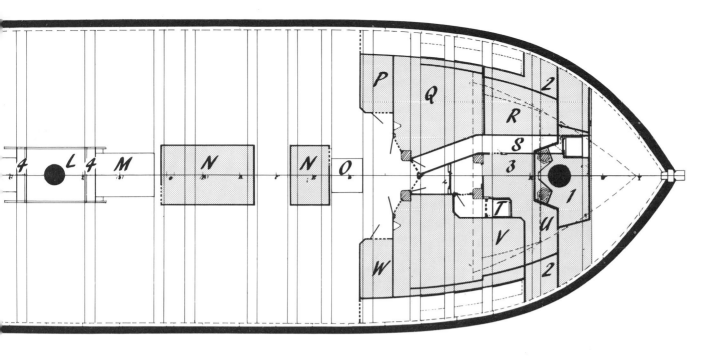

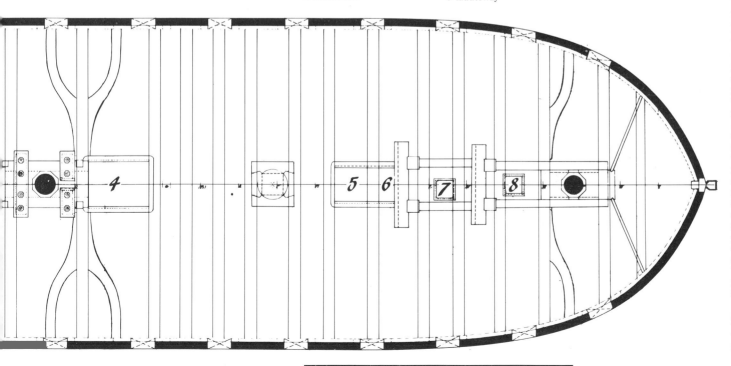

Figure 108 *Key to diagram*

1 hatchway to steward's room
2 fish-room hatch
3 after hatch
4 main hatch
5 fore hatch
6 ladderway
7 scuttle to powder room
8 scuttle to gunners' storeroom

On the other side of the bulkhead, on both sides of the ship, were lockers for storing filled cartridges (bags of gun-powder). Between these was the filling room, where the cartridges were filled. It was plastered with mortar to keep the powder dry. Access to the filling room was through another passage and hatch from the orlop deck. The two separate passages were needed to avoid the risk of the cartridges being accidentally ignited. These were lined with lead.

Next aft were stored barrels of powder, then tiers of cables, and then large casks of water packed in shingle ballast.

On either side of the main mast were the shot lockers, with the pump shafts between them and the mast. In the aft hold were barrels of salted meat and butter. At the base of the mizzen mast was another light room with the powder room adjoining it, again with its own access. There was also a room for 'spirituous liquor', a bread room and a room for storing fish.

The orlop deck contained a considerable number of storerooms which could be securely locked and in which victuals and other valuable or dangerous commodities were kept. There were no fewer than three sailrooms. In one, bolts of cloth would have been stored; in another, the sail-maker would have been constantly at work making and mending, although in fine weather with no action he might have worked on deck. In the third would have been a supply of spare, finished sails, as well as light- and heavy-weather sails when these were not in use. The surgeon's cabin and dispensary was right aft, next to the captain's storeroom, one of the largest on the orlop deck. There were also rooms for blocks and pitch and tar. The total weight of stores, provisions, powder and shot for a 74 would have been little short of 1000 tons for a standard period of six months.

The next deck up was the gun deck (Figure 108), the widest deck of all. It carried the largest guns and also formed the main living quarters for the crew. *Thunderer* had twenty-eight 32-pounders mounted on this deck (see Figure 147). A 32-pounder without carriage weighed about 550 lb, giving a rough total of just over 750 tons if one allows for the carriages. The crew of 650 men plus 150 marines, 900 men in all, would have weighed 162 tons, making a total of 900 tons minimum. The gun deck ran the full length of the vessel from bow to stern, but the space was punctuated by two rows of pillars supporting the upper-deck beams and by the capstan, masts, companion-ways, etc. For men of average height and above it would have been a matter of 'watch your head', especially underneath the beams.

The upper deck (Figure 109) was also a through deck. From aft as far forward as the main mast it was covered by the quarter deck; forward was the forecastle which covered the upper deck as far aft as the fourth gun port. Between the forecastle and the quarter deck the upper deck was open, this section was referred to as the waist, and was where the three ship's boats were stored, one inside the other (see Figure 147). The upper deck also carried its complement of guns, twenty-eight in number, but of smaller calibre than the gun-deck cannons. They were 24-pounders, but only weighed about 10 per cent less than the 32-pounders. The upper deck was where all the ship-handling took place, especially the sails on the main and foremasts, and mooring manoeuvres.

The quarter deck (Figure 110) was the command station for the whole vessel. It was from here that she was conned and steered. Below it were cabins for the officers, and above, far aft, the poop deck, under which was the captain's cabin. This was the highest of the decks.

The forecastle deck (Figure 110) provided shelter from bad weather and was used for small guns, as was the quarter deck. Even the captain's cabin was not sacrosanct in this respect, having as many as four pieces. The cabins were fitted after launching

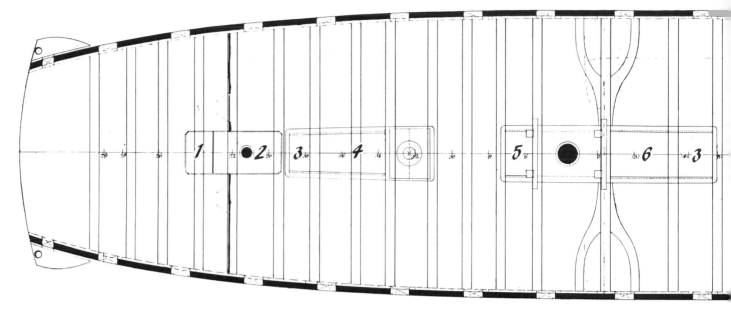

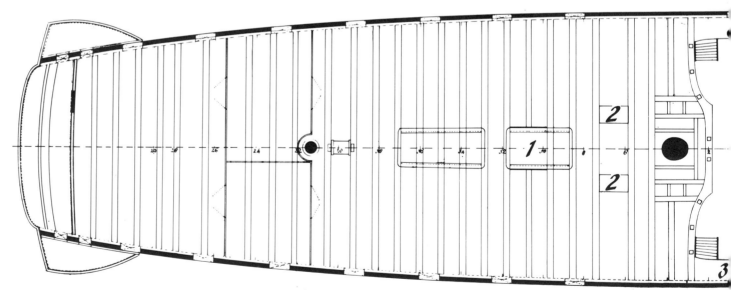

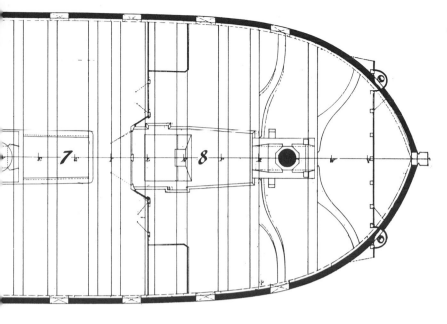

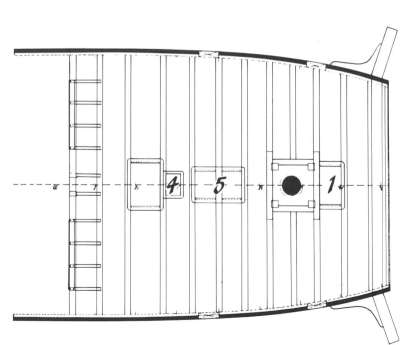

seen on the beam at the after end of the main hatch in the gun-deck plan in Figure 147).

The head ledges and coamings for the hatches were constructed as strongly as possible, the head ledges being 5½ inches thick and the coamings on average 10–11 inches thick. They were made with the ends overlapping and fastened with dovetail joints. The hatch coamings were let into decking and attached with bolts which were driven through the decking and the beams beneath. The gratings for the hatches were made of fir ledges and oak battens, which gave them a decorative appearance.* The battens had to be 2¾ inches broad, and the interstices not more than 2¾ inches square. The gratings themselves were housed in a rebate inside the head ledge and coaming. Small hatchways called scuttles were used extensively for ventilation and to let light into the lower decks. On the forecastle there was one over the galley stove, and sometimes another abaft over the galley chimney.

At this stage of construction there were still a number of jobs to be done. The pumps and pump wells had to be fitted in the hold, and the limber boards and garboard strakes put in place. Lids had to be made for the gun ports. These were of 3½-inch-thick English oak and fastened with substantial iron hinges (see Figure 120). They were sealed round the edges with leather and raised and lowered by means of a block and tackle from the deck to which they were fitted. Normally the gun ports were kept closed until the ship was in action and the guns had to be run out, but in fine weather, with no enemy in sight, the gun-deck ports would be opened to improve the ventilation. In heavy weather the leeward ports had to be kept closed, otherwise water would enter the gun deck as the vessel heeled. French ships at the battle of Quiberon Bay in November 1759 are said to have failed to observe this elementary precaution in the heat of battle and so paid a heavy price. The accident with *Royal George* (see page 34) probably would not have occurred had her leeward gun ports been closed.

Part of the interior fittings were the *bulkheads, palleting* and *partitions*. All the separate compartments were made of deal, the work being done by joiners. Bulkheads ran across the ship at the after and forward ends of the gun deck and across the upper deck, closing off the waist. The palleting in the hold was a raised floor, laid over the keelson, to keep the contents of the bread room and powder magazine dry

---

*This was somewhat at odds with one of their functions; men were tied to the gratings for lashing, one of the commonest forms of punishment at this time.

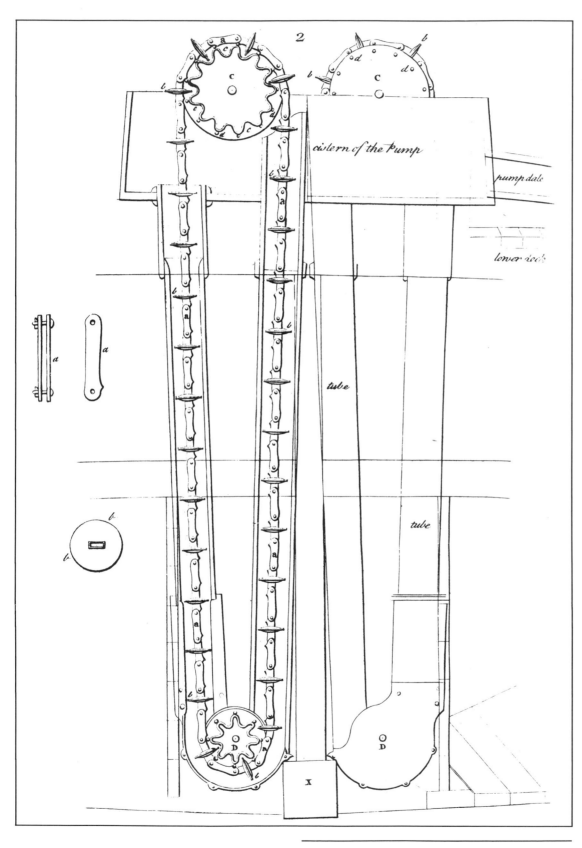

cistern of the pump

pump dale

lower deck

tube

tube

111 An essential feature on all wooden ships was an efficient method of pumping the ship free of water. Water collected in the well, or wells, situated in the bilges, to which all the limbers led, and from there it was brought to the deck by pumps. Suction pumps were used only on the very smallest vessels due to their unreliability and the limited height to which the water could be raised. In the eighteenth century the Navy used the chain pump almost universally. This consisted of a long chain which passed over sprocket wheels on deck and in the well and travelled in a wooden tube. Valves or dishes were set on the chain at regular intervals, and these fitted the tube more or less exactly. They passed down one side of the tube and up the other, taking the water with them as they rose. The pump was operated by a roller or winch worked by several men at a time. It discharged much more water than the primitive suction pumps of the day and was much less fatiguing to operate. However, Falconer was very critical, having the following to say about it: 'This machine is nevertheless exposed to several disagreeable accidents by the nature of its construction. The chain is of too complicated a fabric, and the sprocket-wheels, employed to wind it up from the ship's bottom, are deficient in a very material circumstance, viz. some contrivance to prevent the chain from sliding or jerking back upon the surface of the wheel, which frequently happens when the valves are charged with a considerable weight of water, or when the pump is violently worked. The links are evidently too short, and the immechanical manner in which they are connected exposes them to great friction in passing round the wheels. Hence they are sometimes apt to break and burst asunder in very dangerous situations, when it is extremely difficult or impractical to repair the chain' (William Falconer, *An Universal Dictionary of the Marine*, 1769).

However, Falconer goes on to describe the pump shown in Figure 111, which was a very much improved model built by a Mr Cole under the direction of a Captain Bentinck. The superiority of this pump over earlier models was considerable. The links of the chain were each made from two plates of iron bolted together, while each valve consisted of two circular plates of iron with a piece of leather between them to make a seal with the sides of the wooden tube. This pump was said to have a chain that worked more freely and was less exposed to damage by friction. The chain, moreover, was secured on the sprocket wheels by tension and could not jump off when the valves were heavy with water. The pump could easily be taken up for repair or when it became choked – usually with shingle ballast – and it coped with a greater volume of water than the older version, and needed fewer men to work it.

The new pump was put on test to compare its performance with that of the old one and a report was submitted by Rear Admiral Sir John Moore and twelve captains and eleven lieutenants. The results were as follows:

New pump
Four men raised 1 tun of water in $43\frac{1}{2}$ seconds
Two men raised 1 tun of water in 55 seconds

Old pump
Seven men raised 1 tun of water in 76 seconds
Four men raised 1 tun of water in 81 seconds

The report commented that the pump could be taken up for repair in only two and a half minutes and that it could be cleared of sand and gravel in four to five minutes.

In the mid- and late-eighteenth century French warships were still using an older type of pump made from a bored-out tree trunk. This can only have added to their inefficiency in heavy weather and would have proved a serious handicap in dealing with any leaks sustained in action

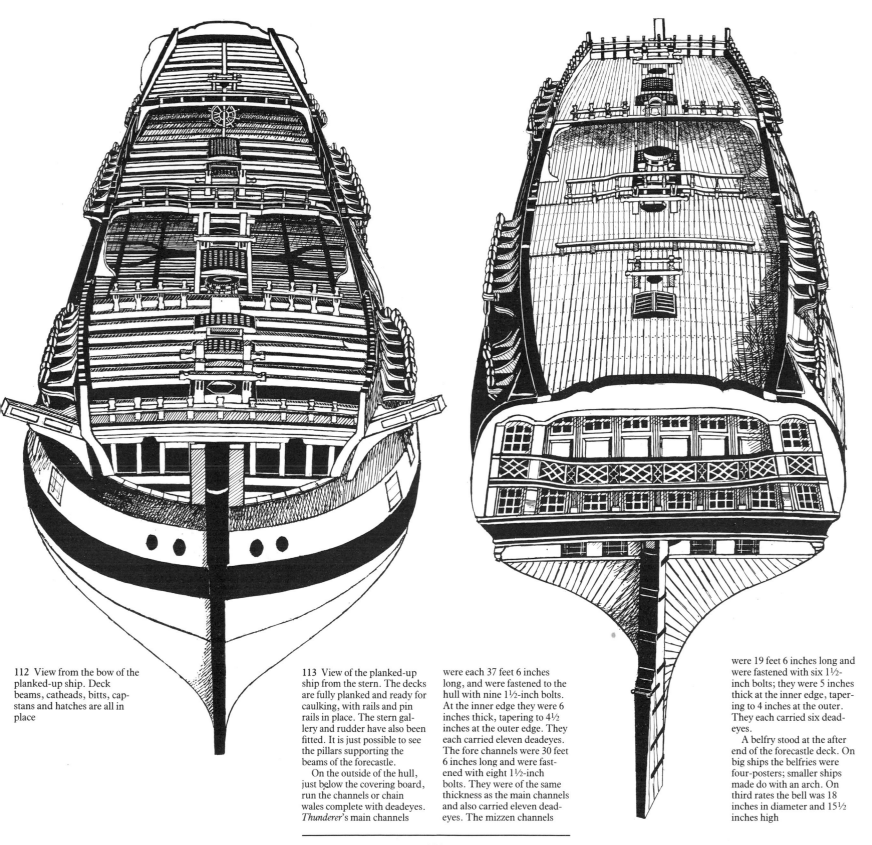

112 View from the bow of the planked-up ship. Deck beams, catheads, bitts, capstans and hatches are all in place

113 View of the planked-up ship from the stern. The decks are fully planked and ready for caulking, with rails and pin rails in place. The stern gallery and rudder have also been fitted. It is just possible to see the pillars supporting the beams of the forecastle.

On the outside of the hull, just below the covering board, run the channels or chain wales complete with deadeyes. *Thunderer*'s main channels were each 37 feet 6 inches long, and were fastened to the hull with nine 1½-inch bolts. At the inner edge they were 6 inches thick, tapering to 4½ inches at the outer edge. They each carried eleven deadeyes. The fore channels were 30 feet 6 inches long and were fastened with eight 1½-inch bolts. They were of the same thickness as the main channels and also carried eleven deadeyes. The mizzen channels were 19 feet 6 inches long and were fastened with six 1½-inch bolts; they were 5 inches thick at the inner edge, tapering to 4 inches at the outer. They each carried six deadeyes.

A belfry stood at the after end of the forecastle deck. On big ships the belfries were four-posters; smaller ships made do with an arch. On third rates the bell was 18 inches in diameter and 15½ inches high

(see Figure 102). The bread room was lined with fir, and the magazine and passageways were lined with lead. The quaintly named *manger* (see Figure 147) was a small compartment which extended athwartships on the fore part of the gun deck, immediately below the hawse holes. Without it, water would have found its way onto the gun deck as the ship plunged into the seas or when the hawser was being drawn in. Scuppers fitted in the manger took the water off as quickly as it collected.

Other work to be finished on the outside was at the bow, and consisted of fitting the *catheads*, *beak* and *gripe*. The *catheads*, which projected on either side of the bow, acted as a crane for the anchor, which could be hauled up by means of tackles and securely stowed clear of the ship's sides – a procedure known as 'catting the anchor'. On the model of *Bellona* (Figure 86) the catheads actually have faces of cats carved on their ends.*

*Parker, the leader of the Nore Mutiny, who was hanged from the yardarm, was ordered to jump from the cathead to complete the job.

Below the cathead was the *beak*, a strongly constructed platform which projected forward of the hull just below the bowsprit. It was used for sail handling and taking soundings, and also contained the heads or latrines for the crew, the ship's motion through the waves generally ensuring a sufficient supply of clean water to keep the heads hygienic. It must have been a fearful place to visit in rough weather, however. For the officers there were heads aft in the wings of the transom, where they were obviously more private and comfortable. The after segment of the beak was decked over, while the forward platform was covered with a grating which allowed the sea free access to the area yet gave the crew a secure footing. The beak, which extended down to the knee of the head, was the foremost timber in the structure.

Below the beak was fitted the forefoot or *gripe*. This was a piece of elm which was joined by a scarph to the forward extremity of the keel. It probably acquired its name from the fact that it is frequently said of sailing vessels that the foot of the bow grips the water.

The gripe curved upwards in a sort of knee or crutch and was a form of protection for the bow. It was bolted through with six 7/8-inch bolts and could easily be replaced when worn.

The finishing touch at the bow was the figurehead, in *Thunderer*'s case a beautifully carved representation of Zeus, the supreme god in Greek mythology and, aptly for this ship, god of the weather, especially thunder and rain. John Henslow, who was one of Sir Thomas Slade's assistants at the time *Thunderer* was being built, is reputed to have drawn the figurehead on the spot. The drawing which he made at Woolwich is shown in Figure 115. The figurehead was attached to the beak and the knee of the head.

At the stern the *taffrail* (or *tafferel*) and *quarter pieces* were then put in place. The taffrail, which was the top part of the ship's stern, was a large, curved piece of wood, usually ornamented with carvings. The quarter pieces formed the outline of the stern on each side (see Figure 113).

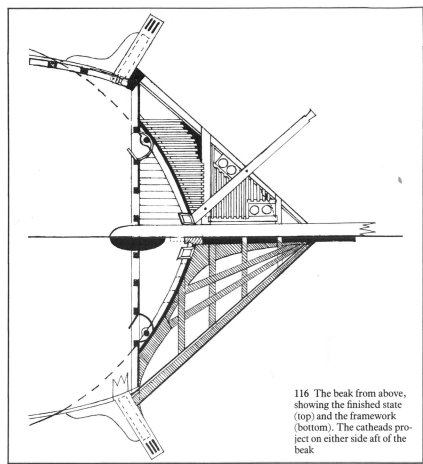

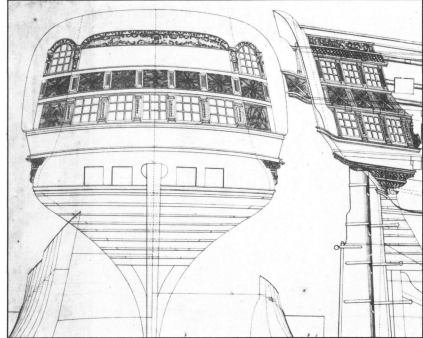

114 Decorations of bow, stern gallery and quarter of a 74. From M. Stalkartt, *Naval Architecture*, 1781. Photo: Science Museum, London. The artist has drawn George III as the figurehead and the royal coat of arms appears on the gallery rail

115 *Thunderer*'s figurehead, a representation of Zeus, drawn by Sir John Henslow when he was assistant to Sir Thomas Slade. National Maritime Museum, Greenwich

116 The beak from above, showing the finished state (top) and the framework (bottom). The catheads project on either side aft of the beak

117 Detail from the draughts for *Hero* showing the decoration of the stern and quarter. National Maritime Museum, Greenwich. Despite the abandonment of overall decoration, there was still a strong feeling that the captain's quarters deserved special treatment

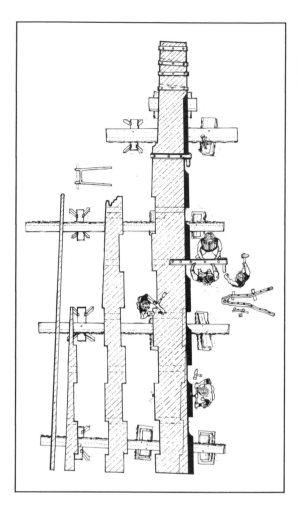

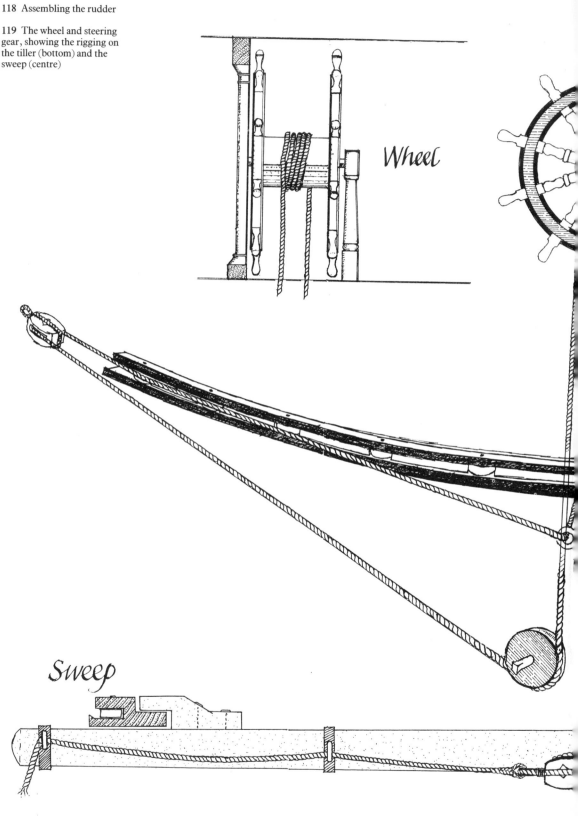

118 Assembling the rudder

119 The wheel and steering gear, showing the rigging on the tiller (bottom) and the sweep (centre)

Wheel

Sweep

After the 1740s ships ceased to be heavily ornamented and many shipwrights who had been trained as woodcarvers found themselves out of work. Some undoubtedly found employment on the great houses of the period, making stairways and carved wood panelling. Heavy ornamentation and gilded work went out of fashion because it was costly, while the practice of adorning ships with wooden statues, as can be seen on the *Wasa* in Stockholm, was recognized as undesirable since it added a great deal of top hamper. There are even tales, probably apocryphal, of ship's captains divesting themselves of the huge amounts of ornamentation by heaving them over the side at the first opportunity. In the second half of the eighteenth century the only parts that were decorated were the figurehead and sides of the beak, and the stern and quarter galleries. There is evidence that shipwrights spared little to make these as colourful as possible. *Thunderer*'s figurehead of *Zeus* is elaborate enough for anyone's taste. Examples of the kind of decoration still in use in the

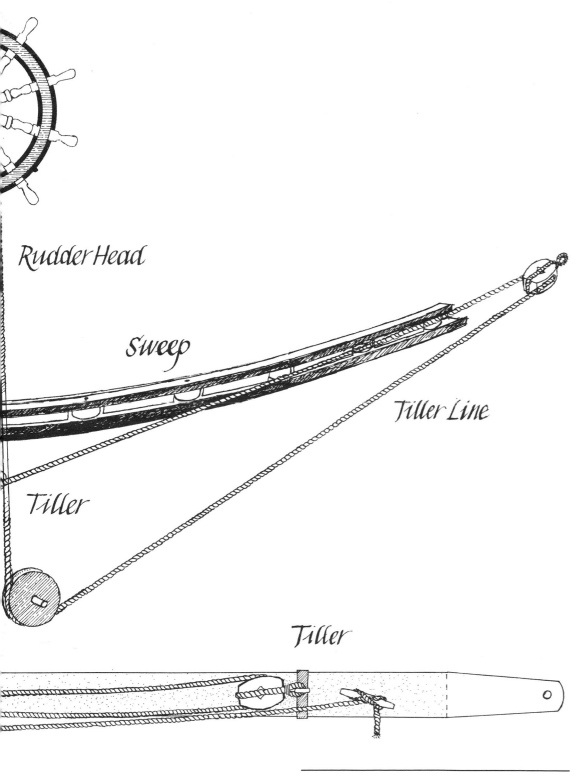

Rudder Head

Sweep

Tiller Line

Tiller

Tiller

1780s, despite the move towards austerity, are to be seen in Figure 114. This engraving appeared in a book on naval architecture dated 1781 – probably a last fling by the designers. The covering or arch over the gallery was always regarded as a suitable place for decoration, but, in this case, figures have been suggested for the quarters as well. The carvings would probably have been painted in bright colours: blues, reds, greens and, of course, gold.

In the 1760s the hull was not painted, but payed with a mixture of resin, oil and red ochre, with the wales black. Inside, on the gun deck, everything was purportedly painted red – a suitable colour to disguise any blood that might be spilt.

The *rudder* consisted of the rudder stock – the foremost timber – which was made from a single piece of oak, and the fan or blade, made from tabled pieces of elm and fayed onto the stock. The stock was bearded (chamfered) on both sides so that when the helm was put hard over, the leading edge cleared the sternpost by three-quarters of an inch. Occasionally the after edge of the sternpost was also bearded, which meant that less bearding was necessary on the rudder itself. The whole rudder was then trimmed and bolted together between the slots for the pintle straps. A false rubbing plank was nailed to the back and heel of the rudder to protect it from wear. This could easily be replaced when worn.

The head of the rudder had to project far enough above the upper deck to receive the tiller. It was bound with five iron hoops and had two slots into the lower of which the tiller was fitted. Athwartships the head was 2 feet 2 inches, fore and aft 2 feet 4 inches. The lower hances fore and aft were 4 feet 3 inches, while the heel fore and aft was 5 feet 10 inches. The thickness of the siding agreed with that of the sternpost. The back of the rudder was 3½ inches thick, the sole of the heel 6 inches thick. The rudder had to be short of the keel by 9 inches at the forward edge and by 11 inches at the after edge.

For hanging the rudder there were seven pairs of pintles and braces, like giant hinges, the two longest pintles being 2 inches longer than the others. The braces were of various lengths, depending on their position on the stern. The straps of the braces and the pintles were 4¾ inches broad, and the pintles 1½ inches long and 3½ inches in diameter. The braces were fastened to the sternpost with clench bolts, and the ends secured with dump bolts. A chain led from either side of the counter to the back of the top pintle where it was attached by a ring. This was a precaution in the event of the rudder being smashed or lifted from the pintles in a storm. If such a disaster occurred, the rudder would not be lost at sea. If the tiller broke, the ship could still be steered by the chains. They also served to stop the rudder waggling about when the vessel was at anchor.

Until the eighteenth century, wheel steering was unknown. Even the largest warships were steered by means of a *whip staff*. This was a long pole which was connected to the tiller at right angles at gun-deck level and passed through an opening in the upper deck. The upper deck itself acted as a fulcrum to give leverage on the tiller. Keeping a ship on course in heavy weather by this cumbersome method must have been a difficult task, requiring several men to control the whip staff. What was worse, it was situated aft of the mizzen mast on the upper deck, which meant that the helmsman could not see where

120 The hull nearing completion. Falconer provides a succinct account of the final stages of fitting out the hull: 'The hull being thus fabricated, they proceed to separate the apartments by bulkheads or partitions; to frame the port-lids, to fix the catheads and ches-trees; to form the hatchways and scuttles and to fit them with proper covers or gratings. They next fitted the ladders whereby to mount or descend the different hatchways, and built the manger on the lower deck, to carry off the water that runs in at the hawse holes when the ship rides at anchor in a sea. The bread-room and magazines are then lined, and the gunnel, rails and gangways fixed on the upper-part of the ship. The cleats, kevels and ranges, by which the ropes are fastened, are afterwards bolted and nailed to the sides in different places.

'The rudder, being fitted with its irons, is next hung to the sternpost; and the tiller, or bar, by which it is managed, let into a mortice at its upper end. The scuppers, or leaden tubes, that carry the water off from the decks, are then placed in holes cut through the ship's sides; and the standards, represented in the midship-frame, bolted to the beams and sides above the decks to which they belong. The poop-lanthorns are last fixed upon their cranes over the stern, and the bilge-ways, or cradles, placed under the bottom, to conduct the ship

steadily into the water whilst launching' (William Falconer, *An Universal Dictionary of the Marine*, 1769).

After 1715 stern lanterns were of a straight-sided pattern that remained standard for the rest of the century. Foreign lanterns were rather more ornate.

The name did not appear on the stern of English vessels until 1771.

In the foreground at the quayside is a gin, a machine for driving piles. It consisted of wooden scaffolding with a wheel at the top over which a rope was rove. This was then wound round a winch with handles on either side of the scaffolding and thence connected to a windlass. From the other end of the rope, suspended by an iron monkey (a block with a quick-release catch), was a beatle. This could be of different weights, according to the size and length of the piles that were being driven; it usually varied between 8 and 13 cwt. As the beatle, in being hoisted, hit the cross piece near the wheel, the monkey automatically released it, and it dropped onto the upper end of the pile, forcing it into the ground. Meanwhile the monkey, overhauling the windlass by its own weight, descended onto the beatle and hooked itself on again. In all eight or nine men would have been needed to operate the gin. The pile being driven here is for attaching the large tackle used in launching (see Figure 123)

he was going. He received instructions by relay from the quarter deck. Also, in bad conditions the gun deck would have shipped a lot of water through the tiller port, which was a fairly wide opening. Thus, it was a major improvement when it was decided to raise the rudder head so that it passed through an opening in the counter (the overhanging part of the stern). The head was then housed on the upper deck, thus eliminating the entry of water on the gun deck.

A further major improvement was the introduction of tiller ropes and a wheel, using the double-block system shown in Figure 119. The rope, which was untarred to facilitate its movement through the sheaves, led from the tiller head to a block on either side of the ship on the gun deck. From there it ran back to two central blocks, then up through the upper deck to the spindle of the wheel on the quarter deck, which was faceted in the same way as the capstan barrel. So that any slack could be taken up when required, the rope was not attached directly to the tiller, but was rigged on either side of it with tackles. Thus, if the rope stretched or shrank, it could easily be adjusted.

A final important feature was the *sweep*. This is the long curved piece of timber that can be seen in Figure 119. It extended in an arc for the full sweep of the tiller and was fixed, i.e. it did not move with the tiller or the wheel. Its function was to keep the tiller lines taut when the helm was put over. Since the tiller travelled in an arc under the deck, putting the helm hard over meant that the line on that side would go slack. If this was not corrected, the whole arrangement would cease to function properly as the rope, being slack, would simply have run round the drum on the wheel. The sweep prevented this from happening as its curve kept the rope under tension the whole time. Even so, it was necessary for a sharp eye to be kept on the steering mechanism, especially in heavy weather, to make sure that the rope was not fraying or that the helm was not out of balance.

Falconer has the following comment on the importance of keeping the steering gear in good working order:

As the safety of a ship, and all contained therein, depend, in a great measure, on the steerage or effects of the helm, the apparatus by which it is managed should be diligently examined by the proper officers. Indeed, a negligence in this important duty appears almost unpardonable, when the fatal effects, which may result from it, are duly examined.

By this stage the caulking was complete, the final operation before the vessel was launched.

The Thames at Rotherhithe, 1824. Oil painting by Thomas Whitcombe, 1752–1827. National Maritime Museum, Greenwich

9
THE LAUNCH

Launching a ship the size of a 74 was a nerve-racking occasion for the whole dockyard. The bigger the vessel, the more chance there was of something going wrong: she could topple sideways or foul the slip. The enormous first rates were built in graving docks where possible, so launching them was a less hazardous operation, simply a matter of opening the gates and letting the tide flow in.

Steel, in 1805, had the following to say:

The launch of a ship, or machinery by which she is safely conveyed into the water, after she is completely built, is a grand piece of mechanism, and requires every consideration: as in the first place, to ascertain exactly with what declivity the ways may be laid, which should be as great as possible, or according to the depth of water wherein the ship is to be launched and according to what height is required for laying the ways, so as to keep her forefoot from striking against the groundways.

Thunderer was launched, on 19 March 1760, by what Steel describes as the 'old method'. At the time, the largest ship to have been launched in this way was the first rate *Britannia* of 100 guns, at Plymouth.

First, *bilgeways* or *ways* had to be installed. These were wooden rails, 10 feet apart, down which the cradle supporting the ship slid. They extended from the bows right down the slip and into the water. They were firmly attached to the groundways, care being taken to ensure that there was no fastening protruding that might impede the smooth passage of the cradle. According to Steel, the bilgeways were made from decayed bowsprits (not literally rotten, but simply discarded because of rot) encased in planks. The casing was made from East Country (Baltic) plank, 4 inches thick on the top and 3 inches on the sides. The ways were approximately 2 feet 6 inches wide. The whole construction was firmly fastened with 1-inch bolts and 7- or 8-inch nails or spikes. An alternative method of making the ways was to use large baulks of fir mounted on blocks, all securely

fastened to the groundways (see Figures 121 and 122). Shores from the side of the slip prevented any lateral movement of the ways, which were heavily lubricated with soap and tallow so that the cradle would run smoothly.

On top of the ways was constructed the *cradle*, made of thick planks of fir for the base, the underside of which was also liberally treated with soap and tallow, with *spurs* enveloping the bow and stern of the ship to support her as she slid down to the water. There were four spurs forward and five aft, and they were forelocked through the hull with three 1½-inch bolts at the head and heel so that they could easily be released once the vessel was safely afloat. The distance between the spurs was approximately 4 feet, and they conformed exactly to the shape of the vessel.

At the end of the bilgeways beneath the stem was a pair of *drivers*, similar to spurs, but standing in the fore–aft direction. Between these was attached the

driver screw, a simple jack with two wooden screws, which was used to set the ship in motion.

To prevent the cradle from moving until required, a block was bolted to the fore end of the base of the cradle. The shores from the slip each terminated in a long baulk of timber, the fore end of which was hinged. This engaged the block on the base of the cradle and was kept in place by a wedge with a rope attached so that it could be withdrawn at the appropriate moment. At the after end, the ship was further supported by a series of oak shores, about 8 inches square, between the edge of the footways and the main wale on either side of the hull.

At this stage the ship was ready for launching, except for one important item: the false keel. This was a 6-inch-thick piece of elm which protected the main keel and could be replaced as often as necessary. It also served to protect the heads or clenches of the keel bolts. The false keel was made in eight pieces scarphed together, and was inserted in stages as the top wedges on the blocks were knocked or split out. It was fastened to the main keel by iron staples, similar to dogs, which were driven into the sides of both the keel and the false keel. These staples could easily be removed when the false keel needed renewing. Once all the splitting blocks or wedges had been knocked out, the whole weight of the vessel rested on the cradle.

All the preparations having been made, the ship was now ready to be launched. This took place at high tide so that the ship had the minimum distance to travel before she floated, thus reducing the speed with which she entered the water. Before the tide reached its full height, the lower parts of the ways were liberally daubed with tallow and oil or soap. A rope was taken from the stern to a ship moored in the river, and anchors were set ready to be dropped if necessary. The Ensign, Jack and pennant were flown

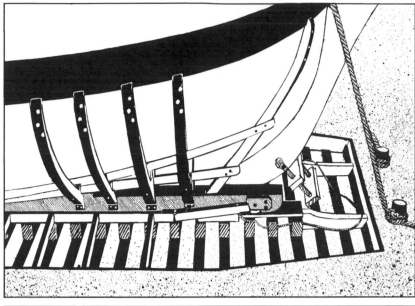

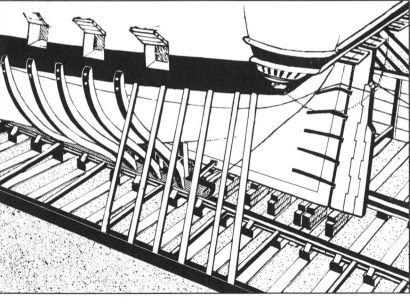

◄121 The launching cradle at the bows with the driver screws in position

◄122 The launching cradle at the stern

123 The launch.
'The Master Shipwright of His Majesty's yard at Woolwich having acquainted us that His Majesty's ship *Thunderer* building at that yard is in such forwardness that she will be ready to launch on Wednesday the 19th March (when she will be in a capacity to receive men), we desire you will acquaint the right Honourable the Lords Commanders of the Admiralty therewith and that we have ordered her to be launched at that time accordingly in case she shall then be in all respects ready for it, and hope it will meet with their Lordships' approbation' (Letter from the Navy Board to the Admiralty, 1760)

from three staffs, one set in each mast hole. To signal the moment of launching a bell was rung. The shores and stanchions supporting the ship were knocked away and the screws applied to get her moving. A ship usually began to slide as soon as the shores were removed, but occasionally extra force had to be exerted. For this, tackles were rigged from the forward part of the cradle to a bollard on the side of the slip near the stern. It was then a case of all hands to the ropes to get her started.

After being launched, the ship was towed out to the moorings in the river to await being taken to the graving dock for the sheathing to be applied. This consisted of 1-inch-thick fir planks which were nailed over the bottom planking with a layer of hair and tar in between. The purpose was to give protection against all manner of fouling, particularly marine borers such as the teredo worm, the sheathing being replaced as it became worn. Copper took the place of wood in the 1780s, after experiments had shown that it was more effective, and its use continued for as long as wooden vessels were being built.

The vessel was then graved with a mixture of brimstone, pitch, resin and tallow, the equivalent of modern antifouling paints which have replaced it to some measure.

124 Rigged model of *Hercules/Thunderer*, 1795. National Maritime Museum, Greenwich. Models
were not usually rigged when they were built; the rigging in the case is a modern addition

10
FURNITURE AND ARMAMENT

Once afloat, with her sheathing applied, a ship was ready to be fitted out with her furniture and equipped with guns and ammunition. Her stores and provisions had also to be loaded. Steel provides a table showing the weight of guns, stores, provisions and men in relation to the hull (see page 114).

A ship's furniture consisted of her masts, spars and rigging. A 74 such as *Thunderer* had three masts: the mizzen aft, then the main mast, and towards the bow the fore mast. Each of these was constructed in three sections: the lower mast, the top mast and, the highest of all, the topgallant mast. The top masts and topgallant masts were pole masts, i.e. cut from single trunks, but the lower masts, because of their diameter, had to be 'made', i.e. cut from lengths of timber tabled together along their length rather than from a single piece. This was also the case for the lower spar of the bowsprit, which was in two sections. The mizzen, main and foremasts each carried three yards; the mizzen also had a lateen spar and the bowsprit a yard. *Thunderer*'s masts, spars and yards totalled twenty-three in number.

The height of a ship's masts was related to her length and beam. David Steel describes how this measurement was calculated:

The length of the lower deck of a 74-gun ship is 176 [feet], the breadth extreme 48 feet 8 inches; added together they make 224 feet 8 inches; the half, or 112 feet 4 inches, is the length of the mainmast; which being determined, the other masts, yards, etc., bear the following proportions. Fore-mast, 8/9 of the mainmast; mizzen mast, 6/7 of the main mast.

According to Steel, the main yard was 8/9 of the main mast, i.e. the lower section of the main mast; the main topsail yard, 5/7 of the main yard; and the topgallant yards, 2/3 of the topsail yards. He even lists the diameters of all masts and spars for all types of naval crafts, right down to barges, pinnaces and yawls with

sprit sails, and provides fractional tables for determining the size of timber for the various pieces.

In his 1797 article in the *Encyclopaedia Britannica*, Steel also gives a detailed account of the materials used in making the main mast of a 74-gun ship (see page 115). As can be seen, fir, oak and elm were all used in the construction, the total cost of which was £513 6s 2d.*

By way of comparison, Admiralty records show that the main mast of *Royal Sovereign*, built in 1740, cost £466 19s 2d, of which the labour charge was £75, almost exactly the same as for the 74-gun ship in 1797. Apparently twelve men worked on *Royal Sovereign*'s mast, completing it in sixty days.

The timber for the masts was stored in the mast pond, a process which enabled the fir to season very slowly, thus reducing the risk of its twisting or

splitting. The immersion in salt water also pickled the timber, making it resistant to rot. Once seasoned, the trunks were floated to the ramp of the mast house (see chapter 4), where they were allowed to dry out before being used. The timber for pole masts was first trimmed to square section, equivalent to the required diameter, then rounded with an adze. For made masts, however, the trunks were cut into square sections, then tabled together, before being rounded up. The joins were reinforced with cross setts and through bolts every 5 feet along the length of the mast, which was then *woolded*, tightly bound with rope, of thirteen close turns, each turn being held by woolding nails with leather beneath the heads to prevent them from cutting the rope. On a 74's mast, 3-inch rope was used. Clasp hooks or iron bands were fitted between the wooldings.

Next the mast was floated to the rigging house where two crab-type cranes were used to hoist it from the water. The rigger fitted cleats, eyebolts, etc., as required and a minimal amount of standing rigging. The mast was then floated out to the sheer hulk for stepping in the warship. Since the masts were very heavy, the hulk had up to three spars or sheers for lifting. These were lashed at the heel to the rails and deck of the hulk; at the head of the sheer was lashed a fourth spar, which projected like a sprit, and this was lashed at its lower end to the hulk's mast. Four large blocks and tackles ran from the sprit to the head of the hulk's mast and these enabled the sheers to be raised or lowered, thus giving the two lifting blocks a wider range of distance from the hulk. The mast had to be swung up over the deck until it was immediately above the mast opening, and then manoeuvred until its foot engaged the mortice in the stepping on the keelson.

The masts were maintained in position by stays and shrouds, which were made from tarred rope. On

*In order to lessen the cost and weight of masts, it was proposed around this time to make them hollow.

any sailing vessel there are two types of rigging: *standing rigging*, the stays and shrouds, which hold masts, yards, spars and bowsprit in place, and *running rigging* by which the yards and sails are adjusted. Running rigging includes halyards for hoisting and lowering the sails, sheets, bowlines and clew lines for setting them in relation to the wind, and brails and bunt lines for furling them. According to Steel, the rigging for a 74/80-gun ship weighed 30 tons, which must represent many miles of rope.

The rigging was prepared in the rigging house, which at Woolwich was situated next to the mast pond. This was equipped with a windlass at one end and posts at intervals for stretching and serving (binding) ropes. On either side were workbenches at which riggers were busy on smaller jobs. Certainly commonly needed pieces of rigging were usually kept in stock. The different sizes and lengths of rope required for each piece of rigging for each rate were laid down in a table of dimensions.

Rigging a 74-gun ship was a complicated and expensive process. The time allowed for the job was fourteen days, and Steel gives the cost of labour as £106 (£112 in the winter). The cost of *Thunderer's* rigging and stores was £6111 9s 7d. The rigger's main job was to splice and worm (bind with yarn) the shrouds, and to fit the hundreds of deadeyes and blocks through which the running rigging was threaded. Much of this work would be done aloft. He also worked closely with the sailmaker, fitting yards and bending (attaching) sails.

---

125 'The different pieces which compose the Main Mast of a 74 Gunship, etc.', from David Steel, *Elements of Mastmaking, Sailmaking, Rigging, etc.*, 1794. Photo: National Maritime Museum, Greenwich

The Weight of Hull, Furniture, Guns and Ammunition, Officers' Stores, Men and Provisions for an 80-Gun Ship*

Weight of the Hull.

	Nº of Ft.	Nº of lbs.	Tons.	Lbs.
Oak timber at 66lb. to the cubic foot	48497	3200802	1428	2082
Fir timber at 48lb. to the cubic foot	4457	213936	95	1136
Elm timber at 52lb. to the cubic foot	520	27040	12	160
Carve work and lead work		4651	2	171
Iron work, rudder irons, chain plates, nails, &c.		88254	39	894
Pitch, tar, oakum, and paint		17920	8	
Cook room fitted with fire hearth		16123	7	443
Sum -		3568726	1593	406

Weight of the Furniture.

	Nº of lbs.	Tons.	Lbs.
Complete set of masts and yards, with the spare geer	161000	71	1960
Anchors with their stocks, and master's stores	39996	17	1916
Rigging -	69128	30	1928
Sails, complete set, and spare	32008	14	648
Cables and hawsers	73332	32	1652
Blocks, pumps, and boats	62056	27	1576
Sum -	437520	195	720

Weight of the Guns and Ammunition.

	Nº of lbs.	Tons.	Lbs.
Guns with their carriages -	377034	168	714
Powder and shot, powder barrels, &c.	116320	51	2080
Implements for the powder	6500	2	2020
Ditto for guns, crows, handspikes, &c.	21573	9	1413
Sum - - -	521427	232	1747

Weight of the Officers Stores, &c.

	Nº of lbs.	Tons.	Lbs.
Carpenter's stores -	20187	9	27
Boatswain's stores -	21112	9	952
Gunner's stores - -	8964	4	4
Caulker's stores -	5200	2	720
Surgeon and chaplain's effects	11096	4	2136
Sum - -	66559	29	1599

Weight of the Men, &c.

	Nº of lbs.	Tons.	Lbs.
Seven hundred men with their effects, including the officers and their effects -	316961	141	1121
Ballast - -	1478400	660	
Sum - -	1795361	801	1121

RECAPITULATION.

		Tons.	Lbs.
The hull - -	3568726	1593	406
The furniture -	437520	195	720
Guns and ammunition -	521427	232	1747
Officers stores -	66559	29	1599
Provisions -	1792870	800	870
Weight of the men and ballast	1795361	801	1121
Sum - -	8182463	3652	1983

Weight of the Provisions.

	Nº of lbs.	Tons.	Lbs.
Provisions for six months for 700 men, with all their equipage	858970	383	1050
Water, casks, and captain's table	933900	416	2060
Sum - - -	1792870	800	870

*From David Steel, *Elements of Mastmaking, Sailmaking, Rigging, etc.*, 1794.

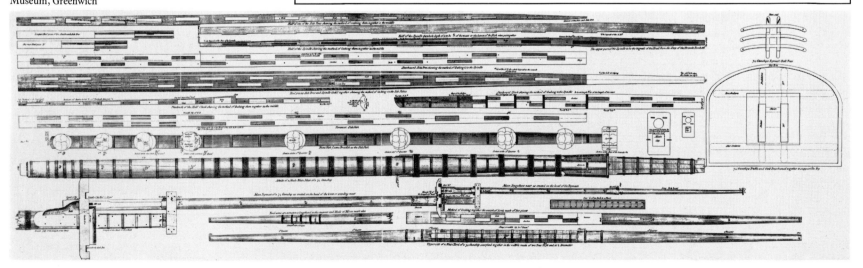

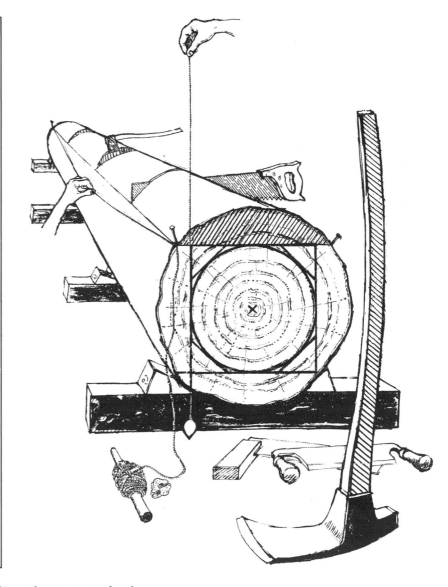

Materials for The Main Mast of a 74-Gun Ship			
Fishes for a spindle, 21 inches, 2 nails of two masts,	£101	3	11
Two side fishes, 22 inches, 2 ditto	133	10	9
Fore and aft fishes, 22 inches, 2 nails of one mast	66	13	10
Fish 21½ inches, 1 nail of half a mast,	29	8	5
On the fore part			
Iron 3 qrs 19 lb	1	5	9
Aries load baulk, 2 loads 22 feet	12	2	5
Breadthning 2 loads 7 feet	11	1	1
Dantzic fir timber			
Cheeks 4 loads 2 feet	20	18	4
Iron, 5 cwt 2 qrs 24 lb	8	0	0
Knees, elm timber, 13 feet	0	15	2
Iron, 2 qrs 14 lb	0	17	6
Hoops and bolts on the body, 13 cwt 1 qr 16 lb	18	15	0
Tressel-trees, straight oak timber, second sort, 2 loads 10 feet	10	2	4
Iron, 3 qrs 10 lb	1	3	6
Cross trees, straight oak timber, second sort, 1 load 12 feet	5	14	0
Iron, 2 qrs 2 lb	0	14	6
Cap, elm timber, 1 load 24 feet	4	6	0
Iron, 2 cwt 14 lb	2	19	6
Fullings, bolsters, bollins, and Dantzic fir, 1 load 2 feet	5	7	8
Workmanship	78	6	0
	£513	6	2
Main topmast of a 74 gun ship	50	16	3
Main top-gallant mast*	8	11	0

*This latter would, presumably, have been a pole mast.

Each mast had a lower sail or course. Above the courses were the topsails, with the topgallants above them; highest of all were the royals. Between the masts were the staysails. In addition, the main and fore masts both carried studding sails on the courses, topsails and topgallants. These were used in fine weather to give a greatly increased sail area, and were set on spars which were withdrawn and housed when not in use. Quadrilateral-shaped sails were extended on yards, while triangular-shaped sails were spread on stays, although a small number of such sails were occasionally set on a yard, which would have been the case with a lateen sail.

The scene of sailmaking in the yard was the sail loft, which had a floor of very smooth wood. The sails were made from flax canvas of varying weights according to their position and purpose on the rig. The heaviest canvas was used for the main sails and for heavy weather sails. Each sail was made up of a number of panels designed to give it the required shape and make the best use of the widths in which the sailcloth was supplied. This method of sailmaking is followed to this day. The sailcloth was laid out on the sail-loft floor and marked with charcoal lines for cutting out.

As with everything, the Navy was most particular in its requirements. All sails had to have a double, flat seam throughout and be sewn with best English twine of three threads. The number of stitches to the yard had to be between 108 and 116. The twine for the larger sails had to be waxed by hand with beeswax mixed with a sixth part of clear turpentine.

126 Making a pole mast. The tree trunk was first stripped of its bark, using a draw knife, then secured on wooden blocks with wedges and cut to the required length. The diameter of each end of the mast was drawn on each end of the trunk with compasses (masts normally taper towards the top). The circle was squared vertically to the outer edge of the trunk with a plumb line, and horizontally with a set square to the plumb line. A string was stretched down either side of the trunk joining the points at each end where the horizontal line came to the outer edge of the trunk. The string was then chalked and flicked against the side of the trunk, producing a chalk line along the entire length. Saw cuts were made at intervals to the chalk line and the first flitch (the shaded area) removed with an adze. The mastmaker would stand astride the tree, swinging the adze between his legs.

This process was repeated for the remaining three sides of the trunk, producing a squared length of timber. The corners were then marked with a chalk line and adzed off, leaving eight sides. Again the corners were trimmed, using a draw knife, giving sixteen sides, which were then rounded off with a plane

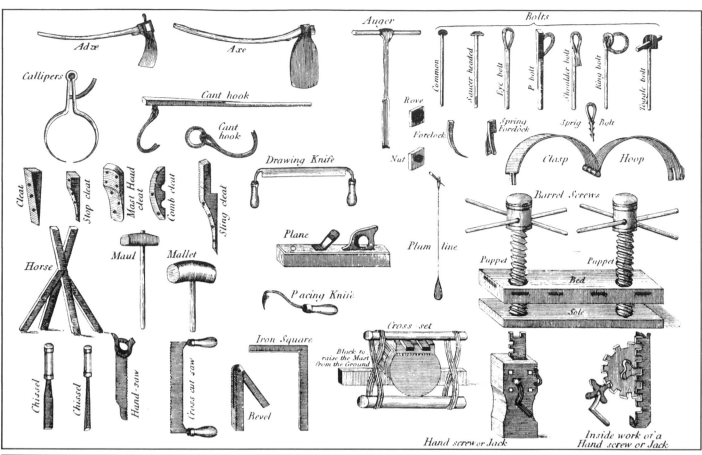

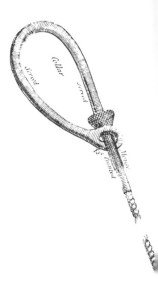

128 The main stay. From ▶ David Steel, *Elements of Mast-making, Sailmaking, Rigging, etc.*, 1794

Sheer Hulk

127 'Tools for Mast Making' and 'Sheer Hulk', from David Steel, *Elements of Mastmaking, Sailmaking, Rigging, etc.*, 1794. Note the setts for holding a made mast together while the woolding and iron bands were applied.

Two methods of stepping the mast are shown: in the foreground a sheer hulk is being used for stepping the main mast of a first rate; in the background a smaller vessel, equipped with sheerlegs, is having its own mast stepped. Sheer hulks were generally old ships which had been cut down to gun-deck level. They were sometimes fitted with a man-powered treadwheel for tilting boats for careening, and had several capstans fitted on deck for stepping ships' masts.

Part of a sheer hulk can be seen on the extreme right in Figure 16

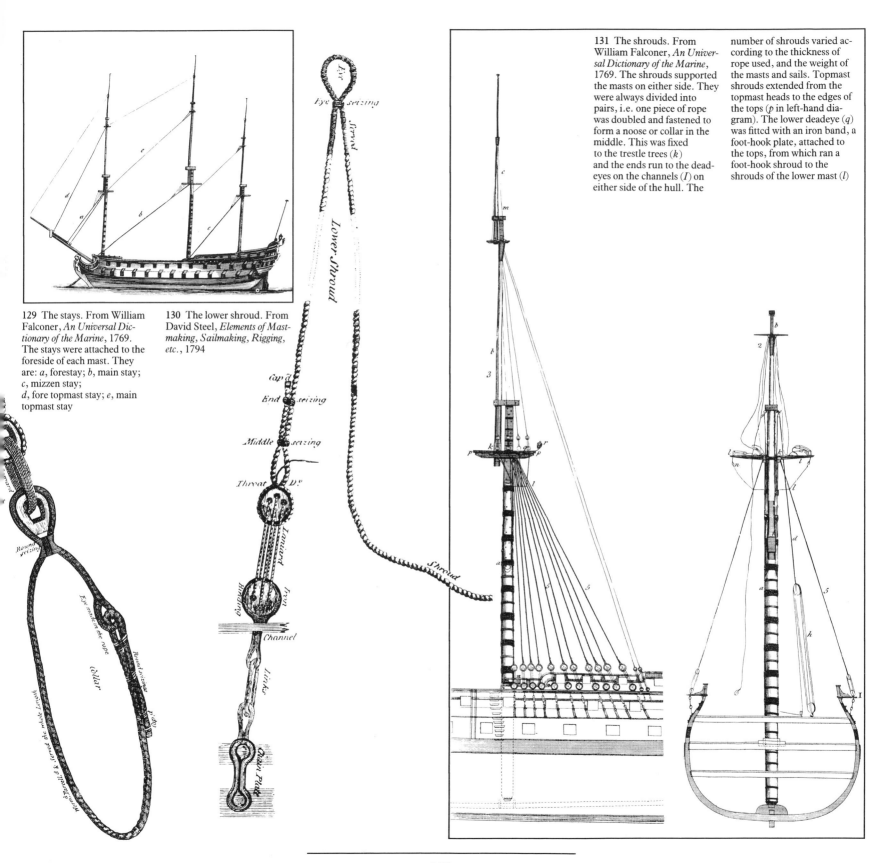

131 The shrouds. From William Falconer, *An Universal Dictionary of the Marine*, 1769. The shrouds supported the masts on either side. They were always divided into pairs, i.e. one piece of rope was doubled and fastened to form a noose or collar in the middle. This was fixed to the trestle trees (*k*) and the ends run to the deadeyes on the channels (*I*) on either side of the hull. The number of shrouds varied according to the thickness of rope used, and the weight of the masts and sails. Topmast shrouds extended from the topmast heads to the edges of the tops (*p* in left-hand diagram). The lower deadeye (*q*) was fitted with an iron band, a foot-hook plate, attached to the tops, from which ran a foot-hook shroud to the shrouds of the lower mast (*l*)

129 The stays. From William Falconer, *An Universal Dictionary of the Marine*, 1769. The stays were attached to the foreside of each mast. They are: *a*, forestay; *b*, main stay; *c*, mizzen stay; *d*, fore topmast stay; *e*, main topmast stay

130 The lower shroud. From David Steel, *Elements of Mastmaking, Sailmaking, Rigging, etc.*, 1794

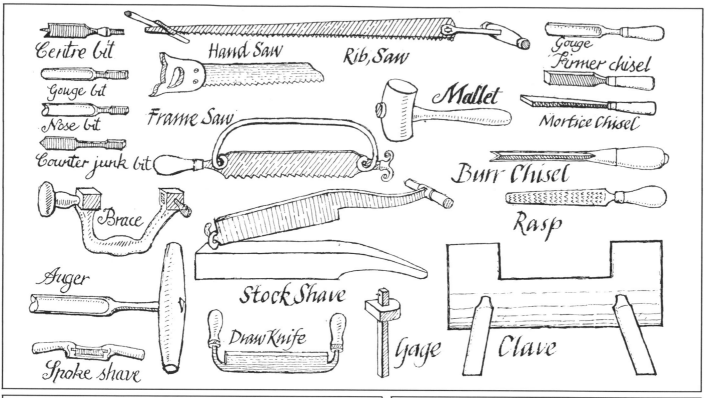

Centre bit

Gouge bit

Nose bit

Counter junk bit

Hand Saw

Rib Saw

Frame Saw

Brace

Mallet

Gouge
Firmer chisel

Mortice Chisel

Burr Chisel

Rasp

Auger

Stock Shave

Draw Knife

Spoke shave

Gage

Clave

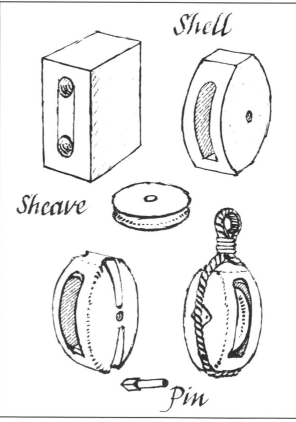

Shell

Sheave

Pin

132 Blockmaking. Each block consisted of three pieces: first, the shell, which was made of elm, ash or beech, was mortised out to admit up to four lignum vitae sheaves, or wheels, over which the rope ran. The sheaves were held in place by a pin, also of lignum vitae, which allowed the sheaves to spin. The pins were later made of iron.

The roughly shaped block was wedged in a work bench known as a clave. An auger was used to bore the mortises in the shell, and the waste material was cleaned out with a mortise chisel and a burr chisel – a V-shaped chisel for cutting out square corners. The pin hole was bored out with a brace and bit. A frame saw was used to cut the very hard lignum vitae for the sheaves. All blocks were rounded so that they had no sharp edges or corners. This was done with a stock shave or with a rasp and spoke shave. Finally, the block was scored with a gouge to make a hollow to hold the rope strop by which the block was attached to the rigging.

Blockmakers also made deadeyes, parallel and wooden cringles and bull's eyes.

The largest block, for the main tack, was 10 inches deep, with sheaves 1 foot 1 inch in diameter and 3½ inches thick. The diameter of the pins was 1⅞ inch. The largest deadeye, on the main channel, was 1 foot 4 inches in diameter and 9 inches thick. A 74 required 922 blocks in all

133 'The Patent Block-Mill', ▶ from David Steel, *Elements of Mastmaking, Sailmaking, Rigging, etc.*, 1794. Photo: National Maritime Museum, Greenwich.

Until the invention at the end of the eighteenth century of a blockmaking machine by Sir March Isambard Brunel (see p. 39n.), blocks were made by hand. They were cut to length and shaped by means of a saw and lathe driven by a horse mill. Shown here is Taylor's block mill. The Taylor brothers, of Southampton, were the main suppliers of blocks to the Royal Navy in the second half of the eighteenth century

A double Friction wheel

Lever   5   5   Lever

Patent Block Mill.

119

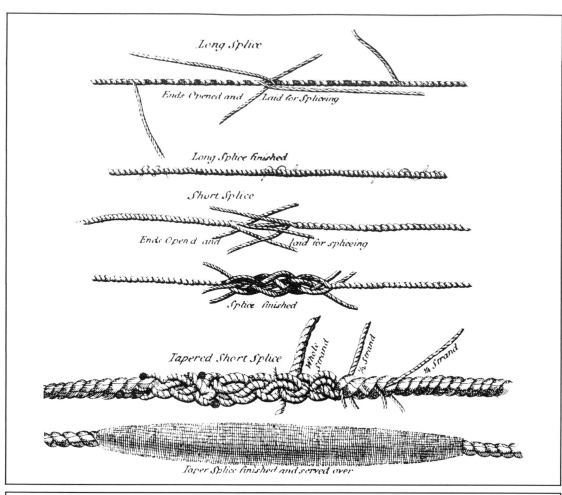

134 Methods of splicing ropes. From David Steel, *Elements of Mastmaking, Sailmaking, Rigging, etc.*, 1794

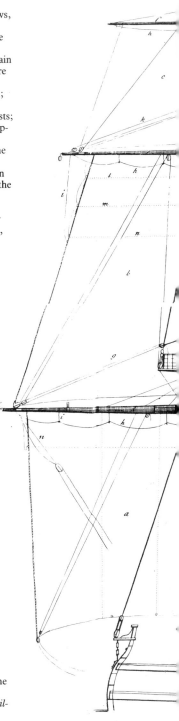

136 The sails for a three-mast ship. From William Falconer, *An Universal Dictionary of the Marine*, 1769. The left-hand diagram shows, *a*, course or lower sail; *b*, topsail; *c*, topgallant. The right-hand diagram shows: *d*, main sail; *e*, topsail; *f*, main topgallant; *g*, foresail; *h*, fore topsail; *i*, fore topgallant; *k*, mizzen; *l*, mizzen topsail; *m*, mizzen topgallant. Between the main and foremasts; *o*, main stay sail; *p*, main topmast stay sail; *q*, main topgallant stay sail. Between the main and mizzen masts; *r*, mizzen stay sail; *s*, mizzen topmast stay sail. Between the foremast and the bowsprit; *t*, fore stay sail; *u*, fore topmast stay sail; *x*, jib. Under the bowsprit; *y*, sprit sail; *z*, sprit topsail

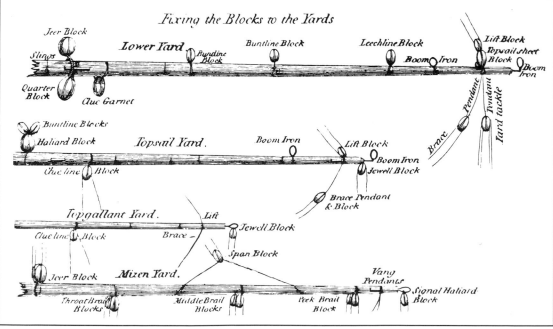

135 'Fixing the Blocks to the Yards', from David Steel, *Elements of Mastmaking, Sailmaking, Rigging, etc.*, 1794

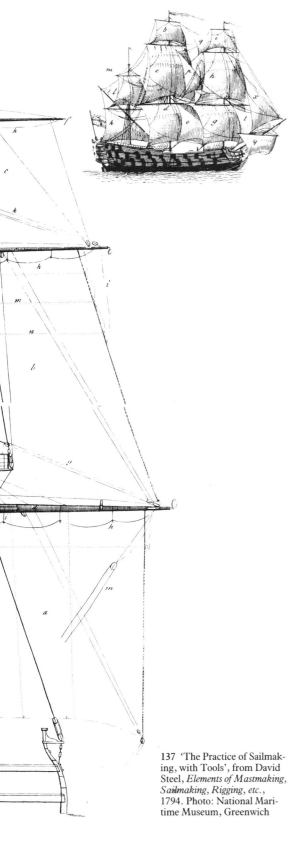

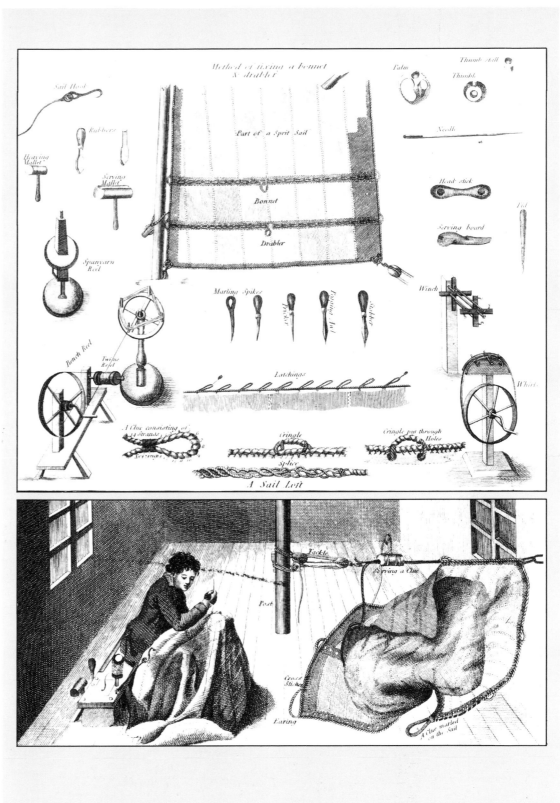

137 'The Practice of Sailmaking, with Tools', from David Steel, *Elements of Mastmaking, Sailmaking, Rigging, etc.*, 1794. Photo: National Maritime Museum, Greenwich

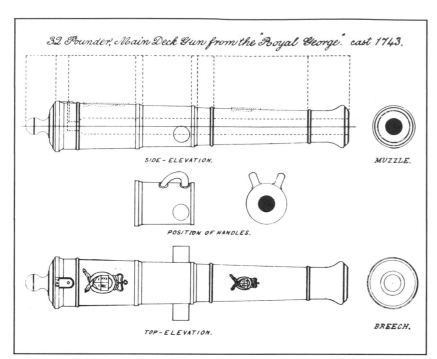

32 Pounder, Main Deck Gun from the "Royal George." cast 1743.

SIDE-ELEVATION.   MUZZLE.

POSITION OF HANDLES.

TOP-ELEVATION.   BREECH.

138 32-pound cannon from *Royal George*, 1756. National Maritime Museum, Greenwich

139–144 Woolwich Arsenal, 1750. Watercolours by an unknown artist. National Maritime Museum, Greenwich.
The choice of Woolwich as the site of the Royal Arsenal was determined by the discovery there of a type of sand particularly suitable for the fine castings

139 Perspective view of the Royal Laboratory

141 The forge

143 Making gunpowder

Once sewn, every sail was skirted round with a bolt rope to strengthen it, and thimbles to which ropes were to be attached were inserted at various points.

Given that every ship had several sets of sails, the sailmaker was an extremely busy man. His work was not confined to sails, however; he also made canvas covers, dodgers (canvas shelters), cot bottoms, hammocks and tarpaulins. He even made basic clothes such as smocks and trousers for the sailors.

Thunderer's armament was founded at Woolwich Arsenal, which lay about a mile to the east of the shipyard. Cannon were made of either brass or iron. Until improvements in iron casting, brass cannon were more reliable, being less likely to burst when being fired and kill their crew. Brass, however, was expensive, and as iron grew cheaper and more plentiful, so it became the preferred material. There can have been few more impressive sights than a deck of freshly polished brass cannon glinting in the sunlight.

In the 1750s there was a range of sizes in regular use by the Navy, ranging from 42-pounders right down to 3-pounders. *Thunderer*'s main cannon were the 32-pounders on her gun deck, supplemented by 18-pounders on the upper deck, and 9-pounders on the quarter deck and forecastle. Like all cannon of the period, they were muzzle loaders, having a solid breech which was drilled with a hole for the touch powder to fire the charge, and smooth bore, the inside of the barrel being a simple, uninterrupted

140 Laboratory Square

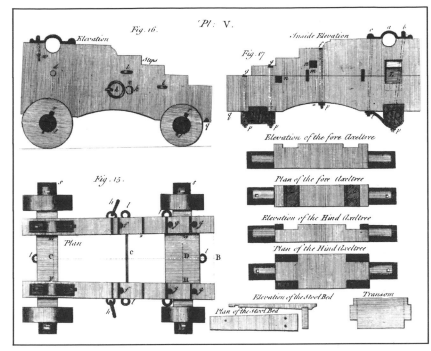

142 Melting metal

144 Making charges

tube which was bored out after casting. Each cannon was mounted on a carriage, being supported by trunnions which projected from the body of the cannon like stumpy arms.

The guns were secured by gun tackles and breechings. The tackles were used to manoeuvre the gun for loading and for pulling it back into position for firing. The breechings, rather like giant springs, took the force of the recoil as the gun was fired.

When a vessel was not in action, the cannon on the gun and upper decks were usually drawn back into the vessel. The breech was then pulled down so that the muzzle rested against the upper edge of the gun port. The tackles and breechings were then secured so that the gun would not move, no matter how rough the sea.

The fighting ship of the eighteenth century was, essentially, a huge floating gun platform, and her design and construction were geared to this one function. Herein lies the reason for the massive nature of her hull. Rarely was strength sacrificed for the sake of manoeuvrability or speed and although, compared with French and Spanish ships, British men-of-war were heavier and more cumbersome, there is plenty of evidence that they could outgun and outfight their rivals. Naval records show that very few British ships were lost in action, while the enemy vessels suffered greatly.

145 Gun carriage. From John Millan, *Treatise of Artillery*, 1768. Photo: National Maritime Museum, Greenwich

146 Detail of midship cross-section of a 74, showing the position of the guns. From William Falconer, *An Universal Dictionary of the Marine*, 1769. Photo: Science Museum, London

147 Plan of the gun deck of a 74. From William Falconer, *An Universal Dictionary of the Marine*, 1769. Photo: Science Museum, London

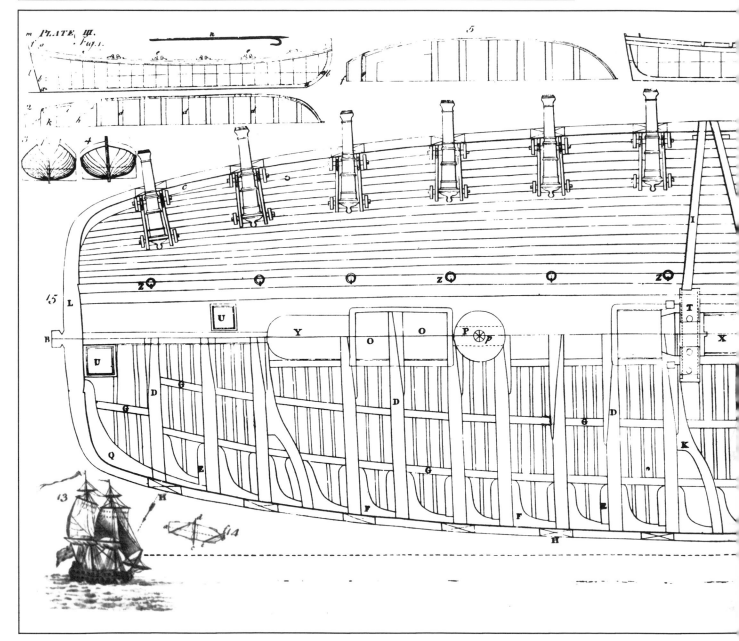

'*Explanation of the figures represented in the Deck*,

A, the principal, or main hatch-way.

B, the stern-post.

C, the stem.

D, the beams, composed of three pieces, as exhibited by D, in one of which the dotted lines shew the arrangement of one of the beams under the other side of the deck.

E, part of the vertical or hanging knee. See also, fig. 16 in the same plate.

F, the horizontal or lodging knees, which fasten the beams to the sides.

G, the carlings, ranging fore and aft, from one beam to another.

H, the gun-ports.

I, the pump-dales, being large wooden tubes which return the water from the pumps into the sea.

K, the spurs of the beams, being curved pieces of timber serving as half-beams to support the decks, where a whole beam cannot be placed on account of the hatch-ways.

L, the wing-transom, which is bolted by the middle to the stern-post, and whose ends rest upon the fashion-pieces.

M, the bulk-head or partition, which encloses the manger, and prevents the water which enters at the hawse-holes from running aft between decks.

N N, the fore hatch-way.

O O, the after hatch-way.

P, the drum-head of the gear capstern.

P p, the drum-head of the main capstern.

Q, the wing-transom-knee.

R, one of the breast-hooks under the gun-deck.

S, the breast-hook of the gun-deck.

T T, the station of the chain-pumps.

V, the breadth and thickness of the timbers at the heighth of the gun-deck.

U U, scuttles leading to the gunner's store-room, and bread-room.

W, the station of the fore-mast.

X, the station of the main-mast.

Y, the station of the mizen-mast.

Z, the ring-bolts of the decks, used to retain the cannon whilst charging.

a, a, the ring-bolts of the sides, whereon the tackles are hooked that secure the cannon at sea.

c a a d, the water-ways, through which the scupper-holes are pierced, to carry the water off from the deck into the sea.

b, b, plan of the foremost and aftmost cable-bits, with their cross-pieces g, g, and their standards e, e.

Thus we have represented, on one side, all the pieces which sustain the deck with its cannon; and, on the other side, the deck itself, with a tier of 32 pounders planted in battery thereon. In order also to shew the use of breeching and train-tackle, one of the guns is drawn in as ready for charging.'

The ship's boats, which Falconer includes in his plate of the gun-deck, were stacked one inside the other on the waist of the upper deck

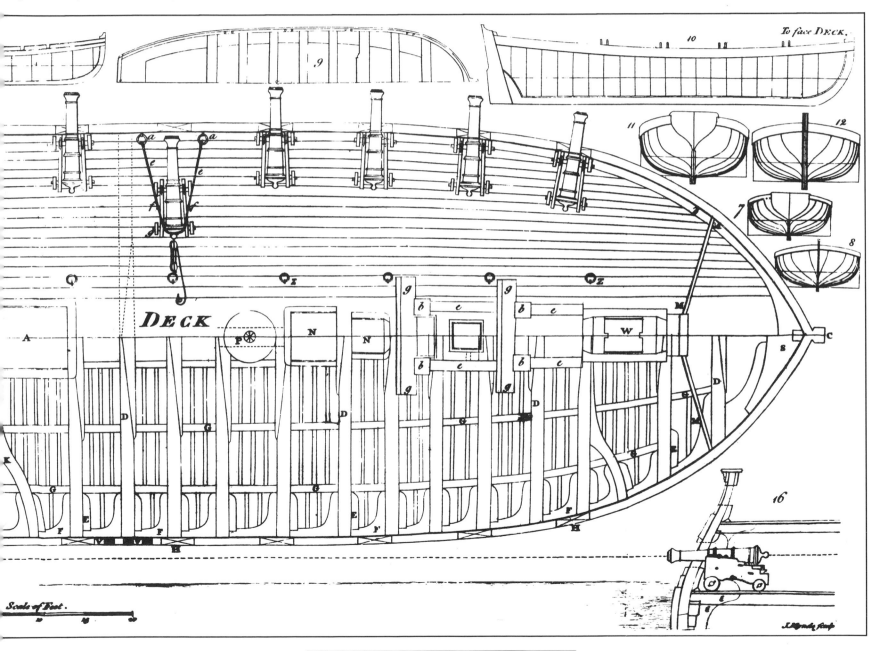

125

EPILOGUE

HMS *Thunderer*, a third rate of 74 guns, was launched on 19 March 1760 at Woolwich Royal Dockyard where she was fitted out. At a Navy Board meeting held on 28 March 1760, at which Lord Anson presided and Messrs G. Hay and G. Elliot were in attendance, it was resolved that Captain Charles Proby should be her captain. It was further resolved that the following officers should serve on the vessel: First Lieutenant Edward Vernon Yates, Second Lieutenant James Stewart, Third Lieutenant Charles Leslie, Fourth Lieutenant Richard Kemp.

On 28 April 1760, the Navy Board decided that the ship should join the Mediterranean Fleet at Gibraltar under the command of Charles Saunders Esq., Vice-Admiral of the Blue.* The vessel sailed from Woolwich at the end of April 1760 for Spithead, where she was stored and victualled before sailing for Gibraltar, where she arrived in the middle of May. She was completely recaulked on arrival. She remained there for some two years, patrolling the Strait and having the occasional not unsuccessful brush with the enemy.

On Friday, 17 July 1761, *Thunderer* was on patrol in the Strait of Gibraltar in the vicinity of Cape Spartel on the North African coast when a number of sail were raised on the horizon. The captain's log tells the story briefly, but quite vividly:†

*Saunders was one of Anson's protégés, having commanded the *Tryal* on Anson's voyage around the world in 1740–44. An outstanding officer, he was in command of the Channel Fleet in succession to Anson in 1758, and commanded the naval squadron in the attack on Quebec in 1759.

†The entry is faithfully reproduced in respect of spelling and capitalization, but punctuation has been added where appropriate and the captain's abbreviations have been spelled out.

Small breezes & cloudy at 2 p.m. Saw 3 sail in the NW. Set all sail & chaced at 6. Two of the Chase I judge to be the French ships of war, the other a Merchant ship under Spanish colours. At 8 cleared ship for Action. At 12 the largest ship about ½ mile from us, the other just in sight to windward. At 12 minutes past one the French ship began to engage (being then within musket shot), which we returned. 45 Minutes past she struck. Proved the *L'Achille* of 62 Guns. During the action one of the 9 pounders on the quarterdeck bursted. The Ships being on board each other, in clearing split & cut away a great part of the flying jib. At 4 the *Favourite* joined us. Employed shifting the Prisoners, unbending the Foretops, shifting the spritsail yard for a crossjack yard, knotting and splicing the rigging. At 8 made

sail towards the *Thetis* and *Modest* with our Prize. Find we have the following men killed in Action, viz.: James Martin, Michael Walton, James Smith, John Smith, Francis Southole, Thomas Field, Robert Basset, Abraham Lawson, James Flower, William Gair, John Pecket, William Crump, Mundy Cormick, Robert Selway, John McGlaughlin, Robert Power, John McGregorymar. Employed shifting the Prisoners, the *Favourite* in Company. At 11 departed this life William Roberts, Hugh James and John Kennet, Seamen.

This rather laconic account clearly underplays what must have been a lively, though short, action. Damage was obviously done to the mizzen mast and rigging, but the number of dead – twenty in all – points to other possible damage which is not recorded. Some of the casualties must have been occasioned when the 9-pounder exploded.

After her service in Gibraltar, *Thunderer* joined the Channel Fleet which was patrolling the Western Approaches and the French coast. In 1763 and 1765 she was a guard ship at Portsmouth. Sometimes she was in the company of distinguished ships such as *Victory* (to which she donated her main yard after a storm had deprived the flagship of hers), and she served her country well, if in an unspectacular fashion.

From 1775 to 1779 she underwent a whole spate of repairs, including a 'great repair' (rebuilding). She was refitted in January 1780 at Portsmouth, from where she sailed for duty in the West Indies.

On 31 October 1780, while on patrol, probably in the area of the Bermuda Triangle, she was overwhelmed by the great hurricane of that year and was lost with all hands.

BIBLIOGRAPHY

Naval Documents

Accounting Department, 1756-59, Public Record Office, ADM 49

Captains' Logs: *Thunderer*, 1760–80, Public Record Office, ADM 51

Henslow Collection, 1750s, National Maritime Museum, HSL/1

Letters from the Admiralty to the Navy Board, 1756–60, Public Record Office, ADM 106

Letters from the Navy Board to the Admiralty, 1756–60, National Maritime Museum, ADM/A

List Books, 1760, Public Record Office, ADM 8

Pay Books (Ordinary and Extraordinary), 1756–60, Public Record Office, ADM 42

Plans of the Dock Yards of the British Isles and West Indies (*The King's Book*), 1774, National Maritime Museum, LAD/11

Progress and Dimension Book, 1620–1912, Public Record Office, ADM 180/3, 2 vols.

Eighteenth- and Nineteenth-Century Sources

Thomas Riley Blankley, *Naval Expositor*, 1750

John Charnock, *History of Marine Architecture*, 1802, vol. 3

John Evelyn, *Sylva*, 1664

William Falconer, *An Universal Dictionary of the Marine*, 1769

John Fincham, *History of Naval Architecture*, 1851

John Fincham, *An Introductory Outline of the Practice of Shipbuilding*, 1821

John Knowles, *The Elements and Practice of Naval Architecture*, 3rd edn, 1822

John Millan, *Treatise of Artillery*, 1768

Mungo Murray, *References and Explanations of Four Prints Exhibiting the Different Views of a Sixty-Gun Ship*, 1768 (*The Sixty-Gun Ship*)

Mungo Murray, *A Treatise on Shipbuilding*, 1754

W. H. Pyne, *The Microcosm*, 1802

M. Stalkartt, *Naval Architecture*, 1781

David Steel, *Elements of Mastmaking, Sailmaking, Rigging, etc.*, 1794

David Steel, *The Elements and Practice of Naval Architecture*, 1805

David Steel, *A Shipwright's Vade-Mecum*, 1805

William Sutherland, *The Accomplished Shipwright*, 1705

William Sutherland, *England's Glory; or Shipbuilding Unveiled*, 1717

William Sutherland, *The Shipwright's Assistant*, 1711

Twentieth-Century Sources

Sir Westcott Abell, *The Shipwright's Trade*, Cambridge University Press, 1948

Robert Albion, *Forests and Sea Power*, Harvard University Press, 1926

Jean Boudriot, *Le Vasseau de 74 Canons*, Editions des Quatres Seigneries, Grénoble, 1973

K. R. Gilbert, *The Portsmouth Blockmaking Machinery*, Science Museum, 1965

W. L. Goodman, *A History of Woodworking Tools*, Bell, 1964

Nigel Harvey, *Trees, Woods and Forests*, Shire Albums, vol. 74, 1981

John E. Horsley, *Tools of the Maritime Trades*, David & Charles, 1978

Frank Howard, *Sailing Ships of War, 1400–1860*, Conway Maritime Press, 1979

Bjorn Landström, *The Ship*, Allen & Unwin, 1961

C. N. Longridge, *Anatomy of Nelson's Ships*, Percival Marshall, 1955

R. A. Salman, *Dictionary of the Tools Used in the Woodworking Trades*, Allen & Unwin, 1975

R. A. Salman, 'Tools of the Shipwright, 1650–1925', *Folklife*, vol. 5, 1967, p. 19

Anthony Sanctuary, *Rope, Twine and Net Making*, Shire Albums, vol. 51, 1980